JY si on p. 77

JY si on p. 77

THE UNSTOPPABLE IRISH

Figure 1. Bernard Ratzer (cartographer), *Map of New York Showing the Extent of the Great Fire,* 1776. Engraving. New York Public Library.

To The Dorymates with best regards and admiration,

DAN MILNER

[signature]

The
Unstoppable Irish

*Songs and Integration of the
New York Irish, 1783–1883*

University of Notre Dame Press
Notre Dame, Indiana

Published in the United States of America

Library of Congress Cataloging-in-Publication Data

Names: Milner, Dan, author.
Title: The unstoppable Irish : songs and integration of
the New York Irish, 1783/1883 / Dan Milner.
Description: Notre Dame, Indiana : University of Notre Dame Press, [2019] |
Includes bibliographical references and index. |
Identifiers: LCCN 2019002907 (print) | LCCN 2019003433 (ebook) |
ISBN 9780268105761 (pdf) | ISBN 9780268105754 (epub) |
ISBN 9780268105730 (hardback : alk. paper) |
ISBN 0268105731 (hardback : alk. paper)
Subjects: LCSH: Irish—New York (State)—New York—Music—History
and criticism. | Irish Americans—New York (State)—New York—Music—
History and criticism. | Irish—New York (State)—New York—Songs and
music—History and criticism. | Popular music—New York (State)—
New York—To 1901—History and criticism. | Irish—New York (State)—
New York—History. | Irish Americans—New York (State)—New York—
History. | Immigrants—New York (State)—New York—History. |
New York (N.Y.)—Emigration and immigration—History.
Classification: LCC ML3477.8.N48 (ebook) |
LCC ML3477.8.N48 M55   2019 (print) | DDC 305.8916/207471—dc23
LC record available at https://lccn.loc.gov/2019002907

IN MEMORY OF JOE "BANJO" BURKE

1946–2003

You may not have heard him sing
But those who did cannot forget his voice
And how he made it soar.

CONTENTS

LIST OF ILLUSTRATIONS

ACKNOWLEDGMENTS

Writing is a lonely pursuit, but in the end it takes many people to make a book. Not coincidentally, nearly everyone who helped with *The Unstoppable Irish* is a librarian, a singer, or a teacher. Some are all three.

As this book is about to be published, I thank my loving wife, Bonnie Milner, for gracefully enduring my seven-year preoccupation.

Five fine scholars made time in their busy schedules to read the manuscript and provide many helpful suggestions. They are John Fagg, senior lecturer in American Studies at the University of Birmingham, England, and author of *On the Cusp: Stephen Crane, George Bellows and Modernism*; Bill Keogan, teaching librarian at St. John's University, New York; Patrick McGough, lecturer on all things Irish at Queens College (CUNY); Rob Snyder, director of American Studies at Rutgers University–Newark and author of *The Voice of the City: Vaudeville and Popular Culture in New York*; and William H. A. Williams, retired professor of history and author of *'Twas Only an Irishman's Dream*. I also remember fondly the late Leo Hershkowitz, retired professor of history at Queens College (CUNY) and author of *Tweed's New York: Another Look*. I visited Leo frequently while working on this book, and the first words he always spoke were, "Are you finished?" Bless you all!

My research efforts were greatly aided by the assistance of Paul Mercer at the New York State Library; Grace Toland, former chief librarian and now director of the Irish Traditional Music Archive, Dublin; Peter Knapp of the Watkinson Library, Trinity College, Connecticut; Nancy-Jean Ballard, former Archive of Folk Culture researcher at the Library of Congress; Brendan Dolan, formerly of the

Tamiment Library at New York University; and Arlene Coscia and Dorothy McGovern of St. John's University Library. Various personnel at the New York Public Library, the New York Historical Society, the Hay Library of Brown University, Providence Public Library, and the Bobst Library of New York University also aided my research efforts. Thanks also to Steve Roud, who generously made available from his private collection a copy of the Glasgow ballad sheet "Skibbereen"; and Marion Casey of Ireland House, New York University, who kindly gave me a copy of "Patrick's Hearty Invitation to His Countrymen."

Over the years, I have regularly discussed songs with a network of like-minded friends, some of whom are no longer living. Sharing their company has been a great pleasure, and hearing their insights ever informative. They are John Baker, Jackie Boyce, Jon Campbell, Luke Cheevers, Jimmy Crowley, Jeff Davis, Gabriel Donahue, John Doyle, Bill Dunlap, Gina Dunlap, Mick Fowler, Barry Gleeson, Martin Graebe, Len Graham, Ken Hall, Frank Harte, Lou Killen, Sean Laffey, Maurice Leyden, Margaret MacArthur, Jim MacFarland, Jimmy McBride, Geordie McIntyre, Alison McMorland, Don Meade, Mick Moloney, John Moulden, Tom Munnelly, Deirdre Murtha, Lisa Null, Andy O'Brien, Robbie O'Connell, Mike O'Leary-Johns, Jerry O'Reilly, Sandy Paton, Mick Quinn, Tim Radford, Mike Risinger, Ian Robb, Fergus Russell, Martin Ryan, Grace Toland, Evelyn "Timmie" Vitz, Shay Walker, and Peta Webb.

I thank my colleagues at St. John's University for their interest in this project, especially Bob Pecorella, Judy DeSena, Phyllis Conn, and Paul Gawkowski.

Last but not least, my gratitude to Eli Bortz and Matt Dowd of the University of Notre Dame Press for their steadfast support.

New York City
June 2018

Introduction

Those in power write the history, those who suffer
write the songs.
  —Frank Harte, *An Phoblacht*, 7 July 2005

The Unstoppable Irish traces the changing fortunes of New York's
Irish Catholics, commencing in 1783 and concluding a hundred years
later with the completion of the initial term of the city's first Catholic
mayor. During that century, Hibernians first coalesced, then progressed slowly and painfully in uneven fashion from a variously dis-
missed, despised, and feared foreign group, ultimately to receive acceptance as constituent members of the city's population. This book
presents evidence that the Catholic Irish of New York gradually *inte-
grated* (came into common and equal membership) within the city
populace, rather than *assimilated* (adopted the culture of a larger host
group). Assimilation had always been an option for Catholics, even
in Ireland. In order to fit in, they needed only to adopt mainstream
Anglo-Protestant identity; but the same virile strain within the Hibernian psyche that had overwhelmingly rejected the abandonment of
Gaelic Catholic being in Ireland continued to hold forth in Manhattan,
and the community remained largely intact.

A novel aspect of the book is its use of song texts in combination
with period newspaper reports and existing scholarship to develop a
fuller picture of the Irish Catholic struggle. Because they have been

long recognized as a highly verbal and passionately musical people, it follows that songs should provide special insight into their attitudes and popularly held beliefs. Largely folk songs, street songs, and early variety theater lyrics, the examples quoted here are principally products of working-class people or members of the middling class who had risen through the trades. They are important because they articulate issues and voice viewpoints from a street-level perspective. Their words are imperative to integration discourse because they were circulated without significant direction from the shaping channels of church, government, and the music industry. Here, song texts make the act of integration more vivid and its stages more discernable.

From 1664, the year England seized New Amsterdam from the Dutch and renamed it New York, all people born in Ireland were regarded as Irish regardless of their ancestry; they were segregated by class, however, and evaluated on the basis of their religious preference. By the late seventeenth century, the Catholic Irish of Manhattan had become a severely repressed and marginalized minority, having been denied various civil and religious liberties since the Glorious Revolution. Following the American Revolution, the equality mentioned in the Declaration of Independence was not immediately conferred on Roman Catholics. Many Americans believed adherence to a mainstream Protestant religion was a fundamental ingredient of American identity and a requirement for full participation in the new republic. Test oaths and other discriminatory means delayed the attainment of uniform religious and civil rights for nearly four decades, while the acquisition of political power, social respect, and equal economic opportunity took far longer. The epoch of group integration—"a two-way accommodation of host and immigrant" (Gibney and Hansen 2005)—was necessarily long because group advances were often followed by setbacks, crises, even disasters. Not until the close of the 1783–1883 study period was it clear that Irish Catholics could not just take but hold their place as equal members of New York's citizenry. Successful strides typically engendered public approbation, while missteps threatened to corroborate wild charges made by antagonists—who may have known the Catholic Irish only through stereotypes and aloof observation—that they derived from an inferior race (Knobel

1986, 88) and were inherently incapable of amalgamating into the American populace.

The Unstoppable Irish is not about the Catholic Irish of the *entire* United States. Its concern rests solely within the tight confines of New York City, America's preeminent and most populous urban center from about 1800 and one of the nation's oldest, having been founded in 1624. Because New York is an American anomaly—established by Dutch interests rather than English, tied equally to Europe and to the United States, possessing a world outlook no less than a regional or national view, long a beacon for immigration, densely populated for centuries, and for most of its life a trader, manufacturer, financier, and trendsetter—constructions reflective of the vast nation as a whole are not necessarily applicable to the hyperurbanized archipelago in the Hudson River estuary. The effects of the city's unique history, extraordinary geography, and massive concentration of humanity bore on Manhattan's Catholic Irish. They are a distinct group, not just because of their religion and whence they came, but also because their new environment was unique within the new nation (Bayor and Meagher 1996, 534–42).

This book contends the critical era of Irish integration in the City of New York begins on 25 November 1783, when British forces finally evacuated Manhattan after the American Revolution, and ends on 2 January 1883, with the successful completion of William R. Grace's initial tenure as mayor of New York. The identification and validation of an Irish Catholic integration period carries considerable social importance because Hibernians were the first large non-Protestant European minority group in New York; consequently, they were the "trailblazers" of urban, ethnic America (McCaffrey 1997). Long considered "clannish" (Ellis and NY State Historical Association 1967, 284) and treated as suspicious "outsiders," they refused to cast off "foreign" Catholicism and assimilate. Their insistence on integrating as a group of equals, despite being neither from Great Britain nor Protestant was new and, once realized, has served as a model for immigrant groups that followed.

Catholic Irish New Yorkers were not uniform, of course. Some were strict conformists, some practiced a religion mixed with Celtic folk beliefs, while others, more cultural than religious Catholics, rarely attended a church service. The macroview shows that male immigration predominated early on, whole families often left together during the Great Hunger, and single women predominated after the Civil War. In the postwar period, the numbers of second-generation residents eventually exceeded those of the Irish born. The majority were members of the working class (laborers, laundresses, servants, and skilled and semiskilled workers). Below them lay an underclass that was either unable or unwilling to provide for itself in a large, strange, churning, urban place—people who found little acceptance from the city en masse or even the Irish community in general. There was an ever-growing middle class of business owners, who had ascended through a combination of hard work and good luck; during the post–Civil War period, many second-generation women became professionals, particularly teachers and nurses; and there was always a small upper class composed of the talented and fortunate. Variation within the group also existed with regard to the acceptance of American identity. Some immigrants were traditionalists, who hoped to live in Manhattan as they had in Ireland. Others, for example those who joined with African Americans to create new American popular entertainment forms such as minstrelsy (Crockett 1835, 48–49) and tap dance (Anbinder 2001, 172–75), embraced the mode of the metropolis.

Customs and mores were considerably different for women and men. Drinking on the job by men was tolerated, sometimes even officially encouraged, because in certain New York industries until the 1850s it was regarded as an invigorator for tired workers (Stott 1990, 142–44). Such behavior, however, would have meant dismissal in virtually all principally female occupations, except for some in the sex and entertainment businesses (McNamara 2002). While men formed many of their opinions in male-only barrooms, women were not permitted to vote. However, a commonality existed, in that the rural peasantry of Ireland during the era "rarely consumed alcohol except at fairs" (Stott 1990, 180), implying Irish immigrants from the countryside were at risk for alcohol abuse in New York because they were generally unaccustomed to the heavy-drinking culture pervasive in urban centers. There was also a basic dichotomy between the habits, opinions, concerns, and interests of the first and second generations: the former firmly believed they had earned US citizenship through hard application or military service, while the latter had birth certificates to prove their citizenship and ardently regarded themselves cocreators of the Manhattan lifestyle. Despite their many differences, virtually all group members held certain tenets. First, they believed allegiance to the Catholic religion (whether practiced or not) was as essential to their being as Irishness, a factor that greatly delayed their acceptance by Protestant New Yorkers; and, second, they regarded themselves as exiles in America, a people banished from their homeland by English oppression.

Historians of Irish America have not employed songs extensively in their analyses. Wherever possible, *The Unstoppable Irish* presents folk, street, and variety theater song lyrics as historical documents to display and illuminate the complex processes of integration. The term *folk song* presupposes the "complete absence of all officialdom, all influence exercised from above" (Krappe 1964, 154), a quality largely within the nature of printed street ballads and of many early Irish American popular song lyrics. Mick Moloney (2006, 381) observes songs have "always played a central role" in Irish culture; and this is particularly true among the highly oral, remarkably musical Catholic Irish of nineteenth-century Manhattan. William H. A. Williams (1996, 3) believes songs played a highly important function in the integration of the Irish into mainstream American society, being "within the realm of popular culture . . . where much of the 'negotiation' between the Irish and Anglo-America took place." While the surviving corpus of early Irish American song lyrics does not necessarily conform *unequivocally* to Krappe's ideal of unmediated expression, it certainly provides powerful access to attitudes prevalent among working-class Irish Catholics without direct influence from religious and political leaders. Conversely, community reception has acted as a filter to keep out untrue lyrics—songs that reflected period group beliefs were accepted and retained, while those that did not vanished quickly. The songs quoted and discussed here were composed mainly by laboring-class male authors: unpaid, unremembered folk poets; anonymous "scribes" in the broadside industry, who wrote and sometimes also sold topical song sheets; and popular performers in music halls, many of whom grew up in working-class surroundings.

Virtually all were observers with a street-level perspective—listeners with "ears to the ground."

Dialogue between songs and integration history has been sought throughout and sustained where possible. But songs can only be used if meaningful examples exist, and a song was not made about every event. Some incidents may have seemed too small, too mundane, hugely embarrassing, or too dull to make for compelling song topics. Even more substantially, not every song that was composed entered the communal repertoire or survived the passage of time, either in memory or on paper. The result is that many potentially important songs were lost. Traditional ballads and songs brought from Ireland were not always in the English language. So many immigrants origi-nated in predominantly oral, Irish-speaking areas that a significant but inestimable number of folk songs gradually faded away because they were neither written down nor adopted by future generations in the new metropolis. Irish-language songs occasionally appeared in Man-hattan song print media and ethnic newspapers, but English lyrics were the standard because the Irish language reflected the traditional culture of Ireland, which was itself in the process of being overtaken by commercial culture. English-language songs were the norm also be-cause Irish singers over time increasingly sang not just to Irish-born audiences but to mixed gatherings that included second-generation Irish Americans and non-Irish listeners.

Popular song retains some characteristics of folk song but with important differences. An entertainment medium generally preferred by nonelites, it is typically composed for an audience that is larger and wider than a particular ethnic community. But while folk song is refreshed and sustained by gradually evolving tradition, popular song is driven more by contemporary change, although, importantly, its texts are static. While popular song often expresses the values of the broad community, it is also about making money from music-making (W. Williams 1996, 3–4), especially through paid performances and the mechanical duplication and commercial distribution of songs. This does not mean that performers are typically without scruples regard-ing repertoire; rather, they tend to prefer performing songs that elicit a better audience response. Also, songs that do not sell well usually disappear quickly.

Popular songs of the period were circulated in three print forms: broadsides, songsters, and sheet music. While commonalities exist among them, each holds characteristics that bear unique implications. The broadside ballad (also known as the song sheet, ballad sheet, or penny ballad) was a transitional format halfway between traditional folk song and commercial popular music. Its composers were largely anonymous, working-class people, albeit ones who were usually compensated either financially or, in the case of amateurs, through the recognition attached to publication. Broadsides were printed on one side of a piece of usually poor quality paper and typically sold for one cent. Designed as ephemera, they nearly always contained the words to only one song, though as many as three might appear on a single sheet. Purchasers learned the words and discarded the sheet, sometimes using it for decoration or in the toilet. Song sheets almost never incorporated musical notation but commonly included mention of a well-known tune that could carry the words. They were sold in novelty and printed-goods shops, as well as in the open air on city streets (Charosh 1997, 468–70). "Tony Pastor's Combination Song or a Bunch of Penny Ballads," published on sheet music by Oliver Ditson and Company in 1863, is a "list song" of broadside song titles that were popular when it was composed. The opening stanza sets the scene at a typical Manhattan outdoor point of sale:

As you walk through the town on a fine summer day,
The subject of my song you have met on the way;
On railings and on fences, wherever you may go,
You will see the Penny Ballads stuck up in a row,
The titles for to read, you may stop for awhile,
And some are too odd, they will cause you to smile;
I've noted them down, as I read them along,
And I've put them together to make up my song.

Outdoor ballad hawkers demonstrated their wares while selling them, so purchasers could both buy the ballad sheet and learn the melody directly from a source singer. Irish immigrants were numerous among New York's song sheet sellers.[1]

Broadsides were common in Ireland between 1760 and 1920 but enjoyed greatest popularity there between 1780 and 1870, according to John Moulden (2006, 9, 12). Colin Nielands (1991, 209) writes that English was overwhelmingly the language of Irish ballad sheets, noting specifically that fewer than 2 percent of nineteenth-century Irish broadsides had Irish-language or macaronic English Irish texts. Such songs were occasionally printed in Manhattan; for example, publisher H. De Marsan printed "Cross-Keen Lawn" [*sic*] with English-language stanzas and a chorus in Irish. Broadsides were published in New York as early as colonial times but enjoyed a shorter heyday (1850–70), continuing with some currency into the early twentieth century (Charosh 1997, 465–70; Wolf 1963, iii).

The songster was a second popular song print format, typically containing forty or more songs and selling for as little as ten cents (a "dime") in the years 1850–90. Songsters were usually inexpensive, paperbound, pocket-sized booklets or "good-cheap" hardbound books with higher pricing. In twentieth-century, recorded-sound parlance, broadsides were "singles," while songsters were "albums." The latter were often tied to specific themes or to the repertoires of specific singers; for example, *The Double-Quick Comic Songster* (1862) was published during the Civil War and contains only lyrics by John F. Poole, while *James O'Neill's "Candidate for Alderman" Songster* (1876) includes lyrics by various composers, though most were made popular through O'Neill's performances. Considerable content overlap existed between broadsides and songsters, and long-loved songs straight from tradition could appear in either format. Lyrics in both print forms, for example, might comment humorously and wisely on current events. Broadsides, however, were more frequently realistic, while songster material was somewhat more inclined to escapism, romance, or poetical aspirations. Also, because both formats were known in Ireland and America, songs produced in either country could migrate easily across the Atlantic seaway.

Sheet music, containing musical notation as well as lyrics, was a third popular song print format. Generally, more content overlap existed between broadsides and songsters than between either of those and sheet music. Comparatively, sheet music was by far the most expensive commodity based on a cents-per-song ratio. Produced for posterity in large size, it required both textual and musical literacy and presumed instrumental ability; consequently, it carried higher status and cost. Though it had long existed, the wide popularity of sheet music developed later than broadsides and songsters, when increased affluence and education began changing American tastes and habits and more people were entering the middle class. It was particularly tied to the arrival of the piano on the domestic scene. But sheet music was not a vehicle exclusively for parlor songs. Minstrel songs were printed in this format, as well as the output of the hugely popular, realism-inclined team of Edward Harrigan and David Braham, whose output included the 1883 song "On Board of the Muddy Day" about a "trim built scow" that carried "garbage down from the city to the sea." William H. A. Williams (1996, 5) cautions about an important characteristic of Irish-themed sheet music, "Being commercial items, ultimately intended for musical entertainment in the home, there were certain topics inappropriate for songs. Significantly, this meant the most vicious of anti-Irish (and anti-Catholic) propaganda did not generally appear. . . . At the same time, songwriters virtually ignored certain things that were very important to the Irish but that might have offended, disturbed, or puzzled mainstream audiences."

The Unstoppable Irish investigates the incorporation of a displaced, foreign, rural people into a hostile, urban environment. Chapter 1 (1643–1783) is a prologue to the main body. It argues that integration of the Catholic Irish in colonial New York was impossible because the conditions necessary for community settlement did not yet exist. Suffering from the anti-Catholic legacy of the Reformation, Gunpowder Plot, and Glorious Revolution, the Irish were by 1700 a small and severely repressed minority. Chapter 2 (1783–1844) shows that certain rights enumerated in the Declaration of Independence were withheld from New York Catholics after the Revolutionary War, because many Americans regarded membership in a conventional Protestant religion to be a fundamental requirement of full citizenship. Nearly forty years transpired before uniform civil rights were granted, but toleration was thrown backward after the Napoleonic Wars, when increasing immigration from Ireland took place. Chapter 3 (1845–59) examines the dual effects of Ireland's Great Hunger and America's Second Great Awakening. While destitute, rural Irish peasants attempted to settle in a city for which they were entirely unprepared, nativist mobs intent on arson threatened their neighborhoods in hopes of driving "foreign" religion and people from Manhattan. A strengthening Catholic Church led by John J. Hughes provided leadership through this trial by fire. Chapter 4 (1860–65) sees Irish Catholics presented with a clear opportunity to achieve equality through active participation in the Civil War. Colonel Michael Corcoran of New York's Sixty-Ninth Regiment was proclaimed nationally as an early war hero. But after two years of carnage on the battlefield and suffering on the home front, mobs largely composed of Irish Catholics took to Manhattan streets, engaging in brutal mayhem because the basis for war appeared to have changed and the wealthy were being given ways to avoid conscription. During the period seen in chapter 5 (1866–83), Irish laborers fought a costly battle on the streets of Manhattan against their ancient Orange enemies, William M. "Boss" Tweed went to prison, and Tammany Hall adopted a new business model. The number of Manhattan-born Irish finally surpassed that of immigrants, and just as New York's Hibernians became more Americanized, the city as a whole took on a greenish patina. As a great migration of immigrants from southern and eastern Europe was beginning, the Irish gained standing when County Laois native William R. Grace was elected New York's first Catholic mayor. Throughout these five eras, song texts illustrate the changing status of the Catholic Irish. In some instances, songs clearly swayed, even led, public opinion. Fewer songs appear in earlier chapters because fewer songs were printed, while larger numbers were published during and after the Civil War. In general, lyrics written by Irish New Yorkers reveal anxiety early on, moving from pride to lament during the Civil War, and later develop a sense of confidence.

Just as the Catholic Irish changed greatly during the integration epoch, so too did New York City. Originally occupying only the southernmost tip of Manhattan, it grew over time from a small trading post to a metropolis covering the entire island. In the process, it incorporated outlying villages to the north (Harlem, for example) into the larger body. In 1873, the appellations of Manhattan, New York City, and New York County were interchangeable. The following year, the southwestern section of Westchester County (the West Bronx) was appended to New York. But it was not until the municipal consolidation of 1898 that Brooklyn, Queens, Staten Island, and remaining sections of the Bronx were finally joined. This fact is particularly important because much of the accreted territory remained farmland, forest, or wetland well into the twentieth century; however, it was the tight, urban confines of nineteenth-century Lower Manhattan that played the formative role in shaping the New York Irish community and character. New York is also known as the Empire City, a moniker that gained currency once it had capitalized on the location of its truly magnificent natural harbor—at the meeting point of the North Atlantic European-American trade route and the Hudson River, Erie Canal, and Great Lakes waterway into the interior of America—and was well on the way to becoming a commercial industrial giant.

Many books have been written about the City of New York (its official name). The first was a combination geography and history of the Dutch colony during its first three decades. Thousands of volumes have since followed, and many more are sure to come because New York is ever changing and always fascinating. It is so huge a topic that no one author, no one book can ever give it full justice. *The Unstoppable Irish* is about only one of the city's innumerable facets, albeit a large one. If readers find these pages memorable, it probably will be because the narratives and songs of Manhattan's Hibernians are truly compelling. However, it might also be because herein they find insights into the countless other immigrant groups who continue to follow in their path.

CHAPTER ONE

Prologue

Colonial New York

Before I was *Born* in the dear *Irish nation*,
I never saw *here* such queer *Baderation*,
Such *Murder* of Ink, and such *Blood-shed* of *Paper*,
It makes all the *Brains* in my *Belly* to caper.
— "*Mr. Lawrence Sweeny*, Esq.;
Vehicle General *of* News . . . 1769"

In the autumn of 1643, the French missionary Isaac Jogues landed at New Amsterdam after a six-day journey down the North (Hudson) River. He came almost straight from hell — *almost* only because he had spent an intervening month and a half under the protection of the commandant at Fort Orange (Albany), 142 miles upstream. Jogues and twenty-two French and Huron companions had been ambushed and captured the preceding year by a war party of over a hundred Mohawk Iroquois. Badly beaten and horribly mutilated, they were staked to the ground with hot coals cast on them, their bodies punctured repeatedly with sharp augers. A few of the party were summarily executed, while others were slowly burned alive (Martin 1885, 71–110).

After thirteen months in captivity, he was finally ransomed by the Dutch at Fort Orange, who acted as proxies for their French allies (Martin 1885, 149–52).

Father Jogues was the first Catholic priest ever to walk the streets of officially Calvinist New Amsterdam. That distinction, plus reports of his terrifying ordeal and the horrific deformities he bore, raised considerable interest among the townsfolk. Violent, fatal disputes had already raged between New Amsterdam's European settlers and their Native American neighbors. Of course, the savage taking of civilian life was hardly unique to the Americas. Contemporaneously in Ireland, thousands were meeting grisly deaths.

Jogues wrote of the nineteen-year-old settlement, "On the island of Manhate, and in its environs, there may well be four or five hundred men of different sects and nations: the Director General told me that there were men of eighteen different languages; they are scattered here and there on the river, above and below, as the beauty and convenience of the spot has invited each to settle" (Jameson 1909, 259–60). A weeping Polish man, a Lutheran, came to the priest and kissed his mutilated hands as he repeated the words, "Martyr of Jesus Christ!" A Portuguese woman showed him pictures of the Blessed Virgin and of Aloysius Gonzaga, a fellow Jesuit, beatified a few years earlier. But the meeting that pleased him most was his encounter with a "good Irish Catholic, who arrived during his stay from the Virginia coast" and who made it his "first and urgent duty . . . to approach the Sacraments" (Martin 1885, 153–54).

Two Early Irish New Yorkers

Father Jogues did not record the Irishman's name, so the chance encounter was a matter of interest even before historian Leo Hershkowitz (1996, 12) gave it increased currency with a mention in the classic essay collection *The New York Irish*. In 1966, journalist Edward Robb Ellis (60) pointed to Hugh O'Neal, stating he "married a Dutch widow the very year that Father Jogues paid the city a short visit." Ellis's date and details, however, were incorrect. O'Neal wed the widow of Adriaen van der Donck, a wealthy lawyer and author of the first book known to have been written about what is now New York, *A Description of New Netherland*. But van der Donck did not die until 1655, twelve years after Jogues's visit. Further, after the nuptials, the couple repaired to Hugh O'Neal's home in Patuxent, Maryland (Brodhead 1853–87, 1:533).

Anonymous for centuries, the "good Irish Catholic" has recently been identified (Milner 2011). Born somewhere in Ireland, circa 1613 (Riker 1999; Stillwell 1887), he is referred to in English and Dutch documents by various, similar-sounding names, an inconsistency not particularly meaningful because the importance of standardized spelling dates only from the mid-eighteenth century, when the first edition of Samuel Johnson's *Dictionary of the English Language* (1755) was published. Moreover, the Irishman moved between three cultures, and most surviving documents relating to him were written by colonial officials, rather than his own hand. But during the Duke of York's proprietorship, when an atmosphere conducive to Catholicism prevailed, New York's first Irishman signed and gave his name as William Goulding or Gouldinge (Brodhead 1853–87, xiv, 535, 622).[1]

Perhaps the most fascinating immigration stories are those of people who traveled circuitous routes to reach the places where they finally settled. As indicated in Jogues's note, Goulding arrived from Virginia; however, he had sailed there not from Ireland but from England. On 21 August 1635, a twenty-two-year-old passenger manifested as William Golder became one of 152 "Persons to be transported to Virginia by the *George*, Mr. John Severne, after examination by the Minister of Gravesend" (Coldham 1988, 163). His name and age appear on the passenger list immediately after that of his master (Hotten 1874, 124). Goulding was the indentured servant of Edward Abbes, a man fifteen years his senior.

Indentured servitude was a standard practice used to populate American colonies, both Dutch and English. A *servant* was in actuality an all-purpose employee, whose passage was paid by a sponsor, either fully or in part. Servants incurred an obligation to work a certain number of years, but similar to slaves they could be bought and sold. During the term, the employee received food and clothing and learned farming or a trade. At the end of the contract, the servant became a free person, might be granted some land, and could acquire the right to vote subject to the laws of the jurisdiction (Morison 1965, 82). When master and servant agreed, it was a boon to both parties. When they did not, it was likely a constant, sore vexation. Song sheets printed in London, as early as 1612, alternately extoll the virtues of Virginia,

> Where Capons are so cheap, and Eggs are in such plenty
> Also such Fowl and Fish, and other things most dainty:
> As Pigs, Veal, Lamb, and Venison, if Travellers speak truly,
> Which is the cause so many go, and travels to Virginny.
>   ("A Net for a Night-Raven," Bodleian, 40 Rawl. 566[165])

and lament a servant's existence in the colony,

> I have play'd my part, Both at Plough and Cart,
> In the Land of Virginny, O:
> Billets from the Wood, Upon my back they load,
> When that I was weary, weary, weary, weary, O.
>   ("The Trappan'd Maiden," Bodleian, Douce Ballads 2[219a])

Indentured servants in the early English colonies of America came from a wide variety of social segments within Ireland and Britain. The majority were voluntary émigrés—free persons who wished to settle on the far side of the Atlantic to better their circumstances but who could not afford the price of passage. Involuntary servants constituted the other large group and included "those sent under the arbitrary exercise of royal prerogative or by court sentences," among them outright criminals, paupers, vagrants, and dissolute persons, as well as many poor children (Ballagh 1969, 34–35). Included in the latter mix were many political prisoners. Samuel Eliot Morison (1965, 82) writes, "James I began, and Oliver Cromwell and the later Stuart kings continued, the business of transporting to the colonies Scottish and Irish rebels taken in civil wars. . . . Most of these unfortunates were sent to the West Indies . . . but some went to Virginia, Maryland, and New England." Goulding's relocation from Ireland to England, and subsequent emigration to America, therefore, could have been by design or because of poverty, a result of antigovernment activity or punishment for a petty crime. In any case, it was almost surely related in some way to the large-scale, sectarian-based land redistribution ongoing in Ireland.

Goulding and his master appear to have had a satisfactory relationship in the vicinity of Elizabeth City, near where the James River empties into Chesapeake Bay; but it did not last long because Abbes died the following year. Unresolved is the date on which the Irishman finally became free. Key to that question is the length of his indenture, which could have varied between two and eight years with a three-to-five-year term considered average (Ballagh 1969, 49–50; Kenny 2000, 9). Exactly where Goulding resided in the years immediately before his arrival in New Amsterdam is not known. Employment prospects in Virginia were good because labor was very much in demand, but given the colony's profitable tobacco culture most men preferred to become freeholders, and land grants were frequently stipulated in contracts between servants and masters (Ballagh 1969, 84–85). What is certain, though, is that in 1641, the Virginia House of Burgesses began a legislative campaign that barred "popish recusants" from holding office and likewise disenfranchised Roman Catholics (Billington 1964, 7). As Virginia turned hostile, Manhattan stood open and accommodating.

The image of William Goulding given by Father Jogues is just a snapshot of a faceless young migrant freshly landed at New Amsterdam's seaport, but because Dutch authorities kept good records much more is known about him than the vast majority of Irish who immigrated to America during the seventeenth century. Estimates range from fifty to a hundred thousand, with about three-quarters of the total thought to have been Romanists (Kenny 2000, 7; Miller 1985, 137). According to historian Kevin Kenny (2000, 7), "Virtually no evidence has survived on these Catholic settlers. . . . Mainly young, single, rootless males, they seem to have blended into the general population rather than establishing themselves as a separate ethnic group in America."

The concept of "exile" or "banishment" from the native land has suffused the literature of Ireland and Irish America for centuries (Miller 1985, 3–8). "Exile" appears often in Irish song lyrics and other literature, sometimes deployed with considerable poetic license. Goulding, an educated person, was not a willing emigrant but a true outcast. After establishing himself in Virginia, he was driven from that new home by a second scheme for religious persecution. In cosmopolitan New Amsterdam, he received communion from the mutilated hands of a future saint. But once Father Jogues departed for France, the Irishman was again on his own, severed from his religion. Catholics, along with other high church Christians, experience God principally through sacraments delivered by ordained clergy. With little hope of ever again receiving absolution and communion, Goulding faced the prospect of a life of lonely prayer well beyond the reach of the church. In response, he chose a path that led to his assimilation into the diverse Protestant population of mercantile New Amsterdam.

In New Amsterdam, the Irishman's primary identity was that of an Anglophone. Shortly after Father Jogues heard his confession, he came in contact with one of the more extraordinary women of early colonial America, Lady Deborah Moody, a "woman of considerable wealth and education" from Wiltshire, England (Stockwell 1884, 1). Moody was an Anabaptist who had been admonished by the court in Salem, Massachusetts, for opposing the practice of infant baptism, and in June 1643 she and some like-minded followers decided to move to the more liberal New Amsterdam. William Goulding became a member of her group.

Catholic-to-Protestant conversion certainly was no great rarity in seventeenth-century Ireland. Setting aside issues of belief, it was a pragmatic solution that secured the ownership of land and conserved family wealth. But it was also an extreme measure that represented far more than the acceptance of a foreign religion. The act symbolized the embrace of an alien oppressor in full view of one's neighbors, and it embodied the repudiation of the ancient culture, native language, and living community. In more open and accommodating, Dutch-administered New Amsterdam, Goulding felt no such social pressure. Marrying a woman who emerged as a free-tongued street preacher, he had no alternative other than to accept her religion. In isolation, his decision was simple, natural, and his own. He chose the practical, logical option—he assimilated. Homesteading with the Moody group in Gravesend, he showed leadership in public affairs, elevating himself to a position of respect in a frontier American community that lay

Figure 2. New York a Small City on Manhattan Island, North America, 1667. Copied for *D. T. Valentine's Manual,* 1851, by G. T. Hayward, 120 Water Street, New York. New York Public Library.

perilously close to the European beachhead. The Irishman's reward was broad acceptance in an English-speaking enclave dominated by radical Dissenters (Milner 2011).

As the known parts of his persona are connected, William Goulding becomes increasingly important. Likely from an esteemed Irish family, and possessing a particular facility in property trading, he stands as a rare, identifiable figure entirely consistent with the mass silhouette of thousands of anonymous seventeenth-century Catholic Irish immigrants, in that he arrived in bondage, he was harassed for his beliefs, and his travels took him farther and faster than his reviled religion could keep pace. In attempting to mitigate his challenges, he adopted many of the ways of his neighbors, and in that sense he may be seen as a prototypical New Yorker (fig. 2).

During the seventeenth century, few Irish people lived in New York, even though it was a very cosmopolitan place. Records kept during the period of Dutch control (1624–64 and 1673–74) identify only four permanent Irish residents (Riker 1999). In 1664, an English fleet seized New Amsterdam in the name of James Stuart, Duke of York. Twenty-three years later, James's governor wrote tellingly to the Committee of Trade in London, pointing out great ethnic diversity within the colony,

> I believe for these 7 years last past, there has not come over into this province twenty English Scotch or Irish familys. But on the contrary on Long Island the people encrease soe fast that they complain for the want of land [and] many remove from thence into the neighboring province [Connecticut]. But of French [Huguenots] since my coming here several familys come both from St. Christophers [St. Kitts] & England [and] a great many more are expected as alsoe from Holland are come several Dutch familys which is another great argument . . . that a more equal ballance may bee kept here between his [Majesty's] naturall born subjects and foreigners which latter are the most prevailing part of this Government. (O'Callaghan 1849, 60)

Such ethnic variety, together with low Romanist numbers overall, was beneficial to Irish Catholics at first. They were less visible, less enviable, and less likely to be perceived as a threat by the overwhelmingly Protestant population. But despite their small numbers, they came under suspicion immediately in 1683, when James appointed a Catholic, Colonel Thomas Dongan, to rule his vast North American holding.

In contrast to William Goulding, Dongan was deeply rooted in the Irish aristocracy (fig. 3). His mother was a member of the Talbot family, and two of his maternal uncles—the Roman Catholic archbishop of Dublin and the lieutenant governor and Earl of Tyrconnell—were the most prominent individuals in Ireland. So notorious was the latter that he was made the butt of a wildly popular English antipapist song called "Lilliburlero," the melody of which has sometimes been attributed to Henry Purcell (Simpson 1966, 449; Wilgus 1982, 227). "Lilliburlero" preceded Dongan to New York, making him deeply suspect, likely hated, and certainly feared even before his arrival. The song mocks Irish Catholics with garbled, ignorant dialect. It also accuses them of plotting to withdraw the fundamental document of British constitutional monarchy (the Magna Charta) and to overthrow English supremacy in Ireland as a prelude to threatening Great Britain.

Figure 3. Colonel Thomas Dongan Governor of New York, 1682, afterwards Earl of Limerick. Print. Emmet Collection. New York Public Library.

Ho Brother Teague dost hear de decree,
Lillie Burlerlo Bullen a-la,
Dat we should hab a new Debittie,
Lillie Burlerlo Bullen a-la,
Lero, Lero, Lero, Lero,
Lillie Burlerlo Bullen a-la,
Lero, Lero, Lero, Lero,
Lillie Burlerlo Bullen a-la.

Ho by my shoul it is a T____t, [Talbot]
And he will cut de Englishman's troat.

Ho by my soul de English do Prat,
De Law's on dare side and Chreist knows what.

But if Dispense do come from de Pope,
Weel hang Magno Carto and demselves on de rope.
                    (Bodleian, Wood 417 [168])

Dongan encountered a host of problems on his arrival in New York, most related to the duke's authoritarian policies; but fortunately, he also bore the good news that James had instructed him to "create an elected assembly and to revise the province's tax structure" (Lankevich 1998, 27). While Dongan created controversy by bringing with him a small group of English Jesuits, who opened a school for children of all religions, at least for the merchant elite, "the religious uneasiness abated once the community leaders recognized that Dongan was no fanatic"; they then concentrated on the "commercial privileges he could dispense" (27).

Dongan had intended to stay on at his Staten Island estate when his term of service ended, but that proved impossible. Unlike Goulding, who made peace with his God privately, because Catholic religious services did not exist in Manhattan at the time, Dongan for reasons of class and calling was inextricably tied to both the Catholic Church and the Stuart cause. Faced with no other choice, Goulding could assimilate into a community of English Anabaptists; but religious conversion was never an option for Dongan. Once the Glorious Revolution consigned the Duke of York, now James II, to banishment, the retired governor was looked on in New York as his agent provocateur, someone who might attempt to turn the province into a base for recapturing the crown. After the fiercely anti-Catholic militia leader Jacob Leisler seized control of the colony in the names of William and Mary, he pointed to Dongan as the devil, centering his entire attack on Dongan's Catholicism rather than on his Irishness: "He circulated stories to the effect that the 'papists' were gathering around Dongan on Staten Island and terrorizing the Protestant inhabitants of that island. He charged Dongan with fitting out his brigantine with guns, ammunition and provisions and of collecting a force of 'papists' from Boston and other places. Dongan's pretended preparations Leisler pictured as a menace to the lives of all Protestants in the colony" (Kennedy 1930, 108).

Dongan was hounded from New York, removing any potential for the coalescence of an Irish community in seventeenth-century Manhattan. Ironically, he fled to London, where he was allowed to live in peace and where he eventually inherited the earldom of Limerick, an indication that New York exceeded even London in its hostility toward Catholics. In Manhattan, the threat of a demonic, Catholic "other" allowed British and Dutch, elites and laborers, to realize their commonality. In 1696, Governor Fletcher stated only nine Catholics were left in Manhattan (Shea 1878, 26); and in November 1700, New York passed An Act against Jesuits and Popish Priests, a statute that made the presence in the colony of a Catholic cleric a crime punishable by life imprisonment or death (Davis 1985, 194; Rosenwaike 1972, 11).

The contrast between Goulding and Dongan shows Irishness was less an obstacle to settlement than Catholicism and that British colonial policy was aimed at discouraging Romanists from living in New York. Dongan's difficulties are evidence that to be a Catholic was to be anti-Christian and a traitor, who would deliver the land into the hands of France or Spain. Thereafter, the entire population became an anti-Catholic army, and only misguided, desperate, or compelled Roman Catholics journeyed to the city on the Hudson River estuary.

The New York Conspiracy of 1741

Among the compelled were Irish soldiers serving in the king's regiments. In recognition of Manhattan's strategic importance at the base of the Champlain-Hudson water route between the St. Lawrence River and the Atlantic Ocean, New York was unique among the North American colonies in that British troops were regularly stationed there during the entire period of royal rule (Kammen 1975, 307). "In 1700," writes Hershkowitz (1996, 12, citing E. B. O'Callaghan 1858), "Four companies of soldiers with 150 from Ireland arrived. Governor Richard Coote [Earl of Bellomont], of County Sligo, remarked that the 'recruits that came from Ireland are a parcel of the vilest fellows that ever wore the King's livery, the very scum of the army in Ireland and several Irish Papists amongst [them].' Something of a riot occurred and several citizens were wounded. Two 'mutineers' were executed. . . . What happened to the rest of the recruits is not known, though many surely remained in the colony."

Early in 1741, a series of suspicious fires frightened New Yorkers into believing a slave revolt was imminent, probably in conjunction with a Spanish invasion. Reports that blacks, almost all of them slaves,

Figure 4. Harry Fenn, *New York Slave Market about 1730,* 1902. Line photo-engraving. New York Public Library.

had frequently gathered and "talked among themselves and with several whites about seizing freedom, money, and a measure of revenge" gave credence to the conspiracy (Davis 1985, x). The whites included British soldiers named Connolly, Corker, Fagan, Kane, Kelly, Murphy, O'Brien, and Ryan; a prostitute who accommodated blacks and was known as the "Newfoundland Irish Beauty"; and a purported priest and supposed spy said to be in the service of Spain (Lepore 2005, 177–83, 191; Davis 1985, 233–34, 255).

The probe of the New York Conspiracy of 1741 was obscure in its origins, investigated through bribery and intimidation, and prosecuted with terrifying zeal by a "scheming opportunist" (Lepore 2005, 222). Because claims of innocence were ignored, an accused suspect's best hope was to confess—guilty or not—and especially to implicate others. Ultimately, some 175 persons were arrested. Eighteen blacks and four whites were hanged; 13 slaves were burned to death; and 70 were transported to other colonies (Kammen 1975, 213). The investigation quickly concluded once frightened informers began implicating some of Manhattan's most upstanding citizens. There is no doubt that some fires were set and robberies took place. For Manhattan's lowest classes, crime was both a sustainer and a leveler. However, the events of 1741 were not a conspiracy by dictionary definition. Rather, they occurred at the meeting point of Anglo–New York cultural nightmares tied to life in a slave-owning, colonial outpost, where colonists shared space with unequal and resentful foreigners. Their unease was prompted by anti-Catholic "fact-myths" emanating from the Gunpowder Plot of 1605, by living memory of the deadly New York slave insurrection in 1712, by ongoing war with Spain in the Caribbean and along the shipping lanes off the Atlantic seaboard, and by a recent, particularly violent slave revolt in Charleston (Davis 1985; Lepore 2005).

The behavior of the prosecution demonstrated a policy of exacting punishment on the three New York "other" groups that were most feared and despised by city elites: slaves and free blacks, who were believed to enjoy too much freedom; British troops, who were outsiders supported in part by local taxes, who also competed with local laborers by taking part-time work and were often accused of abusing the civilian population (complaints later cited in the Declaration of Independence); and Catholics, prominently Irish, who it was believed frequently intrigued politically with England's enemies. Whether by chance or design, an unexplained fire broke out in the home of the colony's lieutenant governor on 18 March 1741, the afternoon after Saint Patrick's Day. By no coincidence, these same three groups were tightly pressed together at the bottom of the city's socioeconomic pyramid, where they regularly interacted. Their numbers were substantial—the population of New York City at this juncture was close to 20 percent black (Davis 1985).

One place the accused were said to have plotted was the public house of John Hughson, a hostelry where the innkeeper fenced stolen goods; where a priest was said to swear black men into the plot by drawing a ring on the floor with chalk and, standing in the middle of it with a cross in his hand, promising to forgive them their sins; and where patrons, blacks and whites together, danced to fiddle music (Lepore 2005, 136, 192). Hughson (identified by various historians as either English or Irish) was at first considered to be the ringleader, but the prosecution later substituted a more appropriate, better-educated mastermind, a reclusive, itinerant teacher who had lodged with Hughson. His name was John Ury, and it was alleged that he was a Catholic priest because he knew Latin and had considerable familiarity with religious ritual. But Ury was actually a former Anglican minister, who had been cast out from that church for refusing to acknowledge the validity of the succession of William and Mary (Davis 1985, 161–62, 198–99). The unlucky, defrocked minister was found guilty and executed. At the same time, no real punishment was laid on the soldiers, some of whom had engaged in burglary and arson. Three absconded quickly and were never apprehended. The remainder were examined individually and released on the provision they be transferred elsewhere (Davis 1985, 233–35). The soldiers bore names that marked them as Irish Catholics, but they denied such religious affiliation and probably survived for that reason only. Again, a varying pattern can be seen in the perception of Irish and Catholics. Common Irish were misguided fools, but Catholic Irish were cunning traitors.

Eighty years after Jacob Leisler's *coup d'etat*, twenty-eight years after the New York Conspiracy, and just six years before the War of American Independence, an unnamed colonial printer published a thirteen-verse, riddle-filled, song sheet entitled *"Mr. Lawrence Sweeny*, Esq.; Vehicle General *of* News and Grand Spouter of Politics, to His *Humble Petitioners, this* New-Year's *Morning, One o'Clock,* P.M. 1769."* Validating the above assessment, the central character, "Sweeny the Irishman," is portrayed as a wise fool or a rogue or both simultaneously. He is a man behind a mask of drunken riddles, so his exact nature cannot be determined, but it is very clear he is neither to be taken entirely seriously nor to be fully trusted. Still he is not depicted as evil, and he would have been so identified if he were Irish *and* Catholic:

> By Patrick! With Balling and Squalling along,
> Poor Sweeny has silenced the Noise of his Tongue;
> But zounds tho' he *speak* not, he thinks, d'ye' hear
> To *whisper* some Trifles *aloud* in your Ear.
> > *Sing Balinamona ora, a sight of your purses for me.*

. . . .

De'el take me—say I, upon my Salvation,
'Till I *die* I never will *live* out of my Station;
In the Cause of Potatoes, and Freedom I'm hearty,
And I *bate* none I *love*, whatsoever his Party

For the King—Swinney always shall living or dead,
With the *throne* may *fit light* on his Majesty's *Head*:
May his Foes, and our Foes, to their *Rise* have a Check,
And *fall* 'till they *hang* very *high* by the Neck.

(AAS 1769)

Three Songs from the American Revolutionary War

The first Saint Patrick's Day parade in North America, which took place in New York in 1766, was a "military procession" (Cronin and Adair 2002, 10). Historically, such events presented opportunities for recruiters to bolster sagging numbers by proposing enlistment in the presence of uniformed finery. In such an environment, recruiters could quickly sign up those easily impressed, then fall back on trickery, persuasion, inveiglement—and sometimes *force*—to complete the ranks (Palmer 1988, 283).

During the American Revolution, in spring 1778, British commander-in-chief General Sir Henry Clinton sought to lure soldiers into deserting the American forces and joining the Loyalist corps, appealing to the "national attachment of the Irish by inviting them into a regiment whose officers should all be from that country, and placing at its head a nobleman of popular character and ability." Clinton had one in his command, whom he believed to be the perfect leader, writing that Lord Francis Rawdon (subsequently Earl of Moira; fig. 5) would "spare neither expense nor pains to complete its numbers and render it useful and successful" (Nelson 2005, 60). Rawdon had deep pockets. In an advertisement in New York's *Royal Gazette* in 1779, he offered recruits thirty shillings plus a complete military outfit. By March, he had gathered a regiment of 494 men (Murphy and Mannion 1962, 53). That Saint Patrick's Day, the Volunteers of Ireland paraded to the Bowery, preceded by their "band of musick. . . . [Afterward] a dinner was provided, consisting of five hundred covers. . . . The soldierly appearance of the men, their order of march, hand in hand, being all NATIVES OF IRELAND, Had a striking effect, and many of their Countrymen have since joined them." A regimental drinking song, "Patrick's Hearty Invitation to His Countrymen," was created for the occasion and sung en masse to the tune of "Paddy Whack" (Irish Sword 1955, 125–27):

> Each son of St. Patrick, each true-hearted Fellow,
> Come join in our March, and bear Part in our Song;
> The Offer's no bad one, my Lads, let me tell you,
> So give us your Hand, and parade it along.
> At *Yankey* hereafter we'll tickle a Trigger,
> For Clinton, God bless him, will give us the Van;
> Let's first shew our Vigour, on Beef and good Liquor,
> St. Patrick's the Word, and your Fist to your Can.

> Long Life to the *Shamrogue*, long Life to *Shilely*,
> Whoe'er would live happy, to us let him come;
> Our Days are contented, our Nights we pass gaily,
> For all the Girls follow the Sound of our Drum:
> Whoever will join us, must sure be the Winner,
> For Mirth and good Humour is always our Plan.
> Priest, Parson, or Sinner, he's welcome to Dinner,
> St. Patrick's the Word, and your Fist to your Can.

On examination, we see that "Patrick's Hearty Invitation to His Countrymen" is written to be highly inclusionary. Commanding manly Irishmen to cast off the boredom of a stationary trade in favor of an exciting life on the field of battle in the company of daring chums and gay nights in camp, it states men of all creeds and no creed at all are welcome, Catholics included. Still, it is curious that the regiment would invite a priest to dinner in a colony where an antipriest law with capital consequences was still in effect. Was the prohibition being ignored? Did Rawdon believe that prospective Catholic recruits simply would not notice or care? Or was the song just disingenuous, alliterative rhyme? Likely, there was at least some truth in each. William Harper Bennett (1909, 338–40), founder of the Order of Alhambra,

Figure 5. James Heath, *Francis Rawdon, Earl of Moira*. Engraving. Emmet Collection. New York Public Library.

claims mass was said secretively in New York in the years before the revolution. If that were the case, the effect was threefold: first, commanders of Irish troops could willingly turn a blind eye to religious observance because recruits came at a premium; second, the greatest concern of Rawdon's men was survival, something he himself learned in battle; and third, "Patrick's Hearty Invitation to His Countrymen" would have been sung only at official regimental functions. Rather than being a popular lyric, it is more a commercial enticement, one that despite its official origin was unlikely to be beneficial.

The song continues as an open invitation to Irishmen from all parts of the island, as evidenced by the location of the mentioned rivers: Nore (south), Shannon (west), Liffey (east), and Bann (north). At the time of the American Revolution, Ireland was overwhelmingly an agricultural nation but also a populous one. Apart from movement to the cities, there was minimal internal migration, particularly between provinces (Gilbert et al. 2017). New York, a foreign, neutral place, was therefore an important first-time meeting point for many Irish people from far-flung regions of the country. In a force of men expected to

fight as a unit, flashpoints such as county, provincial, and religious fac-
tionalism had to be avoided. The basis of a bonded regiment was a
united Ireland:

> The Harp of sweet *Ireland* has called us together,
> The Rights of our King; and our Country to shield;
> We hope the Assistance of all who would rather
> Than slave in a Trade, take the Chance of the Field;
> To such gallant Fellows, we give Invitations,
> Whether born on the *Nore, Shannon, Liffey,* or *Ban*;
> Whatever their Stations, we'll own them Relations,
> St. Patrick's the Word, and each Fist to the Can.

Further binding elements are the universally admired drink and, de-
pending on the political views of the receiver, the possibly conflicting
patriotic symbols of king and country. The principal attractions are
adventure and alcohol, both known antidotes for drudgery in an otherwise inescapable occupation; however, the mention of prosperity is
noticeably absent.

The final verse is important because it promises each soldier a
youthful surrogate father. So great was his ambition and so heavy was
his purse that Rawdon solely outfitted and maintained his men. Whatever rhymester wrote the song did not neglect the opportunity to sing
the praises of his master and, like him, attempt to curry favor:

> And now my brave Boys, let us toast our Commander,
> The gallant young Rawdon, our Chief of Renown,
> I'll warrant our Foes he will make to knock under,
> Then fill him a Bumper and let it go round:
> With him at our Head, Boys, no Dangers shall fright us;
> It were base to desert such a Chief of a Clan;
> His Name shall unite us, his Bounty requite us,
> His Health is a Toast, so each Fist to the Can.

The following Saint Patrick's Day, Rawdon again feted the Volunteers. By now, the regiment was quartered about fifteen miles distant
from Manhattan at Jamaica in Queens County. Another musical tribute

was offered: "A Song. By Barney Thomson, Piper to That Regiment"
or "Success to the Shamrogue":

Success to the shamrogue, and all those who wear it.
Be honour their portion wherever they go.
May riches attend them, and store of good claret
For how to employ them sure none better know;
Every foe surveys them with terror,
But every silk petticoat wishes them nearer,
So Yankee keep off, or you'll soon learn your error
For Paddy prostrate shall lay ev'ry foe.

.   .   .   .

St. George & St. Patrick, St. Andrew, St. David
Together may laugh at all Europe in arms,
Fair conquest her standard has o'er their heads waved,
And glory has on them conferr'd all her charms.
Wars alarms! to us are a pleasure,
Since honour our danger repays in full measure,
And those who join us shall find we have leisure,
To think of our sport ev'n in war's alarms.

(Crimmins 1902, 34)

"Success to the Shamrogue" offers another hearty helping of bravado,
this time with England, Ireland, Scotland, and Wales in saintly union —
and Saint George notably at the fore. Drink and the promise of female
companionship are again mentioned, though less lasciviously. Significantly, the "Yankee" rather than the rebel is the enemy, suggesting all
Americans are likely traitors.

Though Rawdon fed his men lavishly at least once a year, an annual feast was not enough to buy complete loyalty, just as musical
braggadocio could not buoy their morale continually. A few months
later in battle at Camden, South Carolina, Rawdon's regiment was dis-
integrating before his eyes. He wrote to a subordinate on 1 July 1780,
"Sir: So many deserters from this army have passed with impunity
through the districts which are under your direction that . . . I will give

the inhabitants 10 guineas for the head of any deserter belonging to the Volunteers of Ireland; and 5 guineas only if they bring him in alive" (Crimmins 1902, 32). Colonial forces absconded too but in order to tend to their farms and families. They were stakeholders in America rather than imperial pawns. This discrepancy would not have been missed by Rawdon's Irish deserters, who now saw a civilian existence in America as a better alternative than life in the British military.

New York was an early scene of conflict during the revolution. Patriot bodies began to usurp municipal authority beginning in 1774, and by October 1775, the new Continental Congress recommended the arrest of royal officials. On 6 June 1776, the last British troops, "a hundred or so soldiers from the Royal Irish Regiment," marched down Broad Street en route to a warship waiting in the Hudson estuary (Burrows and Wallace 1999, 225). Given New York's crucial location between New England and the mid-Atlantic colonies to the south, General Sir William Howe had no other choice than to retake the city and restore the old order. On 2 July 1776, British naval transports began to arrive off Staten Island, assembling "the largest fleet and biggest army Great Britain had ever sent from her shores" (Fleming 1997, 186). On 22 August, a virtually unopposed landing was made at Gravesend Bay by fifteen thousand troops (Fleming 1997, 187), and Washington began planning for an inevitable retreat.

In "Dear Molley," the little-known period folk ballad that follows, a colonial emplacement on a high elevation engages Irish soldiers in the king's service as they traverse northern Manhattan's irregular, well-forested terrain. While the official "Success to the Shamrogue" refers to the patriots as "vermin," the Irish narrator of "Dear Molley" calls the Americans "our own relations," with the received meaning of "countrymen," and appears to question the necessity of internecine violence. Battling foreigners on the European continent was very different work than fighting fellow British citizens on their American home ground. The parallel with colonial control of Ireland was only too clear.

The encounter remembered in "Dear Molley" took place during the November 1776 Battle of Fort Washington (fig. 6), when units of the Continental Army and militia situated on a steep hill were attacked by units of the British Army and Hessian mercenaries, who had crossed the Harlem River to Manhattan:

Figure 6. A View of the Attack against Fort Washington and Rebel Redouts near New York on the 16 of November 1776 by the British and Hessian Brigades. Drawn on the spot by Thomas Davies, capt R. R. of artillery. I. N. Phelps Stokes Collection of America Historical Prints. New York Public Library.

Dear Molley Read those lines that I have Riten hear
And when you do that perruse them you can but Shed a tear
When I Relate my Story it will greave your heart ful Soer
When I tell you of our Miserey Sense we Left our Native Shoer.

The Second of November by the Dawning of the Day
At New York we was Landed and ankard in the Bay
To Meat our foes at kingsbridge next morning we marched away
To fight our own Relations in the North America

Who Marched with Resolution to fase our Enemy
Advancing on the Mounting they had a Battery
Down on our Irish heroes theair haughty Calls Did fly
This was Awful welcom in the North Amarica

Who Marched with a Resolution to face our the Rebel Crew
And So Boldly we attacked them tho Men we had but few
Tho they was teen to one brave boys it never be Said we Ran away
But we fought whilst we Could Stand the North Amarica

Then through fields of blood we waided where Cannon Loud
  Did Roar
And Many a war like hero ly Roleing in their goer
And heeps of Mangled Soldiers all on the ground did lay
That was Both kild and wounded in the North Amarica

Your Heart would Melt with pitee to See the Souldiers wifes
Sarching for their Dear husbands with Malenclry Crys
And Children Crying out Mamey arc we may rue the Day
That we Came to Lose our Daddays in the North Amarica.
                          (Kendal 1783, 25–26)

The visceral realism of "Dear Molley" stands in stark contrast with the conniving, jingoistic blather of "Patrick's Hearty Invitation to His Countrymen" and "Success to the Shamrogue." In the panorama of "Dear Molley," the Irish speak for themselves and appear shocked at the reception shown them by their opponents. In common, both sides fight as men of homelands shared by diverse cultural traditions, while each languishes beneath the same dark cloud of colonialism. Though the Irish fight courageously, they are disillusioned, not just by horrific carnage, but also by the realization that they now function as agents of the same foreign oppressor who ruled them at home.

"Dear Molley" exists solely because it was transcribed into a copybook by Joseph Kendal Jr. of Ashford, Connecticut, who wrote above the words, "New York, September the 6 D 1780" (Kendal 1783, 25–26)—presumably the place and date he received the song. The Bodleian Library collection of over thirty thousand broadside ballads includes a number of song sheets containing texts bearing motifs similar to "Dear Molley." The most common title for these lyrics is "Gown of Green," which was sufficiently popular to have spawned a sequel entitled "The Answer to the Gown of Green." Bodleian researchers have ascertained the publication date span of some of these sheets by tracing various clues, such as the addresses of publishers. Following are the dated broadsides, along with the printer and the time range of publication:

Armstrong, W.   1820–24
Evans, J.   1780–1812
Pitts, J.   1819–44
Such, H.   1849–62

Of these sheets, none predates the American Revolution, and only the Evans text (1780–1812) may have been contemporaneous. The fixed spaciotemporal location of "Dear Molley" in close proximity to the action at Fort Washington argues compellingly that it was written by someone who actually witnessed the event.

The "Gown of Green" text (Harding B 16 [106a], Bodleian Library) provides further confirmation that "Dear Molley" was probably the mother of "Gown of Green" (or at least half of it) rather than its child:

As my love and I was walking to view the meadows round,
Gath'ring of sweet flowers as they sprung from the ground,
She turn'd her head and smiling, said, somebody here has been,
Or else some charming shepherdess has wore a Gown of Green.

My love is tall & handsome, & likely to be seen,
Indeed she's very handsome and her age is scarce sixteen,
Indeed sh's [sic] very handsome and her age is scarce sixteen,
In struggling she consented to wear the Gown of Green,

O Polly love, O Polly love, mind what I write to thee,
And when that you do read it, it will cause you many tears,
It will cause you many tears my love & grieve your heart full sore,
For to relate our story when we leave our native shore.

It was early the next morning by the day,
From New York down to Imos, we all did march away,
From New York down to Imos, we all did march away,
To fight our own relations, in the North America.

Through fields of blood we rang'd and cannon's loud did roar,
And many a valiant sailor lay bleeding in their gore,

There's many a valiant sailor did on the deck doth lie
Who was both kill'd and wounded in North America.

It would grieve your hearts with pity for to hear the sailors' wives,
Lamenting for their husbands, & the melancholy cries
The children cries out, mammy, we will make them rule [*sic*] the day,
As they have kill'd my father in North America.

Now some to please their sweethearts will buy them toys and rings,
And some will buy them posies, and all such foolish things,
Let every lad that loves his lass, as I pretend to do,
Give her the Gown of Green to wear and she will follow you.

While "Dear Molley" has a through-composed storyline posing no extraordinary leaps of logic, "Gown of Green" is muddled and presents two, essentially separate motifs oddly stitched together. The first of these is an amorous encounter in a grassy field (hence the green-stained gown), and the second is a confused narrative of sailors involved in a military operation somewhere near New York. The claim that "Dear Molley" was the mother rather than the daughter is legitimized here for the following reasons: there was a crucial battle in northern Manhattan at Fort Washington on 16 November 1776, British Army troops advanced to a point near King's Bridge, and the British troops were fired on by Continental forces from an elevated position (Schecter 2002). "Gown of Green" has an unexplained time leap between verses three and four, and verse four pictures sailors leaving their ship in New York to march to "Imos," a place-name not listed in the extensive *Webster's Geographical Dictionary* (1966). "Gown of Green," therefore, is not an integral or corrupted document but one that was rudely assembled from various sources, most likely by a scribe engaged in the commercial ballad trade. Viewed merely in mercantile terms, the ballad succeeded. But "Dear Molley" is considerably more. It is a rare example of an early Irish American folk ballad that provides a first-person view of a major occurrence in the American Revolutionary War, and one that presents social commentary from the mouth of an Irish witness on the eve of American independence.

Comparing "Dear Molley" and "Gown of Green" provides insight into the intricate and unpredictable relationship between oral folk songs and printed song sheets, two mediums that exchanged information frequently but mainly in undocumented intercourse. It also illustrates the British governmental practice of controlling the national designs of its colonies by employing military units from faraway regions to quell uprisings. The "haughty Calls" of the New York militia also signal that the Irish who decided to stay on (or come anew) would find settlement and integration a long, hard fight even in free, national New York.

During the seventeenth century, when Catholics represented the greater percentage of Irish immigrants, they were the "young, single, rootless males" mentioned by Kenny (2000, 7). The life of William Goulding in New Amsterdam and New York validates that synopsis, and through him can be seen certain of the reasons why early Catholic Irish immigrants tended to assimilate rather than coalesce as a group and integrate en masse—most importantly because for political and logistical reasons their church was unable to keep pace with so many members spreading thinly across an ever-widening Atlantic world. During the eighteenth century, Ulster Presbyterians were the most numerous Irish immigrants in America, but they generally steered for ports south of New York, so their effect on Manhattan life was minimal. At that time, New Yorkers did not differentiate much between the Irish, treating them as a single group, even though their ancestry could have been Irish, English, Scots, or German.[2] The dominant group, however, was the Anglo-Irish (Goodfriend 1996, 40–42). The antipriest law enacted in 1700 (and left in place until 1784) kept Catholic immigration artificially low in colonial New York, so that Hibernians were a minority segment in the Irish numbers. After the Napoleonic Wars in Europe and agricultural restructuring in Ireland, larger immigrant movements headed to New York. They were progressively composed more of Catholics, who were less likely to hail from relatively prosperous commercial ports and more likely to depart from the depressed and now overpopulated rural landscape. In New York, "Their daily increasing numbers magnified their visibility. With their alien ways, Papist religion, frequent destitution, and sometimes even their foreign language, the Irish ethnic village posed an undeniable threat to the relatively homogeneous metropolitan social structure that had existed during the Jeffersonian years" (Walsh 1996, 61).

THE CATHOLIC IRISH thus presented a new image and entered into a different relationship with Protestant Manhattan. Though poverty was common among the new arrivals, Ray Allen Billington (1964, 32–36) believes that they were primarily "opposed because they were Catholics rather than because they were paupers and criminals." In addition, the "toleration which swept the country in the early years of the Republic" was now submerging below latent nativism. The resentment and animosity of Protestant New Yorkers met fierce physical resistance from Irish Catholic laborers and characterized the battle rhetoric of the crucial period of integration, when decisions were being made as to whether the foreign newcomers might gain acceptance on their own terms, be required to assimilate, or be forced into a permanent subclass. A century passed until the status of the Catholic Irish in New York City was resolved. Much—but not all—of its history was recorded in the popular songs of the day. The era of contested settlement and the songs that illuminate it are the main matter of this book.

CHAPTER TWO

The New York Irish in the New Republic

Such things with me do not agree, I'll bear with them no more;
Before I live in poverty I'd fly my native shore.
Our Island is productive, but we need the statesman's aid.
There's no employment for the plough or for the hook or spade.
—"John Malone," Joseph Ranson, *Songs of the Wexford Coast*

The tide of xenophobia has swelled and ebbed throughout American history. During the first century of national control in New York, many Protestant Americans, regardless of ethnic derivation, identified themselves as "Americans" to the exclusion of Irish Catholics, whom they viewed as foreigners—even when they were American born—as though the city and the country had been divinely granted to Protestants, together with a sacred responsibility for safeguarding Paradise from unworthy interlopers.

In a modern study that seeks to establish the origin of American ethnicity, the basic ancestry element tracked by the US Census Bureau's *American Community Survey* (2010), the author asserts that the envisioning of an American people occurred at the time of the revolution when the free American population was "over 60 per cent English, nearly 80 per cent British, and 98 per cent Protestant. . . . In its mind, the American nation-state, its land, its history, its mission, and its Anglo-American people were woven into one great tapestry of the imagination. This social construction considered the United States to be founded by the 'Americans,' who thereby had title to the land and the mandate to mould the nation (and any immigrants who might enter it) in their own Anglo-Saxon, Protestant self-image" (Kaufmann 1999, 439–40). This model requires immigrant *assimilation* and excludes group *integration*. While of interest within a macrocontext, it does contain one oversight, for it presumes the United States at the close of the Revolutionary War to have been a country with a set of social and cultural traditions that were distributed uniformly throughout, rather than a confederation of states with a multiplicity of settlement histories—Anglican Virginia, Catholic Maryland, Quaker Pennsylvania, Dutch New York, and Puritan Massachusetts for example—or a coalition of regions, each with its own binding commonality (Woodard 2011). Certainly, "Anglo-American people" did exist—they were the people who had previously regarded themselves as Protestant Britons nonresident in the United Kingdom—but they existed with considerable geographic variation. In New York City in November 1783, as British forces evacuated and American forces established control, Roman Catholicism was still forbidden by law, while it was tolerated in other jurisdictions (Meagher 2005, 31).

Historian Dale Knobel (1986, xi) observes, "Ethnicity is a social classification. It is neither strictly biological nor precisely cultural. Ethnicity is a category of ascription and self-identification with boundaries defined by custom." If logic were the basis, an American native would be simply a person who was born in the United States. Birth in America, however, was not the sole determining factor. The actual criteria were color (white), origin (northern European and preferably English), and religion (conventional Protestant). Most white people were permitted entrance into American society, but mainstream Protestant credentials were a requirement for full inclusion. In practice, religion was no less a determining factor than skin coloration.

The New Goodwill, and Who Would Rule and How?

Hasia Diner (1996, 88–89) associates American nativist agitation with steadily rising Catholic Irish immigration, which began to cause friction in the 1820s and increased dramatically during the potato blight of 1845–52 and the following decade. But antipathy toward Roman Catholics was ingrained in New York much earlier. As Allen Ray Billington (1964, 1) writes in his classic book *The Protestant Crusade*, "Hatred of Catholics and foreigners had been steadily growing in the United States for more than two centuries before it took political form with the [nativist] outburst of the 1840's and the Know-Nothingism of the 1850's."

In Manhattan, the exclusionist construction of American identity to which Billington alludes was contested from early national days. After the revolution, as the very nature and structure of governance and politics were reconsidered, not all New Yorkers were content to allow the social and political assumptions that sprang from the preceding colonial system to carry over into state and local statutes. The reexamination process was not immediate but evolutionary, owing to a complex mixture of philosophical and practical questions that required pondering, just as political positions and allegiances required negotiation. Interestingly, the split from the United Kingdom had actually nullified certain arguments against Catholics in America, such as the presumption of dubious fealty to the Protestant British monarchy. At the same time, the American credentials of Anglicans became suspect because many members of that church were Loyalists during the revolution, a war that was won only with the help of Catholic France. After a period of eighty-three years, during which the Catholic Church was an illegal group in colonial New York, the question of how it might fit into Manhattan society could now be examined.

At the end of the eight-year-long War of American Independence, most American Catholics lived in Maryland (15,800) and Pennsylvania (7,000), while perhaps 1,500 Catholics lived in New York State and around its immediate borders. Of those, about 200 resided in the City of New York (Hennesey 1981, 73–75). Immediately after the British departure, the population of war-torn and burned-out Manhattan stood at about 12,000. That figure more than doubled between 1783 and 1786 (Rosenwaike 1972, 15–16). The period of postwar reconstruction was also a complex era of reassessment, of sorting out people, practices, politics, institutions, and ideas. What had been forbidden might now be allowed and vice versa.

Nowhere more than New York was the change from Crown to American democratic control so involved, because it was the most

Figure 7. Evacuation Day—Washington's Entrance into New York, November 25, 1783. From a drawing by W. S. L. Jewett. *Booth's History of New York.* New York Public Library.

diverse of all colonies and "probably the least unanimous in the assertion and defense of the principles of the revolution" (W. Jay 1833, 41). The roles of religious institutions in particular were due for examination. Most colonies had maintained established churches and otherwise regulated religious activities within their boundaries. The Church of England was established in much of New York. Most colonies also had some laws detrimental toward Catholics, but the goodwill engendered by the French alliance generally brought about "a favorable attitude toward the Roman Catholic Church on the part of American Protestants, and this was encouraged by Washington, Franklin, and other leading men" (McGreevy 2003, 11; Morison 1965, 292–93).

But the new goodwill was hardly overriding, uniform in application, or especially long lasting, for there was no obvious, direct connection between the root cause of the revolution—American unwillingness to be taxed and regulated without legislative representation—and the promotion of liberal social ideology. In New York, chief among those who sought to prolong discrimination against Catholics, a growing majority of whom were Irish, was John Jay (fig. 8), leader of the

Figure 8. John Chester Buttre, *John Jay, Second Governor of New York.* Engraving. New York Public Library.

conservative faction at the state constitutional committee meeting of 1776–77, an assembly to which no Catholics were called. During the debate over the state constitution, Jay sought to include an oath, which was rejected, requiring that Catholics deny "the power of an ecclesiastic to absolve from sin." He also sought to add an amendment to the provisions on naturalization (then a state prerogative), requiring immigrants to "abjure and renounce all allegiance and subjection to all and every foreign king, prince, potentate, and state in all matters ecclesiastical and civil" (Ryan 1935, 16)—in effect to disown the pope and necessitate the formation of an American Catholic Church (just as the Church of England in America reorganized as the Protestant Episcopal Church). The amendment on naturalization was passed and remained law until it was superseded by the US Constitution. A critical influence in shaping Jay's views was that his great-grandfather, a Huguenot of La Rochelle, was imprisoned and subsequently fled from France to England after the revocation of the Edict of Nantes in 1685 (Jay 1833, 3–5). Thereafter, staunch support for the Protestant cause (including anti-Catholicism) was a family trait. John Jay's great-uncle Isaac died of wounds received fighting alongside William of Orange at the Battle of the Boyne (1833, 6).

Though the new goodwill engendered by the revolution "made overt discrimination against Catholics . . . contrary to the cause of American republicanism" (Duncan 2005, 69), it is noteworthy that nativism did not disappear. A decade later, legislation was introduced into the New York Assembly that would have required election inspectors to administer a test oath to potential voters renouncing civil and *ecclesiastical* foreign allegiances (a precursor to nativist initiatives in the 1840s and 1850s). The bill was aimed at urban Catholics and was the work of rural Whigs, who were countered by city Federalists. Alexander Hamilton, Jay's younger and more progressive Federalist fellow, took the opposing position, arguing that American-born Catholics were unencumbered by "that dangerous fanaticism, which terrified the world some centuries back; but which now dissipated by the light of philosophy" (Duncan 2005, 69–70). Hamilton was a strong nationalist, who well perceived the dangerous implications of creating a potentially divisive religious underclass. He was also a capitalist, who held a positive view of the city's merchant traders, a number of whom were Irishmen and some of them Catholics (Burrows and Wallace 1999, 272–73).

Because the New York State Constitution of 1777 was based on the preceding colonial charter, it was far from an egalitarian document. Electoral rights were granted only to property-owning, white males. The tension between the expectations of working-class citizens for a new republic that benefited all and the aristocratic traditions characteristic of colonial New York boiled over on the banks of the East River in November 1795, when city alderman Gabriel Furman asked two employees of the Brooklyn ferry to take him to Manhattan prior to the scheduled departure time. They refused at first, then complied, but an argument erupted during the passage, and Furman had the two ferrymen, Timothy Crady and Thomas Burk, arrested. Recent emigrants from Ireland, they were charged with insulting an alderman and threatening a constable (fig. 9).

The case was tried before the Court of General Sessions, with the mayor and three of Furman's fellow aldermen—all Federalists—sitting in judgment. Edwin Burrows and Mike Wallace (1999, 323–24) write, "Neither man was allowed legal counsel, there was no jury [and] Furman was the only witness." The judgment was that Burk and Crady should be jailed for two months, with Crady also receiving twenty

Figure 9. Samuel Hollyer, *Old Fulton Ferry House, N.Y.C., 1746*, 1908. Engraving. New York Public Library.

lashes on his bare back (Pomerantz 1938, 264–65). The harshness of the sentence and the authoritarian tone of the proceedings made clear that vestiges of the old order continued to exist, only in different guise. Crown forces had departed New York twelve years earlier, but the city had not made real progress toward resolving the question of who would rule and how; unfortunately, the divide between those who felt only a select few were qualified to lead and those who, like Crady, believed that they were "as good as any buggers" (Burrows and Wallace 1999, 323) was inherently systemic and needed to be resolved through legislative action.

Crady and Burk may have been marked for such cruel and unusual punishment because of their known ethnicity and presumed religion—Catholic Irishmen were still considered troublesome, and the aldermen's actions indicate they believed an example should be made of them—but the case had broader implications. While on the one hand, the ferrymen presented an immigrant issue, on the other, the plight of Crady and Burk was not restricted to newcomers but was relevant to New York working-class society at large. The treatment received by the Irishmen could have been levied on anyone who was not connected to power or money. Crady and Burk fled prison, but their cause remained, ballooning when a Republican lawyer named William Keteltas denounced the proceedings in a city newspaper and petitioned the assembly to impeach the mayor and aldermen. The Federalist-heavy assembly declined and jailed the attorney; however, two thousand supporters rallied around him, chanting "The Spirit of Seventy-Six" along his route to confinement (Burrows and Wallace 1999, 324).

The case of the ferrymen was an important episode in Catholic Irish community settlement because they had yet to be adopted into a sponsor-client relationship by a political party. Catholics represented potential votes, but they also carried the residual stigma of foreignness, still repugnant to many Americans. Supporting issues closely related to Catholic interests risked alienating the core base of any political party. Hitherto, Federalists had occasionally shown a modicum of encouragement for middle-class Catholic Irish members of their organization, but this backing was unreliable and infrequent. The Brooklyn ferry affair marks the first instance when the rights of Catholic Irishmen were defended by Republicans (soon to become Democratic-Republicans and later simply Democrats). Though Catholic Irish numbers were still small, they were rising, causing Republicans "to think in terms of the common adversary they shared with Irish Catholics: Anglo-Americans known as Tories in Britain and Federalists in the United States" (Duncan 2005, 94).

Early Settlement

Beyond political oppression, the antipriest law sought to diminish immigration and encourage religious conversions. Once the statute was struck in 1784, Father Charles Whelan came to New York at the request of the parish council organizing the city's Catholic mother church, Saint Peter's (fig. 10). Whelan was far from a perfect choice. Born in Ireland during the hard days of the Penal Laws, he entered the seminary in France, became a naval chaplain, and was a prisoner of war in Jamaica (Hennessey 1981, 75). The experience of his self-

Figure 10. Saint Peter's Church, Barclay Street, New York. Published by G. Melksham Bourne, 1831. New York Public Library.

imposed exile set him apart. Perhaps Whelan was more fluent in Irish and French than English. Church historian Leo Ryan (1935, 47) characterizes him as "probably cold, gruff and tactless; even disliked by his own countrymen and lacking in ability to preach with effect."

New York's first Catholic congregation was highly eccentric judged by the standards of the Devotional Revolution (Larkin 1972), which characterized Irish and American parishes for more than a century beginning about 1850. Father John Carroll, the vicar apostolic, or direct papal representative in America, found "lack of fervor . . . and a general condition of relaxed morality" (Ryan 1935, 27). From this can be concluded that the practice of Roman Catholicism, a religion intended as "universal" and tightly structured in ritual and duty, varied considerably in practice between the Irish locales where many of New York's immigrants originated and Carroll's own Anglo-Catholic Maryland. His assessment was rooted both in Ireland and in New York. A century of domination had kept the church in Ireland highly fragmented and amorphous (Bottigheimer 1982, 143), with the effect that a large gap existed "between formally structured Catholicism and the traditional religious practices of rural Ireland" (Foster 1989, 165), which contained numerous pre-Christian carryovers. Importantly, for the rural masses, Catholicism was far more a deeply connected element of group identity hardened by colonialism than a living liturgical experience. Therefore, most Catholic Irish immigrants in Manhattan held strong cultural links to their faith but brought little religious knowledge with them (Miller 1985, 72–74).

A second matter was, because New York had never permitted Catholicism to take root, middle-class Catholic New Yorkers had become familiar with certain Protestant conventions, including a great importance being placed on the ability of a cleric to preach and the right of congregations to "call" and dismiss pastors. This familiarity (and subsequent state law) encouraged Saint Peter's lay trustees to set out on a path of parish democratization that emulated the organization of most Protestant religious communities but contravened the Roman Catholic system of governance. Neither of these contradictions could remain unresolved in a hierarchical organization intent on uniformity. The attempt at recasting the Roman Catholic Church in an American national mold represented the most serious threat to its constitution during its history in the United States (McAvoy 1948, 13–14).

A factional fight developed among the trustees once a second priest, Andrew Nugent, landed in New York and was allowed to officiate at Saint Peter's (Ryan 1935, 48). Under the provisions of state law, lay trustees held title to church property, paid the salaries of priests and employees, and managed the financial affairs of a parish (Dolan 1983, 49), but Nugent's supporters sought to go further, threatening "to use legal means to accomplish this end, assuming that the congregation had a right not only to choose clergymen but to dismiss them at pleasure" (Ryan 1935, 49). This unholy row (known as "trusteeism") was resolved only when Carroll journeyed to New York and seized the church building (Ryan 1935, 52–55). He then lectured the city's Catholics that the church hierarchy alone held the right to assign priests. Notwithstanding, another controversy, this one over the rental of pews, a fund-raising method not common in Ireland, then arose. Both trusteeism and pew rental remained as issues between middle-class church boards and poverty-class parishioners through the famine era, owing to the huge financial burden of funding both a physical location for worship and temporal aid for an increasingly poor congregation.

Migration from Ireland was tied to specific events at home and in America. It surged after the failed United Irishmen Rebellion of 1798, sending a gathering of remarkable, open-minded Irish republicans to New York. Indeed, much of the glue that kept Catholic and Protestant Irish loosely bonded during the early period of community settlement was provided by the presence in New York of veteran United Irishmen. Three towering figures arrived between 1804 and 1806. Two of these, Thomas Addis Emmet and William Sampson, were Church of Ireland (Anglican) members, and the third, William MacNeven, was a Roman Catholic. Emmet, who served as attorney general of the State of New York during 1812 and 1813, was an older brother of the executed revolutionary Robert Emmet. William Sampson was a lawyer (fig. 11), who successfully defended the priestly right of secrecy in the confessional (Walsh 1996, 53–60) and who also assisted in the prosecution of the Orangemen involved in the Greenwich Village weavers' riot.

William MacNeven was the only Catholic member of the United Irish directorate and in New York became a professor of obstetrics and

Figure 11. William Sampson. *Booth's History of New York.* New York Public Library.

the chair of chemistry at the College of Physicians and Surgeons. So roundly respected was MacNeven that a prominent monument to him was erected (and still stands) in the northeast corner of Saint Paul's Chapel (Episcopal) churchyard on Broadway.

The number of United Irish refugees was substantial. Their political songs steeped in American and French revolutionary ideology were published in general interest songbooks of the period, such as *The New-York Remembrancer*, a songster printed in Albany, New York, in 1802, by John Barber for Daniel Steele, a bookbinder and stationer. It was self-described as "a collection of the newest and most admired songs, now extant." "Hibernia's Sons," sung to the well-known tune "The Girl I Left Behind Me," is one such song. Terry Moylan (2000, 8) traces its first publication to Belfast (1795) as "The Green Flag." It was also included in *Paddy's Resource*, a songster printed in Philadelphia the following year. Here, the author proclaims independence in the first verse, while he lays out the underlying reason (his indictment) in the second:

> HIBERNIA's sons, the patriot band,
> Claim their emancipation.
> Arous'd from sleep, they wish to be
> An Independent nation;
> United firm like men of sense,
> And truly patriotic.
> They vow they will not pay their pence,
> To any power despotic.
>
> She shame fac'd mis'ry at the door,
> Erin's peasant's starving;
> While landlords, absentees, and knaves
> In England waste each farthing;
> And thus their crimes our country stain.
> Vile robbers and oppressors,
> We hope that yet a time will come
> To punish such transgressors.
> ("Hibernia's Sons," *New-York Remembrancer* 1802)

The United Irish movement was founded in Belfast in October 1791, primarily by middle-class Presbyterians. A second center was established in Dublin a month later by roughly equal numbers of middle-class Protestants and Catholics and "a sprinkling of gentry and aristocracy" (Connolly 2002, 598). It drew its name from the concept that Irishmen of all religions should band together as citizens of a free state, retaining local control of their domestic affairs and granting universal suffrage to Catholic males. The third and final verse closes with a grand, international toast to like-minded fellows around the world: "Good will on earth, and peace to man / Throughout the whole creation." But by the time "Hibernia's Sons" was written and published, the Dublin branch had been suppressed and the United Irishmen had gone underground, becoming ever-more revolutionary. Now an *independent nation* is called for. That the song rejects the payment of taxes to "any power despotic" is reminiscent of the American colonial cry of "No Taxation without Representation." Indeed, the United Irish movement was greatly inspired by the American Revolution. Thus, the affinity between Irish émigrés and their American hosts *should* have been great.

By 1798, membership had reached an estimated 280,000 and the United Irishmen had forged a loose alliance with the Defenders, a Catholic secret society (Connolly 2002, 598). But the government struck preemptively, and the army thereafter dealt effectively with uncoordinated, sequential risings that occurred in various parts of Ireland, and British domination prevailed. Some United Irish leaders fled during the suppression, while others were captured and later exiled to the Continent. The Alien Act of 1798 put forward by the New York Federalist Rufus King, American minister to the United Kingdom, effectively barred United Irishmen from the United States (and imperiled the stay of those already there); but in the friendlier atmosphere that followed the election of Thomas Jefferson (1801–9), many sailed westward to New York, as did "Hibernia's Sons" and other songs bearing egalitarian ideals. Waiting to receive them and make use of their talent and vigor was the Republican Party.

"Erin Go Brah!" is a second United Irishmen song from the pages of *The New-York Remembrancer*. First published in 1792 as "The Exiled Irishman's Lamentation," it is credited to George Nugent

Reynolds, son of a County Leitrim landowner. The lyric's macaronic construction is proof of its cultured origin and also a marker of the presence of Irish Gaelic in New York. *"Erin mavorneen slan leat go brah!"* translates as "Ireland, my darling, goodbye forever!":

> Green were the fields where my forefathers dwelt, O!
> *"Erin mavorneen slan leat go brah!"*
> Though our farm it was small, yet comforts we felt, O!
> *"Erin mavorneen slan leat go brah!"*
> At length came the day when our lease did expire,
> And fain would I dwell where before dwelt my fire,
> But ah! well-a-day! I was forc'd to retire,
> *"Erin mavorneen slan leat go brah!"*
>
> Though all taxes I paid, yet no vote could I pass, O!
> *"Erin mavorneen slan leat go brah!"*
> Aggrandiz'd no great man–and I feel it alas, O!
> *"Erin mavorneen slan leat go brah!"*
>
> Forc'd from my home, yea, from where I was born,
> To range the wide world, poor helpless, forlorn,
> I look back with regret, and my heart strings are torn,
> *"Erin mavorneen slan leat go brah!"*

The complaints were common ones. The usurpation of property by colonial forces turned Catholic Irish people, who had once been property owners, into precariously placed renters, while their taxes supported a government that by statute provided them no say in its policies. The third verse casts the Irish as exiles forced from their homeland by religious, political, and economic oppression, a fixture in Irish history and psyche that would last even after national independence.

Far from the Shamrock Shore

In addition to the establishment of the city's first parish, the settlement of Catholic Irish in Manhattan required the founding of key functional institutions necessary for community interaction and support. These included social gathering places, a vehicle for the exchange of information, a social welfare apparatus, and organizations for group protection. Secular meeting points, a newspaper, benevolent societies, and cadres of neighborhood defenders were established to meet these needs.

Activity in the port of New York grew rapidly after the Napoleonic Wars. Much of the traffic consisted of incoming immigrants from Ireland, where the rural economy was collapsing in a changeover from tillage to grazing (Hirota 2017, 19–21). Many of these newcomers had no local connections and little money for necessities as they searched Manhattan for shelter and work. The Irish were consigned to menial labor both because they arrived "with few skills or resources compared to the native-born or to other immigrants" and because of prejudice (Kenny 2000, 61–62). The new, growing Catholic Irish community looked "inward as it crowded into the increasingly African and Irish tenements of the Sixth Ward. The efforts of Sampson, Emmet [and] MacNeven . . . to maintain the tolerant ideals of 1798 met with growing indifference among the recent arrivals" (Walsh 1996, 61). As the two groups began to part their ways, republicanism increasingly meant separatism for Irish Catholics, while Irish Protestants began using new terms of identity, distancing themselves from their Romanist countrymen by signaling that to be labeled *Irish* was a drawback.

In 1806, an estimated ten thousand Catholics lived in New York City (Pomerantz 1938, 385), roughly one-eighth of the population; by 1818, the estimated number had grown to sixteen thousand, most of them Irish (Rosenwaike 1972, 18). This influx represented the largest migration of non-British whites to reach New York since the English seizure in 1664. The arrival of so many foreign-born, non-Protestant, and often foreign-speaking outsiders was the cause of considerable alarm. To many New Yorkers—especially members of congregations that chose their own ministers—the influx of Catholics was contrary to the flow of the times, for, in line with the ideals that propelled the revolution, domestic and democratic, rather than foreign and hierarchical, religions were preferred.

Changeover in a heavily urbanized place inherently raises issues of territory. Resident American workers now watched as Irish immigrants crowded into the city's plebeian quarters, bringing competition for housing and pressuring wages downward (Ernst 1965, 103–4). In nineteenth-century New York, ethnicity and religion were primary boundary makers of the working-class cityscape. Catholic Irish tended to live together for safety in enclaves and were the foremost group in the Sixth Ward from the 1820s at least until the 1880s (Stott 1990, 204). For unskilled Irish workers, the obvious plan for success in America was to elevate from the chancy status of day laborers and secure better paying positions, but the route was both regulated by the city and jealously guarded by American Protestants, who already held those jobs. Skilled workers faced a somewhat different challenge: mechanization and changeover from craft to factory production. The Irish and their native-born competitors were stymied both above and below, and friction was inevitable.

Neither working-class Catholics nor Protestants shrank from the sectarian violence that attended their occupational and cultural collision. Both sides, fitted with set frames of reference fashioned in their ancestral homelands, were proud to wear their identities and take up weapons on holidays that held special significance. Paul Gilje (1987, 129) writes, "The first serious and violent battle in New York City between the Irish and Americans occurred on the [official] celebration of Saint Patrick's Day, March 18, 1799. The year was significant. Not only had there just been a rebellion in Ireland, supported by the French, but also the Federalists were riding high on a wave of popularity that included an appeal to nativist sentiment." The cause of the riot was a reinterpretation and extension of Pope Day parading: "On St. Patrick's Day they paraded the streets with effigies called Paddies. The practice was intended as a deliberate insult to the Irish because a Paddy was a mock image of Saint Patrick, usually stuffed with straw and made to look ridiculous. In 1799, when the Paddy procession marched along Harmon Street, a rough area near the East River docks, indignant Irishmen attacked it. The ensuing fight resulted in the death of one man and the arrest of several others" (Gilje 1987, 129).

On Christmas Eve 1806, the ire of Saint Peter's Hibernians rose when some fifty members of an anti-Catholic, anti-Irish, Protestant group called Highbinders demonstrated loudly outside the church (Walsh 1996, 52), chilling the congregation when the front doors of the building were forced open. In early national New York, Catholic Irish of all classes tended to live close together in the vicinity of Saint Peter's. Because the town was still compact, the enclave abutted with — even mixed into — working-class areas inhabited by Anglo- and Irish Protestants. The following night, an all-out battle "exhibiting a ferocity unknown in most riots of the previous century" (Gilje 1987, 131) occurred in the neighborhood when the Highbinders came face-to-face with a Catholic group that assembled in defense. Fighting ended only after Mayor DeWitt Clinton arrived with reinforcements (Ryan 1935, 86–87). By that time, a watchman was already dead, likely victim of a historical legacy brought from Ireland that viewed the constabulary as agents of official oppression, rather than as neutrals dedicated to peacekeeping.

The refusal of the Catholic Irish working class to "back down" in the face of Protestant pressure brought about the transference of other violent Old World rituals to the New. Internecine violence between orange and green flared in Greenwich Village on 12 July 1824, the day Protestant Irish Loyalists celebrate the victory of William III (the Duke of Orange) at the Battle of the Boyne over his father-in-law, James II, the last Catholic British monarch. In the Orange tradition, the main event of the day's festivities has been a parade organized around the march of a fife and drum band and an associated Orange lodge. Bonding the Protestant Loyalist community, the celebration holds a mythic character that has long been used for the demonstration of dominance. The parade itself has not been the focal point of Catholic complaint so much as the route of the procession, which purposefully passes through majority Catholic areas, and the themes conveyed in the titles of tunes played. Many, including "Croppies Lie Down" and "Daniel O'Connell in Purgatory," are also songs with explicit texts. If this were not sufficiently oppressive, the instrumental composition of the band includes a huge, rib-rattling lambeg drum, making the insult not only loudly heard but deeply felt.

In Greenwich Village on Boyne Day 1824, a group of Catholic weavers were "woken by the sound of gunfire and music and looked out on a sight they thought they had left behind in their native land," as a fifer sounded the incendiary, angst-instilling melody of "The Boyne Water" through his instrument (Walsh 2004–6, 3). By midmorning, makeshift green and orange flags hung from the upper windows of opposing taverns at the intersection of Sixth Avenue, Amity (present-day West Fourth), and Cornelia Streets (Walsh 2007, 3). Following verbal abuse from both sides, a vicious melee erupted. Separately, four Protestant and five Catholic rioters were later tried and given lenient sentences as an enticement to conform to the standards of their new American environment; however, the desired result was not achieved. In April 1825, transplanted Irish sectarian violence revisited Manhattan, and many rioters were brought before the same judge, who reminded them that they had religious freedom in America and admonished them not to introduce "the riot, the outrage and violence so long practiced in your native land . . . [for it would lay] the foundations for the form of government which you have fled" (Walsh 2007, 14–15).

The weavers' riot replayed a long-standing Irish form of religious warfare known in certain localities as the "party fight." Georges Denis Zimmermann (2002, 19) writes, "In some parts of Ulster, Protestant and Catholic tenants were mingled and contended for the land. . . . At the end of the eighteenth century the Catholic 'Defenders' were opposed to the Protestant 'Peep o' Day Boys' or 'Orangemen.'" "The Lamentation of James O'Sullivan" (Zimmerman 2002, 196–97), a broadside ballad printed in Ireland circa 1830, describes from the Catholic perspective the type of event that inspired the one that took place in Manhattan:

> July the 12th at Stewartstown, most awful to relate,
> The Orangemen assembled their vile deeds to complete;
> Our holy altars to abuse, our chapels to destroy,
> Those tyrants they collected round Cookstown and the Moy.
>
> Our bold undaunted Catholics they quickly did attend,
> Likewise their holy pastor, his altar to defend,
> Although their numbers were but small, those heroes of renown
> Left twenty-two of that vile crew a-bleeding on the ground.

In Greenwich Village, just as in Stewartstown, County Tyrone, it was Orangemen who created the altercation by publicly goading the Catholic weavers. When the presiding judge chose to frame the situation in an Irish rather than American context—meaning that Irishmen were fighting because it was instinctive behavior—the result was worse for the Catholic side, ultimately because Orangemen could adopt American Protestant identity and join the ranks of nativist organizations. This left the still "foreign" greens alone to bear the reputation of being hot-tempered *Irish* scrappers.

As immigration grew and literacy increased, the newspaper became a tangible sign of Irish community settlement in Manhattan. The *Shamrock or Hibernian Chronicle*, the first Irish newspaper in the nation, appeared on 15 December 1810 (O'Connor 1989, 4). It was aimed primarily at the middle class, with editorial content, such as espousal of Catholic emancipation and condemnation of Orange sectarian activities, generally acceptable to most Catholic and Protestant immigrants. It also ran an "intelligence office that farmed out agricultural laborers," hoping to steer rural Irish people clear of New York's urban evils (Gilje 1996, 73). The *Shamrock* survived for a little more than six and a half years—actually, a good run at that time—before falling victim to an overly optimistic business plan and considerable economic change over a short period of time. The War of 1812 began less than eighteen months after the *Shamrock* opened, and the Treaty of Ghent was not signed until early 1815. During that period, commerce fell precipitously and a recession set in, damaging the merchant class, the *Shamrock's* prime market. Though the economy of the city and country rebounded after the close of the Napoleonic Wars, the newspaper had racked up significant debt, owing to cancelled subscriptions and a dearth of advertising (O'Connor 1989, 4). It closed in 1817, even though a period of great economic expansion was already underway.

That same year, two risky but wildly successful initiatives were undertaken, and the initial advantage they brought secured the future of the City of New York for at least two centuries: one was the formation of the Black Ball Line operating between New York and Liverpool, the first scheduled transatlantic shipping company; the second was the passage of the Erie Canal Bill, which destined New York to become the prime change-of-gauge point for European and American cargoes crossing the Atlantic. Canal boats, as well as coastal craft, soon exchanged freight with deepwater ships tied up at Manhattan's docks, and more accurate delivery estimates could be calculated. By 1825, the combined Hudson-Erie water route connected the Atlantic Ocean to the Great Lakes (fig. 12); thus, even while New York grew dramatically as a destination market, its own extended markets expanded vastly in number, size, and geographic spread. The timing was life-saving for some Irish, for as farming changed from crops to livestock and the cash value of agricultural exports to Britain declined, employment was being expanded in rapidly growing New York, benefiting Ireland's excess labor. In the main, it was Irishmen who moved cargoes and material, dug ditches, and demolished and built structures. Women catered to the needs of a burgeoning population of residents and visitors by taking in boarders, serving in hotels and homes, washing laundry, and, at the lowest level, working as prostitutes. This subsistence-level employment was obtained principally at the expense of African Americans (Kenny 2000, 62–63), because the destitute Irish had no choice but to work for lower pay.

Large numbers of immigrant Irish moved through Manhattan on the way north to construct the Erie Canal (Sheriff 1996, 36–37). While it cannot be definitively ascertained what waterway the song "Paddy

Figure 12. Phillip Meeder, *DeWitt Clinton* (mingling the waters of Lake Erie with the Atlantic, 4 November 1825). Wood engraving. New York Public Library.

on the Canal" praises (Wyld 1962, 80), DeWitt Clinton's "Big Ditch" was America's earliest grand example of the artificial river; and, because the construction cost of its 363 miles was completely paid off just ten years after completion, it remains one of the most astounding construction projects ever attempted in United States history:

> When I came to this wonderful rampire, it filled me with the greatest surprise,
> To see such a great undertaking, on the like I never opened my eye.
> To see full a thousand brave fellows at work among mountains so ta[ll],
> To dig through the vallies so level, through rocks for to cut a canal.
>
> I entered with them for a season, my monthly pay for to draw,
> And being in very good humor, I often sang Erin Go Bragh.
> Our provision it was very plenty, to complain we'd no reason at all
> I had money in every pocket, while working upon the canal.
>
> I learned for to be very handy, to use both the shovel and spade,
> I learnt the whole art of canalling, I think it an excellent trade.
> I learned to be very handy, although I was not very tall,
> I could handle the sprig of shillelah, with the best man on the canal.
>
> I being an entire stranger, be sure I had not much to say,
> The Boss he came round in a hurry, says, boys, it is grog time a-day.
> We all marched up in good order, he was father now unto us all,
> Sure I wished myself from that moment to be working upon the canal.
>
> (NYSL Broadside Ballads, SCO BD 971)

The mammoth scope of canal construction is duly recognized in the first stanza. However, certain successive images conflict with period and modern representations of the canallers' daily lives, in that they gloss over the rough living conditions in outdoor camps, which included infectious disease and the daily grind of backbreaking physical work (Sheriff 1996, 36–38, 42, 44). Some are tongue-in-cheek—the "sprig of shillelah" refers to the head-cracking cudgel sometimes wielded in frequent fights and occasional riots along the route with fellow diggers and nearby townsfolk (Sheriff 1996, 39–41). References to systematic on-the-job drinking are also humorous—but such behavior was part of a self-destructive existence that often marked laborers for life and tarnished the group image among outsiders (Kenny 2000, 63–65; Sheriff 1996, 37). Though the canal-era immigrant surge was smaller in absolute numbers than the massive wave of 1845–52, it was nevertheless proportionally very large. Canal laborers, if they didn't squander their earnings, often settled along the route when they found an appealing and accepting locale. This somewhat ameliorated overcrowding in the Empire City and allowed upstate Irish votes to augment those of the metropolis on issues that were decided at the New York State level. But, most importantly, the Erie Canal gave New York City the initial advantage to make it America's preeminent city to this day.

By the time New York's second Irish newspaper, the *Truth Teller*, opened in April 1825, the Erie Canal was partially open and nearly finished, and it could only be successful. A clear sign that the composition and image of New York City's Irish community had changed, the *Truth Teller* was devoutly Catholic, deeply opposed to British government policies in Ireland, and passionately Irish, even though its principal owners were radical English Catholics. The *Truth Teller* was a literate broadsheet, giving some credence to the observation that many Irish residents in the 1830s were still "generally of the better class—of petty manufacturers crushed out by the factory system and sturdy small farmers exterminated by the economically more efficient enclosure system" (Purcell 1938, 583). Overall, the *Truth Teller* sought more to edify than merely recount or entertain, meaning there was a deliberate character to many articles. The poem "Ireland" was published in the 14 April 1827 issue (vol. 3, no. 15) and attributed to a young, female high school student:

Beyond the wide Atlantic; robed in light,
A little island greets the voyager's sight,
Renowned, in ancient days, for heroes brave,
And still renowned for many a hallowed grave,
Luxuriant Plenty clothes the smiling fields,

And Ceres there her richest bounty yields.
Her sons by the productive soil maintained,
Have long to hardy industry been trained:
Her temperate climate no sudden changes knows,
No summer's heat intense, nor winter's snows.

Bereft of Liberty, of all that's blest,
The unhappy native seeks in vain for rest:
Still, in his youth, he bids a hope remain,
That he may yet his Liberty regain;
Boldly he dares the rivalry of strife,
And to his country dedicates his life,
But when old age steals on his withered frame,
And he beholds his country's lasting shame,
He drops a tear upon his trembling hand,
And seeks a refuge in a foreign land.

Rise sons of Erin, in your country's cause,
And free yourself from England's cruel laws!
Rise! And restore the land that gave you birth,
To the proud rank among the realms of earth!
Join, and regain, in one united band,
The long lost rights of your much injured land,
Nor let relentless England's stern decree
Repress again your efforts to be free.
Think on the ancient glory of your land,
To rouse each throbbing soul and nerve each hand!
Let Emmet's sacred shade your hearts inspire,
And warm you with his patriotic fire!
Then shall your tedious days of slavery end,
And Peace again her olive wand extend;
Then shall your land acquire again the fame
She boasted, long ere England knew her name!

Clearly, the ode is more polemic than poetic. The tenor rises
abruptly from the idyllic (if not fully accurate) images of the first verse
to a scene of foreign domination countered by ardent yet unsuccessful

resistance in the second stanza, an obvious reference to the 1798 Rebellion. The Irish common man, who forcefully resisted oppression in 1798, is now weakened by strain and age and is in exile. His once-respected country is not just enslaved but also humiliated. The third verse demands concerted action, and the lines "To rouse each throbbing soul and nerve each hand! / Let Emmet's sacred shade your hearts inspire, / And warm you with his patriotic fire!" proclaim that action should come in forceful revolt. The combative conclusion of "Ireland" is especially noteworthy, because it fails to mention the successful and peaceful political agitation simultaneously being carried on in Ireland by Daniel O'Connell's Catholic Association. Perhaps the zealous and righteous *Truth Teller* hoped to point out that the Catholic emancipation movement had within its quiver arrows that were both blunt and sharp and that the latter might be used if the former failed, making one wonder whether or to what extent the schoolgirl's lines might have been revised between her first draft and the poem's publication—and, if so, by whom. Correcting students' work is, after all, a primary function of teachers, just as newspaper editors often frame content to influence community opinion. The image of a youthful representative of an exiled, oppressed national group—indeed a young lady enthusiastically urging revolutionary force—makes for inspiring romantic nationalist copy.

The *Truth Teller* supported O'Connell at that time. Two years earlier in 1825, the "Liberator" had democratized the Catholic Association when he offered the laboring-class associate membership at the price of one shilling a year, a sum that could be paid in fifty-two weekly installments of a farthing. A vast multitude of farthings produced the torrent of cash needed to expand the campaign and, as McCaffrey (1997, 40) writes, had even more far-reaching consequences: "In Sunday sermons, priests blessed Emancipation as holy and patriotic, and tenant farmers and urban workers flocked to the Association," with the result that, "in agitating for Catholic Emancipation, people found identity and dignity and hope for the future, liberating them from pessimism and despair, the marks of a slave mentality." The New York Irish, however, "were slow in rallying financial support for the Catholic Association" and by the close of 1828 had raised only two thousand dollars for O'Connell's cause (Moriarty 1980, 359). It was then that The New York Friends of Ireland made the remarkable decision to broaden their fundraising approach by reaching out to the "liberal portion of the Protestant clergy" to solicit donations from their congregations (*TT,* 13 December 1828). This move caught the eye of the mainstream press, with reportage divided along party lines. The Whig *New York Morning Herald* opposed introducing the Catholic question into American politics, while the Democratic *New York Enquirer* approved of the charity and attacked the *Morning Herald*'s stance (Moriarty 1980, 362). The Friends of Ireland appeal worked well: "A Baptist minister and a Presbyterian clergyman attended the 1829 Saint Patrick's Day dinner of the New York Friends of Ireland, and the Presbyterian, Reverend Dr. M'Leod, offered a prayer of thanksgiving. Dr. Henry Hobart, Episcopal Bishop of New York, apologized by letter for his absence, endorsed civil and religious liberty, and prayed that Ireland's 'long course of suffering and trial' might end. The meeting also received a communication from a Reverend Dr. Broadhead of the Dutch Reformed Church supporting civil and religious liberty for Ireland" (Moriarty 1980, 364).

That representatives from four of Manhattan's principal religious groups supported political rights for Catholics *in Ireland* shows it was considered a responsible position for many in New York's middle and upper classes. It did, after all, contain the assumption that more Irish would stay at home—and fewer would emigrate. While intensely Irish institutions—newspapers like the *Truth Teller* and membership organizations such as the Hibernian Universal Benevolent Society—strengthened the Irish community, they did, however, also risk delaying Irish integration into the broader American society.

Songs and Social Gathering Places

The songs and secular gathering places of the Manhattan Irish show the community was not just a single stratum of poorly educated, superstitious country people but a multilayered mix that included the accomplished, middling, and deprived; Catholics, Anglicans, and Dissenters; urbanites and country people; and offspring of numerous ancestries. In winter 1783, the Friendly Sons of St. Patrick in the City of

New York, a fraternal lodge, was founded "for the relief of indigent natives of Ireland and their descendants" (Murphy and Mannion 1962, 69–70). Its first public meeting, held 17 March 1784 at Cape's Tavern, followed the British evacuation by only four months. Membership in the Saint Patrick's Society was restricted to "descendants of Irish parents by either side in the first degree, and the descendants of every member *ad infinitum*" (74).

No religious test for admission was applied, and "from the beginning Protestants of various sects mingled harmoniously with Catholics and Quakers," not the least because religious and political discussion and other discordant conversation was proscribed at meetings (Murphy and Mannion 1962, 75). The governor and mayor were both members of the Friendly Sons, assuring it was an organization of social and political importance. Records of the first fifty years have been lost, but society president William Constable left notes from the 1789 Saint Patrick's Day proceedings, showing those seated at his table included General Henry Knox (commander of the Continental artillery during the revolution) and the philosophically opposed politicians George Clinton and John Jay. In a display of fealty, the first toast offered was not to Saint Patrick but to General George Washington (156–57), who was shortly to be inaugurated in New York as the nation's first president under the Constitution. Even though membership was "almost solidly Protestant at this time," significant toasts were offered to "the Assertors and Supporters of Irish Catholics" (seventh) and "the Mother of All Saints" (seventeenth). Additionally, the Friendly Sons soon became the staunch supporters of Catholic emancipation in Ireland.

Music held an important place at Friendly Sons functions:

> Among the pieces usually played during the dinners of the Society were "St. Patrick's Day in the Morning," "Garryowen," "The Sprig of Shellelah," "Cushla Machree," "Savourneen Deelish," "Erin the Tear and Smile in Thine Eyes," "Yankee Doodle," "The President's March" [and] "Hail Columbia". . . . As the national joyousness of the Irish has ever been expressed in song, vocal music also had its place, and among the songs which entertained the diners were such as "The Marsellaise," "Auld Lang Syne," "O Breathe Not His

Name," "The Harp that Once," "Oh the Shamrock," and others calculated to arouse the Irish spirit. (Murphy and Mannion 1960, 172)

From other reports, it can be gleaned that the number of non-Irish guests present at the society's annual dinners was considerable and included the presidents of the Saint Andrew's and Saint George's Societies and the British Consul (Murphy and Mannion 1960, 172). This influenced the highly inclusionary nature of the musical selections performed, which were chosen for their appropriateness at banquets and were not necessarily pieces Friendly Sons' members might have sung or listened to in less formal settings or at home.

Going forward in time, the issue of Irish sovereignty could prove awkward at pan-Irish meetings, for Irish nationalist aspirations were often expressed in song. One such problematic song lyric in circulation during the prefamine era, "The Soldier of Erin," illustrates the point. Included in *The American Comic Songster* (1834, 69–70), printed in New York, it presents Ireland as a constituent unit in the United Kingdom. Oddly reminiscent of "Patrick's Hearty Invitation to His Countrymen," it proposes loyalty to the British monarch as an integral characteristic of the Irish persona:

> Oh an Irishman's heart is as stout as a shillelagh,
> It beats with delight to chase sorrow and wo,
> When the piper lilts up, then it dances so gaily,
> And thumps with a whack, for to lather the foe.
> But by beauty lit up—faith less than a jiffy,
> So warm is the stuff, it soon blazes and burns,
> Then so wild is each heart, of us lads of the Liffy,
> It thumps, dances and beats altogether by turns;
> Then away with dull care, let's be merry and frisky,
> Our motto is this, let it widely extend,
> Give poor Pat but his freedom, his sweetheart and whisky,
> And he'll die for old Ireland, his king, and his friend.

This simplistic view ignored the existence of conflicting loyalties (Republican Catholics versus Loyalist Protestants), an awkward situation that despite high United Irishmen ideals demanded a reinterpretation of Irishness in Manhattan. The histories of the two groups being incompatible, and their future prospects dissimilar, the most viable option was to construct new ethnic identities to delineate the Protestant Irish. As more poor Catholics arrived in New York, divided loyalties eventually urged Irish Protestants to rebrand themselves "Scotch Irish," "British," or simply "American." By 1820, "Irish" largely meant *Catholic* Irish (Rodgers 2009, 37–38).

Songs of the influential Irish poet and arranger Thomas Moore (1779–1852) were very popular in New York among a wide audience that included many Americans of British extraction. This was in large part because America had not yet fashioned its own, distinct popular music and because Moore had risen to great fame in London. His masterwork, *Moore's Melodies* (1808–34), included lyrics both sentimental ("The Last Rose of Summer") and militant ("The Harp That Once through Tara's Halls" and "The Minstrel Boy"), pieces that are national rather than traditional songs but that do draw on Irish folklore and history, and were often set to old airs.

"The Boys of Kilkenny" was a popular song of the era, which has been associated with, but never been proved to be composed by, Moore. One of a large genre of geographically based Irish tribute songs that typically praise the attributes of stout-hearted boys, comely girls, stately livestock, and defining landscape, "The Boys of Kilkenny" was sung in pre–Great Famine New York, appearing in *The Book of a Thousand Songs* (1843). It was earlier published in Edinburgh (1820) and Philadelphia (1839). Only part of its curious history can be fully ascertained. The song is best considered in three sections: (1) verses 1, 2, and 3:

Oh, the boys of Kilkenny are stout roving blades.
And if ever they meet with the nice little maids.
They kiss them and coax them, they spend their money free.
Oh! of all towns in Ireland, Kilkenny for me. [repeat]

Through the town of Kilkenny there runs a clear stream;
In the town of Kilkenny there lives a pretty dame,
Her cheeks like the roses, her lips much the same,
Like a dish of ripe strawberries smothered in cream. [repeat]

Her eyes are as black as Kilkenny's famed coal,
And 'tis they through my boson burned a big hole;
Her mind, like its waters, is as deep, clear and pure;
But her heart is more hard than its marble, I'm sure. [repeat]

(2) verse 4:

Oh! Kilkenny's a fine town, that shines where it stands,
And the more I think on it, the more my heart warms;
For if I was in Kilkenny, I'd think my self at home,
For 'tis there I have sweethearts, but here I get none. [repeat]
                                              (Croker 1839, 209)

(3) and verse 5:

I'll build my love a castle on Kilkenny's free ground
Neither lords, dukes nor squires shall ever pull it down
And if any one should ask you to tell him my name,
I am an Irish exile and from Kilkenny I came.
                                              (LC, amss.as101550)

Thomas Crofton Croker, a much-published Irish amateur historian and folklorist, originally believed the first three verses were "written for and sung on the Kilkenny stage" between 1802 and 1804 by Thomas Moore. But Croker (1839, 206–9) later retracted that claim on "good authority" without citing a source, which might have been Moore himself, as the two were contemporaries and simultaneously residents of London. Croker, however, did not specifically withdraw his theory regarding the place and era of composition. The core first three verses do not vary greatly in print. They are sometimes found alone, but texts containing verses 1 through 4 appear more often. Croker (206) suggested the fourth verse was "probably an adjunct by Moore when he sang 'The Boys of Kilkenny' in England." The last line of verse 4 is sometimes sung as, "For it's now I'm in London and friends I have none," which may support Croker's speculation. The fifth stanza, however, appears only in America. John Andrews, the

Chatham Street broadside printer, published it on a song sheet some-time between 1853 and 1859. The emergence of an additional verse in far-off Manhattan begs the question whether "The Boys of Kilkenny" was a true folk song just then surfacing from the underworld of oral tradition or a composed popular song that through adaptation was being subsumed into the free-and-easy atmosphere of folk culture.

Either scenario is possible, but the following considerations bol-ster the popular song option. First, in the practical eyes of a printer who had a fixed space to fill within the center of the broadside, five verses fit better than four within the song sheet's ornamental border. Second, in the mind of a potential customer, added allure or extra value might be perceived with the inclusion of a longer and seemingly more complete text. Third, the fifth verse is not intrinsic to the lyric—actually, it is not even unique to the song. A very similar stanza is also part of a folk lyric communicated to collector Sam Henry in 1930s Ireland:

I'll build my love a castle at the head of the town,
Where neither lord, duke or earl will e'er pull it down,
And if anyone asks you where you are from,
You can tell them you're a stranger from the County Tyrone.
(Huntington and Hermann 1990, 345–46)

An admittedly speculative reconstruction of the history of "The Boys of Kilkenny" would then be: verses 1, 2, and 3 were either newly composed or adapted from a traditional source, possibly in Kilkenny; verse 4 was written away from Kilkenny, possibly by the lyricist-singer Thomas Moore; and verse 5 was likely a floating component found in other Irish songs, possibly in America. Finally, because of its associ-ation with an immensely popular performer *and* its possible roots in tradition, "The Boys of Kilkenny" may have been sung by upper- and middle-class members of the Friendly Sons of St. Patrick *and* by working-class Irish immigrants in Lower Manhattan.

While middle- and upper-class Irish convened at Cape's, the lower classes gathered in New York's early Irish "groceries," small shops that were modeled on and were emigrant extensions of the shebeens (infor-mal bars) of Ireland. Groceries were central places that functioned as general stores and also served liquor, the primary source of profit.

Many were likewise "arenas of entertainment and conviviality" that offered music and dancing at night (Gilje 1996, 76–77). Humorous, political, sporting, drinking, sentimental, and love songs, along with elegies and old ballads, were among the "party pieces" regularly sung in such gathering places. The grocery was a secular counterpart of Saint Peter's, and its proprietor was regarded with a worldly reverence, not the least because he "often dispensed credit and may have even helped some individuals find a job" (Gilje 1996, 77). Looking ahead to the heyday of Tammany Hall, drinking establishments as well as churches took on great importance with profound social and political implications (Meagher 2005, 88). Another factor contributing to the significance of the grocery within the community was that owner and customer spoke the same language, literally and figuratively. In 1800, half the population of Ireland spoke Irish (Ó Tuathaigh 1990, 157–58). As immigration into New York increased during the nineteenth century, arriving Irish were more rural, more Catholic, and more likely to be Irish speaking. Moreover, when they spoke English, they did so with a heavy brogue, and their conversation pattern bore evidence of what Ó Tuathaigh (1990, 66) calls a "rich and vital oral tradition," suggesting a purchase transaction was likely to be unhurried because the ritualistic verbal interchange carried nearly as much importance as the physical and commercial transaction. Irish grocers understood this relaxed process, while non-Irish New York merchants probably had little patience for it. Even in the early nineteenth century, time meant money in Manhattan.

Immigration songs contained elements easily recognizable and hugely important to all who attended sessions in Irish groceries. Typically, they were embedded with the pain of parting; the adventure and travail of the ocean crossing; the uncertainty and readjustment inherent in settling in a foreign environment; and a deep, lasting longing for people, places, and moments never to be experienced again. Such songs might also inform on certain logistical aspects of the voyage. There is no real way to gauge how many Irish immigration songs were composed, for they mainly existed orally. Robert L. Wright's *Irish Emigrant Ballads and Songs* (1975) contains six hundred pages of overwhelmingly English-language texts, and that is still certainly only a portion, for relatively few traditional pieces were ever set down on paper. Few immigration songs have ever had their full provenance determined because they were created for and belonged to the community as a whole. Nonexistent or patchy paper trails are intrinsic characteristics of the traditional song genre and are accepted by folk song researchers, who are willing to draw temporary inferences from partial information in hopes of uncovering greater detail at a later date. Song researcher Roy Palmer (1996, 2–4) believes mainstream historians, document driven by training, typically see the indefinite nature of traditional song as too tenuous to serve in an evidentiary capacity.

"The Shamrock Shore" (McBride 1988, 136), an emigrant passage song composed about 1825 (Huntington and Herrmann 1990, 101; Moulden 1994, 26) and still sung traditionally on the Inishowen Peninsula of County Donegal, is an example of folk song's often puzzling nature:

> From Londonderry we have set sail it being on the eight day of May,
> Between nine and ten next morning we arrived at Moville Bay.
> Fresh water we had twenty tons for passengers in store,
> Lest we might run short going to New York, far from the Shamrock Shore.

Its second verse mixes the love of homeplace—the city of Derry/Londonderry is referred to in feminine form as though it were a sweetheart—and resolve in starting off for a new land, a monumental adventure:

> When we had taken the last fond look of Derry's ancient town,
> Let misfortune never light on us nor pull our courage down.
> She's the grand female of my heart, she's the girl I do adore,
> May the angels bright shed soft light, around the Shamrock Shore.

Though severe infectious diseases could appear shipboard, this vessel and its passengers are spared and further blessed with a caring first mate, who sees them through their first traumatic bout of seasickness. His kindness is remembered with resounding toasts before a final "*deoch an dorais*" (drink for the door) once the ship has landed in New York:

When we were lying all sea-sick not a passenger was clear,
Quite helpless in our bunks we lay with no one to ease our pain.
Neither father kind or mother dear to lift our heads when sore,
And the sun going down between sea and sky, far from the Shamrock Shore.

Here's a health to Mr. Rifle that was our chief mate's name
When we were lying all sea-sick 'twas him that eased our pain.
We will drink his health full flowing glass and we'll toast him four times four
And it's *deoch an dorais* we will drink "Here's a health to the Shamrock Shore."

Despite headwinds encountered sailing into the prevailing westerlies, the transatlantic journey is made in good time. The emigrants are now landed immigrants. Some may have been neighbors in Ireland, others are new friends, bonded by the rigors and enormous scale of their voyage and the shared excitement and uncertainty of a new life in America:

It's now we're safely landed in four and twenty days,
We take our comrades by the hand and we'll go different ways.
We take our comrades by the hand in hopes to meet once more,
And I hope we'll meet our loving friends all around the Shamrock Shore.

(McBride 1988, 136–37)

A word is missing in the last line ("our loving friends *from* all around the Shamrock Shore"), indicating the travelers hoped to settle in the United States among other Irish immigrants.

Nothing at all is known of the song's provenance before 1827 (Huntington and Herrmann 1990, 101), most importantly the circumstances of its composition. One might logically expect it to have been written in America and sent home to Ireland in a letter, but the words could just as easily have been versified by a returned emigrant or composed by an armchair traveler who had heard emigration narratives.

To folk poets, firsthand experience of an event is not a necessary requirement. In a July 2012 conversation, contemporary Irish American ballad maker Jon Campbell succinctly assessed his role in narrative song creation by saying, "I don't make up the stories; I just make them rhyme." There is no written record of "The Shamrock Shore" having been sung in New York City, where popular culture eclipsed traditional folkways early on, but that fact is typical rather than extraordinary. The reason is that traditional immigration songs are "affidavits" of working-class culture that travel without written documentation. However, their great importance comes in presenting period commentary from otherwise unheard voices. That they cannot always be pinned to a particular place or exact time is unfortunate—even frustrating—but does not necessarily render them inadmissible.

The powerful narrative "Johnny Doyle," which tells the story of the foiled elopement of a wealthy landowner's daughter and a man of lesser standing, is an example of a traditional ballad that was unquestionably performed in New York groceries. Possessing great staying power, it is still heard in similar locations in Ireland today. "Johnny Doyle" is typical of its type, existing in an environment where ample time was available to tell longer stories and where commercial "hooks" were not required to retain the attention of listeners. "Johnny Doyle" existed in oral circulation well before its first known printing on an 1858 ballad sheet at the Poet's Box in Glasgow, where it is described as "a very old Irish ballad." Sometime between 1861 and 1864, two New York City broadside publishers, Henry De Marsan and James Wrigley, printed identical texts of a different variant of "Johnny Doyle." While the Glasgow and New York versions have many similarities, they also have important differences. The Manhattan one appears to be an edited rewrite of a traditional text—and not one particularly well done, for it possesses an awkward wordiness antithetic to the typically distilled, yet often fluid, traditional ballad.

The most significant difference between the Glasgow and New York versions is the issue of religion. In both texts, the young lovers are separated by wealth, class, and an arranged betrothal, but while religious difference is a factor in the Glasgow version, the New York lyric makes no sectarian distinction. The absence of a religious reference in the De Marsan–Wrigley text suggests the possibility that

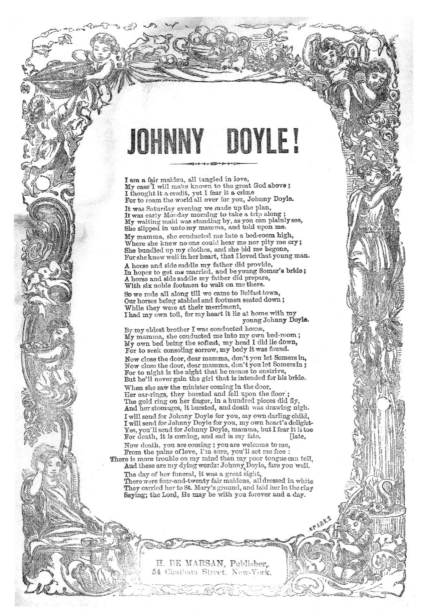

JOHNNY DOYLE!

I am a fair maiden, all tangled in love,
My case I will make known to the great God above ;
I thought it a credit, yet I fear it a crime
For to roam the world all over for you, Johnny Doyle.

It was Saturday evening we made up the plan,
It was early Monday morning to take a trip along ;
My waiting maid was standing by, as you can plainly see,
She slipped in unto my mamma, and told upon me.

My mamma, she conducted me into a bed-room high,
Where she knew no one could hear me nor pity me cry ;
She bundled up my clothes, and she bid me begone,
For she knew well in her heart, that I loved that young man.

A horse and side saddle my father did provide,
In hopes to get me married, and be young Somer's bride ;
A horse and side saddle my father did prepare,
With six noble footmen to wait on me there.

So we rode all along till we came to Belfast town,
Our horses being stabled and footmen seated down ;
While they were at their merriment,
I had my own toil, for my heart it lie at home with my
                                    young Johnny Doyle.

By my eldest brother I was conducted home,
My mamma, she conducted me into my own bed-room ;
My own bed being the softest, my head I did lie down,
For to seek consoling sorrow, my body it was found.

Now close the door, dear mamma, don't you let Somers in,
Now close the door, dear mamma, don't you let Somers in ;
For to night is the night that he means to enstrive,
But he'll never gain the girl that is intended for his bride.

When she saw the minister coming in the door,
Her ear-rings, they bursted and fell upon the floor ;
The gold ring on her finger, in a hundred pieces did fly,
And her stomages, it bursted, and death was drawing nigh.

I will send for Johnny Doyle for you, my own darling child,
I will send for Johnny Doyle for you, my own heart's delight-
Yes, you'll send for Johnny Doyle, mamma, but I fear it is too
For death, it is coming, and sad is my fate.   [late,

Now death, you are coming ; you are welcome to me,
From the pains of love, I'm sure, you'll set me free :
There is more trouble on my mind than my poor tongue can tell,
And these are my dying words: Johnny Doyle, fare you well.

The day of her funeral, it was a great sight,
There were four-and-twenty fair maidens, all dressed in white
They carried her to St. Mary's ground, and laid her in the clay
Saying; the Lord, He may be with you forever and a day.

H. DE MARSAN, Publisher,
54 Chatham Street, New-York.

Figure 13. Johnny Doyle! Published by H. De Marsan. Collection of author.

subject was dropped from the narrative because creed was too controversial a topic for a general audience, especially within an entertainment context, while religious affiliation was integral to Irish culture and sounded a sympathetic chord with Catholic listeners.

Given the oral nature of folk song, it is appropriate to speculate on how a traditional version of "Johnny Doyle" would have sounded at a Manhattan grocery music session as traditional singers performed their signature songs for other community members in a "raw bar" atmosphere. Fortunately, such an approximation is possible. In the late nineteenth or early twentieth century, the mastersinger Hanford Hayes, an Irish-Scots Canadian lumberman born in 1867, learned "Johnny Doyle" from Irish immigrants. They were men who had a generation earlier entered into the forests of Maine in search of work and were of the same cut as those who patronized Manhattan groceries. A field recording of Hayes singing the ballad in 1940 is in the Flanders Ballad Collection at Middlebury College, Vermont (HHFBC_tapes _D06B). Hayes's pace is slow and serious, bearing no hint of stage drama. Notable in his vocal ornamentation are long glides, relics of a now-disappeared singing style. His telling of the story begins and closes with classic third-person ballad narration, but the actual tale is told through first-person statement and dialogue:

> Oh, don't you see the hawthorn that grows in yonder vale?
> Its snowy white blossoms are plain to be seen.
> I heard a fair maid in notes of [sad denial].
> She was deep-lie lamenting for her true love, Johnny Doyle.
>
> "Oh Johnny Doyle, O Johnny Doyle, you're the boy I love well;
> I love you far better than any tongue can tell.
> Yes, I do love you, Johnny, you're the boy that I adore
> It is all to my great grief, I cannot love you more."

The matter of religious difference is subtly put—the young woman's love for Johnny is so great that it supersedes sectarian difference—and the elopement plan is only hinted:

> "Whilst I go to meeting, my true love goes to Mass;
> If I could go along with you, I'd think it no task;

If I could go along with you, I'd think it no toil
This wide world to ramble with you, Johnny Doyle."

It is disclosed that an arranged wedding is to take place:

"My mother she confined me to a room that was high,
Where no one could hear me to pity my sad cries.
She threw me my clothing and bid me be gone;
It was sorely and sadly I did put them on.

"Five hundred pounds then my father did prepare
With horses and coaches that we might ride there;
Six mounted policemen to ride by my side—
It was all for to make me young Sandy Murray's bride.

"We rode along together till we came to the first town,
Our horses to refresh and ourselves to sit down;
While they had their pleasures, I had my toil—
My heart was on the ocean with you, Johnny Doyle."

A startling, perhaps supernatural, occurrence then transpires:

"The minister was the first man that entered the door;
My earrings they bursted, fell down to the floor;
In twenty four pieces my necklace it flew—
It was then, dearest Johnny, I thought upon you."

After the marriage, comes the wedding night:

"The wedding being over, we all returned home.
It was my own mother showed me to my room;
It was there upon my bedside I sat myself down;
It was sorely and sadly my body I found.

"Oh shut the door, dear mother and don't let Sandy in.
He never shall enjoy me though he calls me his own;
He never shall enjoy me though he calls me his wife,
For this very night dear mother, I intend to end my life."

"Oh, hold your tongue dear daughter, what is this that you say?
I will send for Johnny Doyle at the breaking of the day."
"Yes, you will send for Johnny Doyle, and you know it is too late,
For death is approaching, and sad is my fate."

As it is virtually inconceivable that any good might come from so coerced a marriage, the inescapable "died for love" ending takes place but without excessive drama. Still what follows is truly remarkable. There is no scolding moral that tells parents to let lovers choose their own partners. There is no allusion to suicide as a mortal sin. Instead, there is a slight, but even in its economy a complete, condemnation of an entire system encompassing wealth distribution, class rigidity, and religious prejudice, which is proclaimed through one simple two-letter word—*us*:

Oh wasn't it a sad and a melancholy sight
To see four-and-twenty fair maids all dressed up in white:
They carried her fair body and laid it in the clay.
May God have mercy on us, forever and today.

(Flanders 1963, 280–81)

The opposite of De Marsan's clumsy broadside, Hayes's text is on point and economical. Combined with his outstanding vocal performance, it makes for an emotionally thrilling experience, and surely one that could have been heard in a Manhattan grocery session. "Johnny Doyle" tells all who listen that an alien, ascendant society foreign to the lives of ordinary folk was responsible for the death through its preoccupation with avarice and the consolidation of power and its cynical regard for love. In that way, the ballad confirms peasant Catholic Irish community values at home and could do the same in a faraway, industrialized setting such as Manhattan, where a transported society was simultaneously attempting to find its path in strange surroundings while retaining the values of its birthplace. "Johnny Doyle" could be accepted by all in the grocery as a true democratic document. Though its content was an ocean apart from the commercially driven Manhattan that surrounded the community, the grocery performance space was patterned exactly after rural Ireland, where its participants were born. The New York urban experience was altering patrons' lives in a variety of ways, but in certain places in Lower Manhattan, laboring-class traditional modes of conversation, dancing, and singing remained largely unchanged.

Other songs that circulated in New York during the first decades of the nineteenth century display a wide range of origin, emotion, and experience. Divergence of source, approach, and effect is not surprising because some come directly from tradition, while others are composed popular songs not necessarily reflecting the beliefs of an ethnic group but of an individual hoping for some form of credit or financial compensation. Still more are creations fashioned for theatrical or concert performance and may be fantasies having little to do with either Ireland or America. So great was the continuing influence of British entertainment trends in postcolonial America that some "Irish" stage songs presented in Manhattan came directly from England and had little or no real connection to Ireland. Knobel (1986, 91) quotes a word picture of the stage Irishman provided by Maurice Bourgeois (1963):

> The stage Irishman . . . has an atrocious Irish brogue, perpetual jokes, blunders, and bulls in speaking, and never fails to utter, by way of Hibernian seasoning, some wild screech or oath of Gaelic origin at every third word. . . . His hair is of a fiery red: he is rosy-cheeked, massive, and whiskey-loving. His face is one of simian bestiality with an expression of diabolical archness written all over it. He wears a tall felt hat . . . with a cutty-clay pipe stuck in front, an open shirt collar, a three-caped coat, knee breeches, worsted stockings, and cockaded brogue shoes. In his right hand he brandishes a stout blackthorn or sprig of shillelagh and threatens to belabor therewith the daring person who will tread on the tail of his coat.

Irish-themed songs could be alternately sublime, silly, binding, shattering, insulting, sympathetic, capricious, quizzical, endearing, insulting, distant, ethereal, and stirring. Even genuine Irish pieces are products of different milieus—some were produced by the laboring or "lunch pail" class, some by middle-class or "lace curtain" Irish, and others are Orange tinged and at least mildly anti-Catholic. Considerable irony lies in the reality that the lyrics that best represent traditional Gaelic culture are the ones least likely to have been heard by the New York population at large, while the lyrics that were heard by many and contributed most to the stereotype of "Paddy"—the Catholic Irish everyman—were likely to have been created by lyricists unfamiliar or unsympathetic to Irish life.

Songs heard in musical theaters during this period often came from Britain and Ireland, where they had been circulated by "Irish character" performers. "Corporal Casey" is a comic antirecruiting song that appeared in *The Blackbird* of 1820, published by bookseller, bookbinder, and stationer Christian Brown of 290 Water Street, New York City. The 140-page songster describes itself as "a complete collection of the most admired modern songs." "Corporal Casey" is an Irish or British import with a likely stage origin:

> When I was at home, I was merry and frisky,
> My dad kept a pig, my mother sold whiskey;
> My uncle was rich but would never be easy,
> Till I was enlisted by corporal Casey.
> Och, rub a dub, row de dow, corporal Casey,
> Rub a dub, row de dow, corporal Casey,
> My dear little Sheelah, I thought would run crazy,
> Oh! when I trug'd away with my tough corporal Casey.
>
> I march'd from Kilkenny, and as I was a thinking
> On Sheelah, my heart in my bosom was sinking:
> But soon I was forc'd to look fresh as a daisy
> For fear of a drubbing from corporal Casey.
> Och, rub a dub, row de dow, corporal Casey,
> [Rub a dub, row de dow, corporal Casey,]
> The devil go with him, I ne'er could be lazy,
> He stuck in my skirts so, auld corporal Casey.
>
> We went into battle, I took the blows fairly;
> They fell on my pate but they bother'd me rarely:
> And who should be the first that drop't?—an't please ye,
> It was my good friend corporal Casey.

Och, rub a dub, row de dow, corporal Casey,
[Rub a dub, row de dow, corporal Casey,]
Thinks I you are quiet, and I shall be easy;
So eight years I fought without corporal Casey.
                              (*Blackbird* 1820)

In the 1820s, when *The Blackbird* was available for purchase, some New Yorkers still had personal recollections of British recruiting practices in the city during the revolution, while British and Irish immigrants knew of falling prey to recruiting parties during the Napoleonic Wars. Therefore, the recruit's story had real meaning. Everyone in the audience who listened could rejoice in the demise of the martinet corporal, but it was the survival of the mild everyman recruit that made the celebration possible.

"One Bottle More" is a "spree" song that appeared in the *New-York Remembrancer*:

In Candy's, in Church-street, I'll sing of a set,
Of six Irish blades who together had met;
Four bottles a piece made us call for our score,
And nothing remain'd but one bottle more.

Our bill being paid, we were loth to depart.
For friendship had grappled each man by the heart;
Where the least touch you know makes an Irishman roar,
And the whack from shilella brought six bottles more.

Slow Phoebus had shone through our window so bright,
Quite happy to view his blest children of light;
So we parted with hearts neither sorry nor sore,
Resolving next night to drink twelve bottles more.
                    (*New-York Remembrancer* 1802, 46–47)

That "One Bottle More" appeared in a songster of 234 pages, an expensive acquisition in 1802, indicates it was aimed at a middle-class audience. Because the song is specifically located near the courthouse, it may even be describing a notorious evening adventure undertaken by well-known citizens or anonymous members of an important club.

The contents of the twelve bottles are a matter of interest. Twelve bottles of ale, stout, or wine would not have been much of a test for "six Irish blades" to consume in a long night, and locally produced drink probably would have been served from a cask. The contents, therefore, may have been imported spirits, or at least whiskey, transported over some distance. Lastly, the revelers made a plan to repeat their meeting the following night, which would have required, in addition to a strong constitution, considerable discretionary income. The most important characteristic of "One Bottle More" is that it presents an image of Irishmen as likeable, jolly, and free sports. No disputes occur and there is no remorse. So convivial, so satisfactory were the night's proceedings that they are to be repeated anon. But there is no mention whether that plan was actualized.

The Songster's Repository, "Being a Collection of the Most Modern and Approved Songs Selected with Care," was published in 1811 by Nathaniel Dearborn of 171 William Street, New York City. It contains 264 songs, including 25 with some form of Irish content, the largest portion of which can be characterized as "Paddy-the-Irishman" songs. Dearborn cites sources for some of the lyrics. Twelve songs come from the repertoire of six concert or theatrical performers active in Manhattan at the time. Six of these are credited to "Mr M'Farlan," alternately mentioned as a performer at the Haymarket (London), the Theatre Royal (Manchester), and the New York Theater. They are "'Be a Good Boy and Take Care of Yourself,'" "Dennis Bulruddery," "Paddy Mac-Shane's Seven Ages," "Murtock Delarney's Travels and Returns to Ballinafad," "Song in Hit or Miss" (presumably a selection from a play containing music), and "Paddy's Sweet Little Island of Green" (to the tune of "In Ireland So Friskey with Sweet Girls and Whiskey"). The first four are largely rooted in humor contained in their wordplay, and some of these belittle the Catholic Irish, not too surprisingly given that Mac or McFarland is a name more often associated with Irish of Scots background. The following example is from "Dennis Bulruddery":

> When I came to be christen'd my poor mother saw
> On my face our dog Dennis had just laid his paw,
> What's his name, says the clergy, "down Dennis," says she,
> So Dennis Bulruddery he christen'd me.
>
> (*Songster's Repository* 1811, 18–19)

The "Song in Hit or Miss" employs ethnic humor too, in this instance directed at the French. It may have been a song M'Farland used to entertain audiences in England, where insulting anything French was deemed humorous. In the United States, gratitude toward France for helping win the War of American Independence faded quickly after the French Revolution, and the Quasi-War and other irritations chilled Franco-American relations. Thus insulting the French had comic value in America too, at least in front of conservative audiences:

> They talk how they live—why its blarney and stuff;
> For a man when he's hungry can eat fast enough,
> Its not teaching a live man to live, all my eye?
> Let them come over here and we'll teach 'em to die.
> Their frogs and soup-maigre are nothing but froth,
> To our beef and potatoes and scotch barley broth,
> Then what country for living as Erin so fit,
> Hospitality's at home and the birth place of wit.
> (*Songster's Repository* 1811, 20–21)

The Songster's Repository also includes an unattributed vision poem, "The Maid of Erin," in which Ireland is embodied as a beautiful, young, and innocent maiden, who is alas an ocean away. In addition to recalling her physical attractions, the exile remembers that she sang "sweetly" to him, no doubt, of liberty:

> My thoughts delight to wander,
> Upon a distant shore;
> Where lovely, fair, and tender,
> Is she whom I adore.
> May Heaven its blessings sparing,
> On her bestow them free;
> The lovely Maid of Erin!
> Who sweetly sang to me.
>
> .   .   .   .
>
> Although the restless ocean,
> May long between us roar,

Yet while my heart has motion,
She'll lodge within its core.
For artless and endearing,
And mild and young is she;
The lovely Maid of Erin!
Who sweetly sang to me.
　(Songster's Repository 1811, 145–46)

Songs of this ilk are associated with the clandestine hedge schools of Ireland, when Catholic education was severely repressed. In the 1820s, between three and four hundred thousand children attended these informal and uneven institutions, which taught academic basics and attempted to keep alive aspects of Gaelic culture (Connolly 2002, 249). "The Maid of Erin" is an *aisling*, or vision poem, in which Ireland is represented as a beautiful female. Personification of Ireland in womanly form is frequently employed in Irish song literature. Two well-known examples are the nineteenth-century broadside "Erin's Green Shore" and the comparatively recent (1967) song "Four Green Fields," written by the famous balladeer Tommy Makem.

One last song, identified only as "By John McCreery, on the death of the Vice President and Treasurer, of the 'Juvenile Sons of Erin'" is quite different. The Juvenile Sons was an organization established in New York City by members of the United Irishmen (Foik 1915, 262), and the indicated tune is the martial—not mournful—"Gramachree":

Ye youthful sons of Erin weep,
Oh! yes—let tears be shed;
Your two lov'd chiefs in silence sleep,
Rest with the mighty dead:
Go hang your harps on willow trees,
Where night her shadow wings;
Some Sylph, or Fairy in the breeze
May lightly touch the strings.

No—strike the sounding aloud,
And seep the chords along;
Their ghosts delighted from their cloud,

Shall hear the patriot song;
Erewhile, which fir'd their souls with pride—
The song of liberty,
And toss'd the echoes far and wide
"Let Erin's sons be free."
(*Songster's Repository* 1811, 255–56)

Through this grouping of printed songs it can be seen that what it meant to be Irish in New York during early national America was complex, and Irish identity was composed of multiple images, the totality of which was inaccessible in a single frame. To the city at large, the Catholic Irish were signified by a rough, comedic, stage Irish persona. But little about New York is static, and new paradigms were already in development. The American Protestant image of Irish Catholics further eroded during the Great Hunger, while songs supporting an autonomous Irish nation-state, typically one established through armed force and largely funded by émigrés in America, rose in ferocity and number.

In *Paddy and the Republic: Ethnicity and Nationality in Antebellum America*, Knobel (1986, 25–30) argues there were three distinct, successive Irish stereotypes in pre–Civil War America. He develops these images of "Paddy" from everyday print and from the verbal communication of Americans, writing they "encountered the Irish stereotype in diverse doses, in school books and newspapers, in magazines, novels, and travel literature, in politician's speeches and public oratory, and even in the spoken literature of the popular stage." He describes "Paddy" as "a word portrait, a collection of adjectives applied over and over again to the Irish. . . . The words did not merely represent attitudes; they shaped attitudes. . . . Paddy was certainly not a Know-Nothing invention foisted on a gullible public. For the larger number of white Americans, Paddy *was* the Irish: men, women and children" (11). The stereotypical image during Knobel's first period focuses on character, stressing negative behavior that sprung from "'impudence,' 'ingratitude,' 'ignorance,' 'foolishness,' 'wickedness,' 'contrivance,' and the like." Still, he perceives a certain ambivalence, for he quotes Yale University president, Timothy Dwight (1822, 3:375), who claimed, "The national character of the Irish is inferior to no other people . . . not surpassed in native activity of the mind, spright-liness, wit, good nature, generosity, affection and gratitude," continu-ing that "their peculiar defects and vices, I am persuaded, are owing to the want of education, or to a bad one." Dwight's observation was prophetic because much of the developmental work of the Catholic Church in New York in the post–Great Famine decades to come em-phasized education, secular as well as religious (Burrows and Wallace 1999, 750–51)—for the new, disciplined Catholic Church hierarchy believed that without education Catholics would be doomed to be dominated and ultimately absorbed into American Protestantism.

Knobel's first Irish stereotype period begins in 1820 and ends in 1844, essentially a post-Napoleonic period, during which "more than a million Irish immigrants entered the United States" (McCaffrey 1997, 64–65). The start date suggests that the received image of the Irish before 1820 was unfocused (largely seen above), and this is not without reason. Catholic Irish were a minority in New York City at the birth of the nation, and small numbers worked in their favor in two ways. First, as the rolls of the Friendly Sons of St. Patrick indicate, some were successful merchants, who took places alongside Protestant Irish both in business and social affairs. That camaraderie permitted well-connected Americans to construct an impression of Irish people as an economically diverse group of mixed British and Celtic origin, who were members of Anglican, Catholic, and Dissenter religions. Second, Irishmen had gained considerable goodwill for their parti-cipation in the American Revolution—the upper echelon of Wash-ington's forces included four major generals and fourteen brigadier generals of Irish birth or extraction (Maginnis 1913, 99–100), including well-known Catholic leaders as Stephen Moylan and John Barry. Thus, Irish Catholics could be viewed as worthy Americans. In 1783, when General Washington entered the City of New York to establish American hegemony, he had at his side the governor of New York State, George Clinton, whose Presbyterian father was forced to leave County Longford to escape religious oppression enacted by Anglicans (Kaminski 1993, 11). Clinton, who later became the fourth vice presi-dent of the United States, was somewhat supportive of Catholics, who could then be seen as having "men of worth" as friends.

Though coalescence of a Catholic Irish community clearly began with the repeal of the antipriest law and the founding of Saint Peter's parish, the years after the Napoleonic Wars were also important. Propelled principally by systemic agricultural restructuring in Ireland, many more immigrants began arriving, gathering particularly around New York's second Catholic edifice, the new Cathedral of Saint Patrick at Mulberry and Prince Streets, which opened in 1815. New York's Bishop Connolly was quoted in 1818 as saying, "At present there are about sixteen thousand Catholics, mostly Irish," which constituted a tenfold increase from 1783 and made up approximately 13 percent of New York's total population (Rosenwaike 1972, 27, 36). An increase in Irish immigration was generally viewed with apprehension by Protestant New Yorkers, patriotic people who felt threatened in the country their forefathers had founded. This fear increased with the growing vociferousness of the Catholic hierarchy and the militancy of their congregations, who believed they neither could nor must return to Ireland.

The growing swell of poor Catholic Irish immigrants, combined with the associated religious, political, and social controversy, made disassociation with Catholics even more attractive to Protestant Irish. The high ideals of Emmet, Sampson, and MacNeven were discarded. "For most Protestants, *Irish* now was a word filled with negative stereotypes such as superstitious papists and illiterate ditchdiggers" (Dolan 2008, 41–42). The term *Scotch Irish* entered into common usage in the decade 1820–30, during which Catholic emigration from Ireland surpassed Protestant for the first time in more than a century. The Scotch Irish appellation was then adopted by many non-Catholic Irish, sometimes even in instances when their forbearers did not hail from Scotland. Social distance was more important than accurate geography. Others simply identified as British or American. "Irish" became synonymous with "Catholic." Even before the Civil War, it had come to mean Irish Catholic Democrat. In an example of their advance-retreat progress, the Catholic Irish gained political sponsorship while their integration into the New York City mainstream was made impossible for the foreseeable future. In the next phase of their passage, opposition from Protestant Americans was evidenced by torchlight parades and Catholic church burnings, and anti-Irish animosity was loudly and plainly proclaimed in bitter song sheets that could be purchased for a penny on the main thoroughfares of a highly agitated city.

CHAPTER THREE

Irish Famine and American Nativism

When I landed at Swate Castle Garden,
　　　I'd just came from the say,
In my pockets I had not a farthing,
　　　As I stepped out up the Broadway;
I walked up to a lamp-lighter,
　　　The mystery for to unravel,
His hair was cut short like a fighter,
　　　So I shouldered my bundle and traveled.
　　　　　　　— "Swate Castle Garden"

In 1845, the Irish-born population of New York City reached an estimated 70,000 people.[1] During the next phase of integration—the passage
of the Great Hunger and the Know-Nothing era—immigration grew
enormously, nearly doubling to 133,730 within five years and reaching 175,735 by 1855 (Rosenwaike 1972, 41–42). When Irish-born residents are calculated as a percentage of the city's total population—1845
(18.86 percent), 1850 (25.93 percent), 1855 (27.89 percent)—it becomes
clear that famine-propelled inbound migration from Ireland placed tremendous stress on the limited resources of an already-burgeoning city.

Figure 14. Castle Garden, 1850. Wood engraving. Art and Picture Collection. New York Public Library.

Also burdensome were the vast numbers of immigrants who merely passed through New York, many so disoriented and ill-equipped that they lingered for some time while seeking funds to continue their journey and fathoming where to head next. During 1851, the peak year of the Great Famine influx, 163,000 Irish persons landed at New York, more than three times the total of 1847 (Albion 1984, 338, 418).

Prior to 1855, arriving passengers simply walked directly from their vessels onto city streets, but in that year the State of New York opened the first immigrant-landing depot in the United States by repurposing the Castle Garden (fig. 14), a building that only five years earlier had been a theater that hosted concerts featuring Jenny Lind, the famous "Swedish Nightingale." The castle was redesigned to serve both as a place for passenger screening aimed at protecting city and state and as a halfway house for immigrants, a place where they could gather information on accommodation and transportation, rather than being robbed immediately of what few possessions they had. Boldly and callously, earlier Irish immigrants actively participated in such "con games." There were other dangers too. Soon after the "green-horn" narrator of "Swate Castle Garden" (quoted in the epigraph) exits through the depot's gates and begins his tramp northward up Broadway, originally a Native American trail, he encounters a major roadblock to his settlement and integration within the Empire City. In the better-case scenario, the sentry was a Protestant religious zealot, someone who refused to recognize Catholicism as a Christian religion and who thought all its adherents to be devils incarnate; in the worst case, he was a nativist, a fighter who regarded the Irish as subhuman, a species that had to be subdued. Too often, he was a combination of both.

The Great Hunger and Famine-Era Song in Ireland

Shortly before the harvest of 1845, the *phytophthora infestans* fungus infiltrated the landscape of Ireland, causing the loss of one-third of the late potato crop (Gray 1995, 35). The following year, three-quarters of the expected yield was ruined (Connolly 2002, 238). The potato blight occurred annually somewhere in Ireland until 1852. Hardest hit was the country's agrarian peasantry—landless farm laborers and tenant cottiers and smallholders who made up some 4.5 million of the country's estimated 8.5 million inhabitants (Gray 1995, 31). They were people who existed almost exclusively on a diet of milk and potatoes. Desperately poor in the main, illiterate and frequently living in large families, these rural folk constituted the base levels of a feudal, quasi-colonial society. They lacked the means to alter their circumstances, while the agricultural landscape around them turned to rot and their lives to ruin. Subsequent diseases such as cholera, typhoid, and typhus (Ó Gráda 1999, 88) extended the reach of death beyond the rural countryside into towns and cities, and from the laboring class to the middle class and above. Exposure was another cause of fatality. Many landlords hastened the conversion of estates from tillage to pasturage during the blight years, accelerating the eviction of tenant farmers, whom poorhouses were frequently unable to accommodate.

Official efforts to counter the threat of mass annihilation were wholly inadequate, partly because, although the potato crop of 1846 was a nearly total failure, the fungus was not widespread in 1847. Peter Gray (1995, 64) writes, "A combination of circumstances convinced many in Britain (and some in the wealthier parts of Ireland) that the situation had changed for the better. . . . Reports of an excellent Irish grain harvest and continuing massive imports of American food hardened this consensus. Attempts to raise more money in October met with indifference or outright hostility."

Such a response was engendered by prevailing laissez-faire economic thought, but there were darker assumptions—that the Irish had brought the calamity on themselves, and a form of natural selection was at work to reduce gross overpopulation. "Many people in London in the 1840s believed that the famine was nature's response to Irish demographic irresponsibility, and that too much public kindness would obscure that message" (Ó Gráda 1999, 6). Religious hostility was another issue: "Extreme language was common among evangelicals with anti-Catholic leanings, who linked Ireland's plight with its religious 'error' and warned that England's toleration of Catholicism would lead to further punishment of such 'national sin'" (Gray 1995, 37). Politics was an additional factor—or subterfuge. In its first mention of famine in Ireland, the *Times* (25 November 1845, 8) of London crustily laid blame on Daniel O'Connell (whose Catholic Association charged its tens of thousands of members a farthing each in monthly membership) and the Irish people en masse: "The prospect of famine in Ireland has not prevented the collection of the O'Connell tribute. . . . It is equally shocking and extraordinary that the tax should have been levied and paid by a people foreknowing they were squandering the means of life itself in the money they gave. The improvidence, it may be said is characteristic." It continued, "The salve for Mr. O'Connell's conscience is the expectation that England will supply all wants. . . . [He] is willing that Ireland should live with [England] on the terms, what's yours is mine, what's mine's my own."

Food was exported from Ireland throughout the potato blight, although "Irish grain exports were one-third lower in 1846 than in the early 1840s. Even if exports to Britain had been prohibited, Ireland lacked sufficient resources to stave off famine in 1846–47" (Gray 1995, 46). Most importantly, those who were in most need of food had no money to pay for it. Seen in this light, the fault was not specifically that the potato crop failed or even that foodstuffs were exported but rather that government rejected its responsibility to import and distribute adequate provisions until the unstoppable blight had run its course. The question of government blameworthiness in the Great Hunger has been a pervasive issue. McCaffrey (1997, 59) speculates, "If enormous numbers of people in England, Scotland, or Wales had been dying of hunger and fever, British governments might have shown more concern." The suggestion largely removes religion and the Irish Sea barrier as factors affecting government-relief decisions. It leaves at issue, however, other important determinants, such as human distribution, productivity within a changing agro-economic landscape, and geographic location of the most distressed areas relative to the seat of power in London, while leaving in place a laissez-faire attitude and fatalistic outlook. In its 20 May 1846 issue, the *Aberdeen Journal* contrasted contemporary relief efforts in Ireland with measures taken to alleviate a 1783 famine episode in northern Scotland. The article found the former lacking in initiative and stated that quick relief could be provided for Ireland, just as it had been decades earlier in Scotland. The newspaper urged immediate government action in Ireland, laying responsibility for the disaster squarely on absentee Irish landlords.

In fact, a crop failure occurred simultaneously in Scotland during 1847, but coverage in the *Times* (5 February 1847, 12 March 1847) indicates it was confined to the Highlands and Islands and was of insufficient scope and severity to test McCaffrey's speculation. A more appropriate measure would be whether large-scale unrest would have occurred if a serious food shortage struck England's industrial heartland, South Wales, or Scotland's lowland manufacturing region. The best possible estimate is that, if an incident of similar magnitude had occurred in industrial Britain, many people would have died but at nowhere near the ratio experienced in Ireland. In addition, emigration would not have been as massive because British factories needed labor, whereas agricultural Ireland was highly overpopulated. What furthers this conclusion is that starvation in industrial Britain likely would have engendered riot and endangered the economy, thus threatening government stability.

The ghastly nature and incalculable devastation of the Great Hunger did not favor the production of a large song corpus. Cormac Ó Gráda (1999, 215–25) writes, "The Muses might be forgiven for losing their voices during the Great Famine. The rhetoric of fatalism is silence, and as the crisis deepened communal fatalism was an understandable response." Few period lyrics lasted for posterity. That was not entirely because the songs were mainly in the Irish language or because they went unprinted but also because geographic displacement related to famine and eviction disturbed traditional folkways. A combination of "survivor guilt" and a need to move forward and away from catastrophe also quieted the blighted landscape. Ethnomusicologist Gearóid Ó hAllmhuráin (1999, 121–22) observes, "The former intimacy of the *clachan* and the townland was virtually erased, and in its place lay a materialistic world of profit economics and conservative social mores." He continues, "Political ballads and emigrant songs, which were once peripheral, now became commonplace. . . . Some were nationalist ballads that viewed the famine as a callous act of British imperialism; while others . . . recalled the catastrophe in the midst of exile and loneliness." Ó Gráda presents an informed discourse of famine-period song in Ireland, offering examples that display unique characteristics of expression in the Irish language. He also comments on Chris Morash's 1995 collection of verse about the Great Famine, *The Hungry Voice: The Poetry of the Irish Famine*, writing that "the literary provenance of the material inevitably makes it a better representation of well-intentioned middle-class reactions than of popular attitudes in areas where the famine was most intense." Morash also provides four broadside ballads touching "a truly popular chord"; however, as he notes, an inherent incongruity exists in "Dublin newspapers preaching rebellion in English to a largely illiterate and Irish-speaking peasantry" (Morash 1995; Ó Gráda 1999). Moulden (1994, 10–11) and Georges Denis Zimmermann (2002, 237–38) both print a ballad, "A New Song on the Rotten Potatoes," which they date to 1845–47. Its author's tone of suggestion is hopeful but heavily idealistic and far removed from the concerns and inclinations of Irish landowners and power-holding politicians in Westminster:

> You landlords of Ireland I'd have you beware,
> And of your poor tenants I'd wish you take care,

For want of potatoes in the present year
From the cradle to crutch, they are trembling with fear.

See how starvation meets us in the face,
But relief is expected from each foreign place,
Come, sell all your cattle and don't keep a tail,
Before that you'll part with your corn or your meal.

. . . .

Let the Whigs and Repealers all join hand in hand,
And likewise the Tories to come on one plan,
To boldly come forward and never to fail,
And then we will have both our corn and our meal.

. . . .

Do not be down-hearted, but cheer up once more,
The provision is coming from each foreign shore,
Good beer, flour and butter, rich sugar and tea,
From Russia and Prussia and Americay.

It is, of course, a didactic song that pictures how an ideal society might function, and one that bears no evidence the lyricist ever visited a place beset by famine. Many English-language songs of the Great Hunger period are not just geographically and culturally removed from sites of suffering but also unrealistic. Others are nationalist lyrics commenting on the government's ineffective response to the 1845–52 famine as the overriding reason for the separation of Ireland from the United Kingdom.

So many deaths went unrecorded in Ireland that there is no way to know the full extent of human loss. By comparing prefamine population estimates with 1851 Census of Ireland enumeration, and adjusting for natural growth, Gray (1995, 94) estimates the "missing" total at 2.4 million. At least 1.1 million are thought to have died of starvation or disease, with the remainder emigrating (Dolan 2008, 74; Lalor 2003, 456; Miller 1999, 181), the majority to the United States. The Great Hunger was Ireland's holocaust, an event that changed the country forever. But its effects were also profoundly felt elsewhere, including New York, America's greatest port of entry.

Famine-Era Settlement and Song

Largely rural in their homeland, famine-era refugees became a primarily urban people in the United States. Transport construction projects (such as canals and railroads) and other employment opportunities (mills, extraction industries, etc.) spread them over secondary and tertiary cities, and to towns across the countryside. Still, they generally did not gravitate toward farming, a tendency that baffles casual observers. In fact, Irish peasants lacked both a deep knowledge of agriculture—especially in a harsh continental climate, rather than the mild oceanic environment they knew—and the considerable capital required to establish successful farmsteads in the American interior, where land was available.

Census statistics provide quantitative details, but qualitative measures are of no less importance. While the majority of prefamine immigrants were from sections of Ireland that were "modern" (commercially oriented and English-speaking), famine-era immigrants as a group were disproportionately from rural, traditional, often Irish-speaking areas in the west and south of Ireland, especially the provinces of Connacht and Munster, where living conditions were often rudimentary and the view intensely local. Consequently, famine-era Irish with no translatable skills were particularly ill-suited for life in ultra-urban New York. Another major difference between post–Napoleonic War and famine-era immigrants is that the former entered the city when it had a thriving craft-based culture that viewed skilled labor as a relatively expensive input, while the latter, who arrived a generation later, encountered an economy that was adopting market-based industrial principles, which regarded immigrant labor as cheap and easily replaceable. For new arrivals, that meant poorly paid, repetitive, manual work and unstable employment.

McCaffrey's (1997, 71–72) statement that the Great Hunger migration was a tragedy that befell not just the incoming refugees but the Catholic Irish already settled in New York is important in light of these circumstances: "Irish Catholic immigrants of the 1820s, 1830s and early 1840s worked hard and experienced a slight degree of economic and social mobility. They bought houses, built churches and schools, and most lived quiet, decent, respectable lives. . . . the Famine deposited masses of new refugees . . . poor, ignorant and unskilled. America's economy could not easily absorb them, and they pulled down the entire Irish American community from the modest heights of respectability that it had worked so diligently to attain."

The famine-nativist period, therefore, was not simply an extension of the New Republic era in terms of Catholic Irish integration; it presented further and more insurmountable obstacles than existed previously—greater numbers, deeper poverty, carriage of infectious diseases, fewer translatable skills—which resulted in more hostile opposition as the scales of population were tipped increasingly toward people considered to be basely ignorant and controlled by a foreign church. Also, for more than a decade before the Great Hunger, the American Protestant Association had aroused antagonism by making their pulpits "organs for antipapal attacks" (Billington 1964, 220). The famine era is another example of the "two steps forward, one step back" advance of the Catholic Irish during the critical integration period. Adverse timing was a contributing factor as well, in that the presence of large numbers of desperately poor immigrants aroused fear and hatred in the American Protestant working classes, who were themselves already uneasy owing to the pressure of an economic paradigm shift in their disfavor (Gorn 1987, 393).

Middle-class Americans also had concerns about Irish immigrants: "The native middle classes [saw] in them the nucleus of a permanently depressed laboring class. The natives did not foresee the extent to which industry would expand and how important a resource the Irish laborers would be. . . . What they did see was that the Irish did not seem to practice thrift, self-denial, and other virtues desirable in the 'worthy, laboring poor'" (Shannon 1966, 39). At the same time, Knobel (1986, 53) presents another consideration with respect to Irish immigrants, one held by certain, well-educated Americans who, rather than criticizing Paddy for his shortcomings, forthrightly blamed Britain. "The Irish peasantry," wrote W. C. Willard and E. Woodridge, in what may have been the most influential school geography of the mid-nineteenth century, "are in the most wretched ignorance and poverty. They are degraded by the oppression of the landlords; and their stewards or 'middlemen.'" Combined with the absence of "free and tolerant laws," noted another contemporary textbook writer, "such oppression inevitably discourages the spirit of industry."

Finding employment was a prerequisite for famine-dispersed refugees hoping to gain a foothold in New York. In *Immigrant Life in New York*, Robert Ernst (1965) tabulates occupational employment among immigrant groups from the 1855 Census of the State of New York. That data enables basic assessments regarding the quality of employment among Irish-born New Yorkers in the immediate post-famine period. Of the five most populous groups, persons of Irish nativity constituted the largest total number of immigrants (and the highest percentage of employed persons): Irish 175,735 (50.4 percent) vs. Germans—97,572 (46.9 percent), English—22,713 (42.8 percent), Scots—8,487 (48.8 percent), and French—6,321 (47.8 percent). But the Irish fared far worse when quality of employment is considered. They were 88 percent of all immigrant laborers, 86.8 percent of all foreign-born laundresses, and 79.3 percent of domestic servants, but only 36.1 percent of clerks, 32.1 percent of machinists, 25.9 percent of bakers, 14.3 percent of precision instrument makers, and 9.4 percent of immigrant architects. Tellingly, of the 88,480 gainfully employed Irish, 42,570 worked as laborers, laundresses, or servants. The first two, poorly paid and drudge-like occupations, were sensitive to dips in the economy, while the work of household servants, though generally steady and cleaner, was subject to the goodwill of a master or mistress. The lack of a favorable reference could easily destroy an individual's chances for further employment, possibly plunging a chaste woman into prostitution (Howes 2009, 98–102). For Irish men, the best occupational tactic was to learn a skilled trade. Women might hope to become teachers or nurses, but such aspirations were mainly realized by future generations.

New York City in the mid-nineteenth century was a collection of business precincts and related residential neighborhoods. Owing to its unique, narrow, wedgelike landmass, and being nearly surrounded by water, Lower Manhattan's population growth could only expand in one direction (north-northeast)—but not far, because development

Figure 15. Map of the City of New York, 1833. New York Public Library.

was constrained by the time a worker needed to walk from residence to job, work perhaps ten hours, return home, and sleep. This required employed persons, even low-paid laborers, to live in and around the central business district of what was still very much a maritime port city. As the demand for space increased, residential rents rose, while pressure from employers to reduce wages squeezed families' resources. Of the factors determining where the Irish would live, most crucial was balancing proximity to employment with the income required to pay rent. Of secondary but still high importance in a period of fierce economic, cultural, and social competition was safety. As in 1784, with the founding of Saint Peter's, Catholic Irish sought to live in ethnic enclaves gathered around the spire of their parish church and within reach of other community institutions.

In 1836, there were eight Roman Catholic churches in Manhattan, seven below 14th Street and one in Harlem. Eight more churches had been added by 1845, three south of 14th and only one north of 34th Street. By 1855, the number of Catholic parishes had reached twenty-five, with fourteen located at or below 14th Street and six more between 14th and 34th Streets. Of the total in that year, five were ethnic German parishes and one French (Dolan 1983, 13). Not surprisingly, the location of churches with mostly Irish congregations corresponds well with Ernst's (1965, 43) 1855 map of ethnicity within Lower Manhattan political wards. In it, Irish residents make up more than one-third of inhabitants along the East River, from the Battery to Grand Street (First, Second, Fourth, and Seventh Wards), and to the east of Broadway as far north as Houston Street (Sixth and Fourteenth Wards).

In midcentury New York, the Five Points district of the Sixth Ward was "very likely the most studied neighborhood in the world. Journalists chronicled its rampant crime, squalid tenements, and raucous politics. Religious magazines detailed missionaries' efforts to 'save' the district's residents from sin and perdition" (Anbinder 2001, 2). The rich and famous came to Five Points on "slumming safaris" conducted by officials strangely anxious to show off Gotham's worst attributes. These included such contemporary icons as frontiersman David "Davy" Crockett (1835) and English novelist Charles Dickens (1842), who toured Five Points and afterward wrote of the scenes they viewed. But in her unpublished doctoral dissertation, for which she performed quantitative analysis of 1855 New York State Census data, Carol Groneman Pernicone (1973, iv–vii) observes that "25,000 Sixth Ward residents [found] many discrepancies between the actual lifestyle of the poor and the image depicted by the upper classes. Indicators of strong kinship ties—immigration patterns, kin-related households, and the relatively small Irish boardinghouse population—attested to the strong family bonds among the Sixth Ward Irish."

As always in New York's most dangerous neighborhoods, there were many decent, trapped, desperately poor families gathered behind bolted doors, hoping for safe passage through the night. In truth, the destitute viewed by "slumming" celebrities were less likely to be working-class Irish and more likely to be Hibernian representatives of the underclass—victims of desertion and disease, the unfit and least fit for employment, and alcoholics. With no cushion of personal savings or government-supported social safety net, even the slightest misstep could lead to a disastrous fall.

As much as most famine-era Irish would have preferred to live exclusively in ethnic villages, they were not fully able to do so because the vise of high rents and great demand compressed diverse populations to downtown working-class areas. Subletting tenement rooms and taking in boarders were common practices. "Many of New York's African Americans lived in close proximity to the newly arrived Irish" (Burrows and Wallace 1999, 480), promoting many casual encounters and lasting unions. In 1835, ten years before the Great Hunger, David Crockett visited Five Points, noting in particular the revelry enjoyed by blacks and whites together. "It appeared as if the cellars was jam full of people; and such fidling and dancing nobody saw before in this world," wrote Crockett (1835, 48–49), a fiddler himself (Emerson 1997, 71). "I thought they were true 'heaven-borns.' Black and white, white and black, all hug-em-snug together, happy as lords and ladies, sitting sometimes round in a ring, with a jug of liquor between them." He continued, "In my country, when you meet an Irishman, you find a first-rate gentleman; but these are worse than savages; they are too mean to swab hell's kitchen" (Crockett 1835, 48–49), a likely reference to the differences he perceived between his Ulster Scots neighbors in rural Tennessee and the Catholic Irish settling in Manhattan's crowded lower reaches. Crockett's description also bears some resemblance to the carousing (and purported plotting) of greens and blacks together at John Hughson's public house in 1741. Most of all, it reads like an eyewitness account of the birth of the immigrant-native musical fusion known as minstrelsy, America's first popular music.

Famine-era immigrants continued to bring with them songs traditional to their birth locales. Because immigrants were arriving in larger numbers and were from places farther into the countryside than previously, one may reasonably speculate that a higher percentage of Irish-language songs was sung than before. Lyrics specifically related to the Great Hunger must have been brought to Manhattan, but they were probably few in number and have long since been forgotten. English-language lyrics circulating in New York that mention the Great Hunger seem never to be *only* about that catastrophe but rather use the 1845–52 period as an exemplar when speaking of subsequent events or situations. A lengthy song, "The Irish Refugee, or Poor Pat Must Emigrate" (LC digital ID 201690), a precursor of the Fenian song "Skibbereen,"[2] was printed in Manhattan by De Marsan sometime between 1864 and 1878. The broadside cites the air as "Podgee and Rhu" and gives J. S. Berry as the source singer. The Irish Traditional Music Archive (ITMA) in Dublin holds a second broadside that cites the melody as "Apple Praters." The ITMA example may have been published in Ireland, but it is not possible to say that with absolute certainty, for it bears no publisher imprint. Other printings were made in English cities, including London and Manchester, and in Belfast. The De Marsan and ITMA ballads are similar yet hold some intriguing differences. The latter sheet, for example, contains the Irish words *beid-na-husth,* which is set in English on the De Marsan song sheet as "be in no haste." Because *beid-na-husth* is the only Gaelic expression on both sheets, one may speculate that the New York broadside was printed later. In both, the narrator initially opposes the tenant-clearing evictions that began during famine times and continued until the late 1880s:

> The devil a word I would say at all,
> Although our wages are but small,
> If they left us in our cabins,
>   Where our fathers drew their breath;
> When they call upon rent-day,
> And the devil a cent you have to pay,
> They will drive you from your house and home,

To beg and starve to death?
What kind of treatment, boys, is that
To give an honest Irish Pat?
To drive his family to the road,
    To beg and starve for meat?

But the song then presents images that suggest the lyricist might have viewed the Great Famine firsthand:

Such sights as that I've often seen;
But I saw worse in Skibbereen.
In Forty-Eight (that time is no more)
    When famine it was great:
I saw fathers, boys, and girls
With rosy cheeks and silken curls
All a-missing and starving
    For a mouthful of food to eat.
When they died in Skibbereen.
No shrouds or coffins were to be seen:
But patiently reconciling themselves
    To their desperate, horrid fate.
They were thrown in graves by wholesale,
Which caused many an Irish heart to wail.
And caused many a boy and girl
    To be most glad to emigrate.

The song contains both touches of artistry and a certain clumsiness. The place at which the narrator stands, for example, changes irregularly between America and Ireland. However, if one appreciates the song as period listeners would have done, it is more a series of compelling word images with commentary, rather than a through-composed story. The real message in the New York broadside is actually quite clear—political independence for Ireland—as shown in the closing lines:

If ever again I see this land,
I hope it will be with a Fenian band;
So, God be with old Ireland!
    Poor Pat must emigrate.

On the ITMA ballad sheet, though, there is no mention of the Fenians, an organization founded for the purpose of overthrowing British rule by armed force. Its closing lines are instead: "But if ever again I reach this land I hope I'll be a different man / So God be with old Ireland, for poor Pat must emigrate."

This veiled ending comes out of caution for government authorities. The absence of the printer's name and location supports that conclusion, for publishers regularly included contact information because it aided business. Proclaiming Fenian loyalty was of no concern in New York, where Irish nationalist rhetoric was unhindered and became ever louder and angrier. There is no subtlety in De Marsan's "Irish Refugee"; it overrides famine-associated "shame" in support of an overriding goal. In New York City, the Catholic Irish proclaim their wish to rise according to their own model, one that includes a politically autonomous national homeland, underscoring their desire to integrate en masse. However, this aspiration was difficult for most Anglo-Americans to accept, because it was contrary to their own pervasive fealty to England and to their requirement for immigrant assimilation within the larger society.

Politics was an especially crucial agent in the building and advancement of Manhattan's Catholic Irish community. The expansion of male suffrage in the 1830s made machine politics possible in New York. It was supported by a continued inflow of immigrants in need of social services, benefits that nascent labor organizations were unable to provide. "Charity and comradeship were as essential to the boss and his machine as were contracts and commissions. . . . They remained in charge as long as they met the public's demands" (Lankevich 1998, 92).

Daniel Patrick Moynihan, who was born in the Hell's Kitchen neighborhood on Manhattan's West Side and became a US senator and American ambassador to the United Nations, wrote that the two major achievements of the Irish in nineteenth-century New York were building the Catholic Church and taking control of the Democratic Party organization. Moynihan (Glazer and Moynihan 1963, 223, citing Brown 1958) notes, "The Irish role in politics was creative, not imitative." The Tammany machine functioned by distributing patronage in the form of jobs and by navigating city bureaucracy for the benefit of its clients. It also held its own funds, which could be used to deliver crucial necessities, such as food and fuel, in time of need. By force of numbers and political acuity, the Irish eventually took over Tammany.

That the Catholic Irish could command the government of New York City before achieving independence in Ireland seems at first curious. The basis for understanding this arrangement lies in appreciating that the cultural horizon of nineteenth-century Ireland was extremely short. Because Manhattan's many Hibernians hailed mainly from rural places, they understood the importance of local place especially well. For them, the New York City block corresponded with the Irish townland, and they perceived that the electoral ward could be administered like an Irish village, where each person had a place and a role to perform, just as in Tammany-style Democratic politics. Accepting one's duties and rank within the party helped the community at large and also brought increased individual security in an epoch long before the existence of government-provided welfare (Glazer and Moynihan 1963, 226). Characterizing the viewpoint of Irish-led machine politics, Glazer and Moynihan (1963, 224) write, "First, there was an indifference to Yankee proprieties. To the Irish, stealing an election was rascally, not to be approved, but neither quite to be abhorred. . . . Second, the Irish brought to America a settled tradition of regarding the formal government as illegitimate, and the informal one as bearing the true impress of sovereignty." What they do not mention is that, in addition to the Irish village, Tammany reflected prime characteristics of the Roman Catholic Church (Meagher 2005, 58). Each was a hierarchical, membership organization that demanded loyalty and subordination of personal aims for the good of the institution. As churches and clerics accepted donations for services performed, so did their secular counterparts. Priests and political bosses were in general both sober and dutiful in ministering to their congregations, whom they knew well. Whether their faithful flocks were waiting for a place in heaven or merely a better tenement apartment, both church and party expected patience and obedience from them.

"Know-Nothings" and the American Party

In summer 1798, the Federalist-controlled Congress enacted a series of laws restricting foreign entry, making immigrant residence and citizenship in the United States more difficult. Though the Federalists faded away as a political organization, the nativist grain in their party plank was still visible. Indeed, antipathy based on religion and ethnic origin (both elements of "race") has never fully left American life. Hostility toward foreigners, Irish and Germans in particular (for they were the most numerous and visible and were more likely to be Catholic), rose after the national economic collapse and depression that began in 1837.

The hostility was a mixture of prejudice and contested interests that coincided with an ongoing Protestant evangelistic revival known as the Second Great Awakening. The Philadelphia Riots of 1844, which threatened to spread to Manhattan, are a prime example of nativist xenophobia. The Know-Nothing movement, so labeled because members denied the very existence of the organization, originated during this period. Like the Tea Party movement during the presidency of Barack Obama, the upsurge was more a coalition of *anti*party groups holding a spectrum of conservative views than an organization espousing a positive political agenda. In addition to being anti-immigrant and anti-Catholic, Know-Nothings were also likely to be antialcohol, anticorruption, and antislavery. Their positive focus was on what they perceived to be the wholesome American values of times past. In 1854, loosely connected nativist groups formed a national political organization known as the American Party, which sought to restrict immigration, elect Protestants to public office, propose stringent naturalization legislation, and curb the influence of the Catholic Church. Though short-lived, the Know-Nothings were a formidable force. The four-way New York State gubernatorial contest of 1854 is a good measure of conservative sentiment. The winner was "Myron Clark, a Whig with temperance and antislavery sentiments" (Ellis and New York State Historical Association 1967, 231), who received 156,804 votes. Placing third was Daniel Ullmann of the American Party with 122,282 votes, a substantial showing by any measure. In New York City that same year, a sly, aggressive, generally proIrish Tammany Democrat named Fernando Wood was elected mayor, which set the scene for unrest on the streets of Manhattan.

In the early morning hours of 5 July 1857, a large and fierce riot took place along three blocks of Bayard Street between Elizabeth and Baxter Streets. As reported in the *New York Times* (6 July 1857), "Brickbats, stones and clubs were flying thickly around, and from windows in all directions, and men ran wildly about brandishing firearms and clubs of almost every sort. Wounded men were lying on the ground trampled on by the crowds who were driven to and fro. Amidst the din that prevailed, it was almost impossible to tell between whom the fight was raging." The article presents a scenario that began when carousing members of an Irish Five Points criminal group known as the Dead Rabbits attacked a policeman,[3] who ran into a saloon patronized by the Bowery Boys, an American nativist gang. The Dead Rabbits followed him in and rained havoc on the premises. In another incident at 10:00 p.m. the same night, a patrolman was set on as he attempted to disperse a crowd of rowdy men and women. He too escaped and returned with help; however, the entire crowd then turned on the police. By 3:00 or 4:00 a.m., a full-blown riot was in force as the Bowery Boys crossed onto Irish turf and proceeded down Bayard. Nearly the entire neighborhood—women included—rose in defense. The battle ended when a policeman took off his badge and cap, brandished a white flag, and approached each side in succession, persuading them to lay down their weapons. Serious harm had already been done, and the following day's headline in the *New York Times* (6 July 1957) read, "SIX MEN KILLED AND OVER 100 WOUNDED."

Figure 16. Torchlight Meeting of Know-Nothings at New York, 1855. Wood engraving. Art and Picture Collection. New York Public Library.

Drinking was heavy and widespread over the Fourth of July week-end, but rather than being a series of unconnected alcohol-fueled incidents, the events were symptomatic of a building civil war in the Sixth Ward between supporters of Mayor Wood and his Whig enemies in New York State government. In an effort to destabilize Wood by removing a major source of patronage, the state legislature passed the Police Act, which effectively placed city law enforcement under state control and authorized an all-new Metropolitan police force. Wood countered by maintaining the old Municipal constabulary. On 18 June 1857, these two actions caused an interforce brawl outside City Hall, which was memorialized on a J. Andrews song sheet, "Riot in the City Hall Park":

> Some bawled loud and some bawled louder,
> Some wanted to fight with ball and powder,
> Some for Wood and some for King,
> So they made the old City Hall to ring.
>
> At last I heard the Mayor say,
> Here I am and here I will stay,
> I defy Governor King and all his men,
> So now you may take me if you can.
>
> Moreover then I heard him say,
> You had better all get out of the way,
> For the pats will all fight for me;
> You had better go back to Albany.
>
> Then one of the Metropolitan men did say,
> We will take you, Mayor Wood to-day,
> Or we will fight till we are dead,
> And he swung his club high over his head.
>   (NYSL Broadside Ballads, SCO BD1100)

On 2 July, state courts upheld the Police Act, and the Municipals were disbanded. Importantly for Hibernians, the police department had been "one of the few government institutions that hired the Irish in significant numbers for non-menial jobs" (Anbinder 2001, 279). Hardly any Irishmen were appointed to the Metropolitans, but, seemingly, many militant nativists were (Anbinder 2001, 281–82).

Though the *New York Times* certainly knew the cause of the Bayard Street riot, its reports did not highlight the reason, choosing instead to bury the information in a profile of the Dead Rabbits gang in the 7 July issue: "[They] range from eighteen to twenty-five years of age, and they number from one to two hundred members. Their members were increased on Saturday, through sympathy of local pride, and by the circulation of an idle and vicious report in the 'Dead Rabbit' neighborhood that, the Know-Nothings and Black Republicans were coming down to destroy the Catholic Church in Mott Street" (*NYT*, 7 July 1857).

The Bayard Street riot was a transported representation of the "party" or "faction" fights of Ireland, which Hugh O'Rourke (2001) links to recreational violence. Catholic Irish had ongoing animosity toward the nativist camp, which was now exacerbated by the replacement of the Municipals with the Metropolitan police force and the subsequent loss of employment opportunities. Hibernian hackles were raised in anticipation of a challenge to their community, and the Dead Rabbits struck at first provocation. Their actions represented the defense of home territory from an armed, "foreign" power.

Songs supporting both the nativist and Catholic Irish immigrant points of view were published openly in New York City. John Andrews, who printed broadside song sheets between 1853 and 1859 at 38 Chatham Street (Charosh 1997, 469), catered to the Know-Nothing trade during the controversy. Wordsmiths who wrote Andrews's lyrics often employed a popular song template from American blackface minstrelsy, entitled "Jordan Is a Hard Road to Travel." The form was used typically to comment on the issues of the day in a free-wheeling, roundabout, and basely humorous manner. "Jordan Is a Hard Road to Travel, No. 3" is an example:

> There was snakes in Ireland many years ago,
> St. Patrick saw the reptiles a crawling,
> He up with his shelalah and hit them in the head
> And drove them to the other side of Jordan.
> (NYSL Broadside Ballads, SCO BD0552)

But in a succeeding incarnation, "Jordan Is a Hard Road to Travel, No. 6," the format was employed to intimidate Irish immigrants in a very direct way and to rally "Wide Awake" demonstrators.[4] The new song contains neither charm nor wit. Andrews's broadside proclaims the nativist position in hard, direct street language:

> The Irishmen think they can rule
> Over the American people according,
> But the Americans will show them what they will do,
> On this and the other side of Jordan.
>
> .   .   .   .
>
> The Wide Awake white hats are now all the go,
> The Know-Nothings wear them according,
> Only say that you're a "Mick," and you'll get a kick,
> Which will send you to the other side of Jordan.
>   (NYSL Broadside Ballads, SCO BD0554)

"Wide Awake Jordan" by lyricist William C. Marion goes even further, throwing a solid fistful of head bashing and eye blackening intended to carry all the way to the Promised Land:

> No popery—that's a go, and the wide awakes will show
> That they can sing it out according,
> If you want your head broke, just hurrah for the pope,
> And they'll knock you to the other side of jordan.
>
> .   .   .   .
>
> Street preaching am the fashion, it am getting all the go,
> And the wide awakes attend it according,
> So if your fond of black eyes, tell the preacher that he lies,
> And they'll kick you to the other side of jordan.
>
> Our election is coming, and the Irish are a drumming
> Up all the voters that they can depend on,

So perhaps we'll have to fight, for we'll stick to our right,
And we will challenge them to the other side of jordan.
                    (NYSL Broadside Ballads, SCO BD1359)

The mention of street preaching is a reminder religion was a friction issue that coincided with economic and territorial competition. "Wide Awake Jordan" refers to a series of riotous events that took place in 1853 and 1854 in Manhattan and Brooklyn, which were chronicled by city newspapers and summarized by O'Rourke (2001, 135–49). These episodes of religion-based violence were preceded by 1) the contentious 1853 lecture tour of Alessandro Gavazzi, an Italian former priest and notorious anti-Catholic orator, who was sponsored in the United States by the American Protestant Association, and 2) the 1853–54 visit of Cardinal Gaetano Bedini, who was rumored to be complicit in the deaths of antipapal revolutionaries in Italy. In New York, Bedini stayed at the residence of Bishop John Hughes, ostensibly to attend the installation of bishops for the neighboring dioceses of Brooklyn and Newark; but he was also in America "to deal with the [resurgent] issue of trusteeism in parish churches" (O'Rourke 2001, 111–12). Protestant evangelicals, however, believed he had come to eradicate American republican democracy. They demonstrated virulently against Bedini, and an attempt was later made on the cardinal's life (O'Rourke 2001, 112).

Street preaching was not new to New York. In fact, its history dates to the Dutch colonial era, when William Goulding's wife acted out as a gutsy street preacher. The pattern of government response was to treat it as a nuisance proscribed by law. Mainstream clergy were no more sympathetic. On 17 December 1853, the *New York Times* printed a page 1 proclamation by Mayor Westervelt reminding citizens of an 1839 ordinance against public worship in the streets, observing that "recent occurrences seem to require a mutual forbearance and the exercise of careful moderation of our fellow citizens, and especially on abstinence from the unnecessary discussion in public thoroughfares of topics calculated to excite and arouse the passions or prejudices of any portion of our citizens." Such action became necessary after a preacher was arrested on 11 December for usurping "the extensive shipyard of Messrs. Westervelt & McKay." "His loud voice sounded far off, and laborers of all classes flocked to the yard. Shortly after another crowd of persons came there, who were determined to sustain the exhorter should he be attacked by those who were opposed by his religious views. In the course of half an hour there was an assemblage of some ten thousand men, women and children present. The language of the speaker was very severe against Popery, and there being many in attendance whose feelings he touched, they began to initiate an intention of lynching him" (*NYT*, 12 December 1853).

The situation was dire. A violent, religion-rooted riot had nearly occurred on the grounds of a major New York shipbuilding firm, whose senior partner was also the sitting mayor. Westervelt's home was later surrounded by five thousand or more citizens demanding the preacher's release. When that action was not forthcoming, "threats were made that they would burn down the Mayor's house, or blow it up" (*NYT*, 12 December 1853). Adjacent to the mayor's proclamation in the *New York Times* on 17 December was an open letter from Archbishop Hughes to his diocesan flock (fig. 17). In it, the prelate requested that Catholics "avoid all such preachings, and leave the parties who approve of them to the entire and perfect enjoyment of their choice," adding that he believed such combative street oratory to be "a snare." Considering the source, Hughes's missive was sound advice, but one wonders whether there was a tacit "understanding" between the mayor and archbishop. Both had much to lose from a religious war fought across a few square miles of downtown New York. Each was a civic leader and a large property holder, so there was substantial common interest. But there were also great differences in their viewpoints. While both had enforcers on call to resist a violent attack, the state militia fully backed *only* Westervelt's position; so Hughes charged all Catholics to defend their property with force: "If such a conspiracy should arise, unrebuked by the public authorities, to a point really menacing with destruction any portion of your property, whether your private dwellings, your churches, your hospitals, orphan asylums, other Catholic institutions, then in any case of attack, let every man be prepared, in God's name, to stand by the laws of the country and the authorities of the City, in defense of such rights and property" (*NYT*, 17 December 1853, 1).

A *New York Times* editorial in the same edition (17 December 1853, 4) berated the archbishop for using what it regarded as inflam-

Figure 17. The Most Rev. John Hughes, Archbishop of New-York. Print. Emmet Collection. New York Public Library.

matory language. Hughes's carefully worded statement, however, was a very public reminder to the mayor that Catholics were the aggrieved party in the religious controversy and that it was the responsibility of the city to afford them viable protection. Its intention was to reorient official city policy from a neutral direction to a pro-Catholic bent, but the result had an unexpected outcome. Hughes had, in effect, challenged the mayor to step from a ledge onto a lightly tethered tightrope. Westervelt reacted by reaching out instead in the radical Protestant direction. On 18 December, he "sought an interview" with the preacher (now identified as Reverend Daniel Parsons) and "offered his ship yard to the preacher's use for his religious service . . . and assured him that no interference on the part of the police would be made" (*NYT,* 19 December 1853). Westervelt's personal approach to Parsons and the onset of winter combined to cool tempers until spring, when street preaching again became an issue in Manhattan and across the East River in Brooklyn. That series of events is also detailed in area newspapers and has been summarized by O'Rourke (2001, 137–49). Catholics objected to proselytizers preaching Catholic hatred within their ethnic enclave.

In contrast, another song printed by Andrews, "Paddy's Fight with the Know-Nothings" by Tom Robinson, seems to be a sly attempt to discourage Irishmen from voting. Though the song is written in brogue cant, one must question whether a Catholic Irish combatant who was bested in a street brawl would actually compose a song that praises Know-Nothing prowess and discourages his fellows from using the ballot box. Possibly, Robinson was an Orangeman:

> Our party was thirty, all armed wid' big sticks,
> Sure we'd knock 'em about like a thousand of bricks;
> At the villans we went, we "brave men of the hod,"
> An' I gav' a big "Yankee" a belt in the gob.
> "Wide Awake" was their war cry, from near and from far,
> We answered their challenge wid' "Erin-go-bragh;"
> On my eye I then got a we bit of a whack,
> Which laid me right out on the broad of my back.
>
> Wid' sprigs of shelalah so bravely we fought,
> We'd belt them like blazes, so all of us thought;
> But the hard-fisted Yankees they bate us so sweet,
> That all of us Irishmen had to retreat.
> Now I'll tell you one thing an' that you may note—
> I'll keep far away from the place that they vote;
> For I'll tell ye'se the truth, and it's no mistake—
> We found the Knownothings were all WIDE AWAKE.
>
> (Wright 1975, 517)

Andrews's "There's Room Enough for All" sets a different course by urging immigrant tenement dwellers to forsake overcrowded East Coast urban centers for idealized open fields in "rural hills and valleys":

> From poisoned air ye breathe in courts,
>   And typhus-tainted alleys,
> Go forth, where health resorts
>   In rural hills and valleys;
> Where every hand that clears a bough,
>   Finds plenty in abundance,

And every furrow of the plough,
    A step to independence.

Oh hasten then from fevered den, and lodging cramped and small,
The world is wide in lands beside, there's room enough for all.

In this fair region far away
    Will labor find employment,
A fair day's work and a fair day's pay,
    And toil will earn employment:
What need then of this daily strife,
    Each warring with his brother
Why need we in the crowd of life,
    Keep trampling on each other?

Oh, fellow men, remember then whatever chance befal,
The world is wide where those abide, there's room enough for all.
                                (Watkinson Library)

    This rural solution to urban overcrowding and poverty—rejected flatly by John Hughes, who believed that poor, Irish Catholic immigrants needed to gather under the wing of the church within the cityscape to keep body and soul together—was a remedy favored by middle-class Irish as a means of alleviating urban degradation and improving group image overall. It was a long-standing theme in Irish American community discourse. Andrews printed general subject songs, even ones such as this that concerned Catholics more than Protestants, as long as they were not detrimental to American Protestant interests. There was no harm from the perspective of Andrews's main clients in persuading Catholics that the Great Plains were a better place to settle than Lower Manhattan.

    Andrews also published "The Brogue," attributed to John Kiernan, which uses a "Paddy-the-Irishman" character to depict New York as a hostile environment for immigrants:

When I came to this country 'twas late in the fall
Both Cart and Hack-Drivers around me did bawl

From one to another they pushed me about
Saying, "that brogue on his tongue will never wear out."

One chap seized me box and was off in a twack,
I shouted and halloa'd for him to come back,
Says one of the Blackguards he'll come back no doubt,
But that brogue on your tongue it will never wear out.

He ran like the devil up a dirty dark lane,
Says I where's me box sir or what do ye mane,
He stuck up his thum on the top of his snout,
Saying that brogue on your tongue shure will never wear out.

Och! Now I'm a voter, but I don't vote for rogues,
And with Patint Lethurs replaced me Ould Brogues.
(NYSL Broadside Ballads, SCO BD0112)

The "greenhorn" does well eventually, as evidenced by his new patent leather shoes. But does he wear them because he has fallen in with Whigs instead of Democrats? Has he deserted his working-class fellows for the middle class?

Andrews's songs for the mainstream Irish market were largely romances or emigration pieces. These include "Dermot Astore: A Reply to 'Kathleen Mavounreen'" and "The Emigrant's Farewell," which recalls the Great Famine and is unforgiving of the British government's colonialist policy toward Ireland:

I would not live in Ireland now, for she's a fallen land,
And the tyrant's heels is on her neck, with her reeking blood-stained
    hand,
There's not a foot of Irish ground, but's trodden down by slaves,
Who die unwept, and then are flung, like dogs, into their graves.
(NYSL Broadside Ballads, SCO BD0112)

Thus, based on the significant sample gathered, there were no songs supporting the beleaguered Catholics in their fight against nativist oppression. Indeed, at the height of Know-Nothing sway, few mainstream American printers would have found the risk-reward ratio attractive.

In a huge city composed of people with different national origins, societal norms, and needs, one religion could not possibly satisfy all. Indeed, one sect did not satisfy all Protestants. The transference of energy from the English Reformation into ever-more charismatic sects, each seeking to strike a fatal blow against the Church of Rome, meant continuing trouble for the Catholic Irish, who were in turn unwilling to step back from nativist aggression aimed at their ethnic enclaves, owing to the contentious history of their homeland and their stormy passage across the Atlantic. Creed, economics, ancient animosities, and, not the least, red-hot venom and chilling fear on both sides combined to make the famine-nativist period in New York a particularly divisive epoch for all residents.

The saga of New York's Catholic Irish during this period is that of a desperately besieged ethno-religious minority, but not one without hope. The massive, hunger-propelled influx of refugee Irish into the port of New York fueled the flames of contention; however, bolstered group numbers helped the Catholic community withstand the militant nativist onslaught. In 1850, Manhattan was home to 133,730 Irish-born residents. By 1860, that number was 203,740—more than 25 percent of the city's population. In 1854, the American Party won gubernatorial elections in Massachusetts and Delaware. But two years later, divided nationally over the slavery issue, the Know-Nothings gave way to the oncoming Republicans, who had a clear, positive vision with more general appeal. In 1860, the American Party won no congressional seats and quickly disappeared. As overt nativism receded from Manhattan's streetscape, and Catholic Irish found crude shelter and back-breaking work in the city, the Hibernian love of song again gave voice. In 1859, John Andrews sold his broadside song sheet publishing business to Henry De Marsan, who viewed the Irish not as a target but as a market.

Had the slavery issue been resolved without secession and war, New York's Catholic Irish would in all likelihood have been remanded into a permanent underclass. Strangely and painfully, the Civil War presented them with a horrifically violent opportunity to prove themselves, unequivocally and undeniably, as Americans.

CHAPTER FOUR

The Civil War and the
Draft Riots of 1863

I'm a dacint boy, just landed from the town of Ballyfad;
I want a situation: yis, I want it mighty bad.
I saw a place advertised. It's the thing for me, says I;
But the dirty spalpeen ended with: No Irish need apply.
Whoo! says I; but that's an insult—though to get the place I'll try.
So, I wint to see the blaggar[d] with: No Irish need apply.

In 1862, when John F. Poole composed the famous, critically comic song "No Irish Need Apply" (NINA),[1] the phrase was very evident in the help wanted section of city newspapers, where that sentiment was openly voiced:

I started off to find the house, I got it mighty soon;
There I found the ould chap saited: he was reading the TRIBUNE.
I tould him what I came for, whin he in a rage did fly:
No! says he, you are a Paddy, and no Irish need apply!
Thin I felt my dandher rising, and I'd like to black his eye—
To tell an Irish Gintleman: No Irish need apply!

(LC digital ID as10973)

Indeed, the *New York Tribune* printed NINA employment advertising at least as early as 15 May 1851 in help wanted advertisements, such as the following:

INSTRUCTRESS.—Wanted in an Episcopal Family in the country, a Lady competent to teach Music and the English branches. Salary from $100 to $125 a year. . . . No Irish need apply.

The practice continued for at least forty years (*Tribune*, 28 June 1891, 9).

Significant levels of anti-Irish discrimination in hiring also appear in online searches of employment advertising published in the *New York Times*. A search under NINA for the years 1855 and 1865 returns eighteen advertisements, but the practice was far broader than the NINA stricture. When search terms are broadened to include "No Irish" and "Protestant only," the number increases to forty-eight. However, even that larger figure is not an accurate measure of the prejudice faced by Catholic Irish jobseekers, because they were more frequently barred through *positive* preferences, as seen in this 1865 advertisement:

WANTED—TWO SERVANTS, PROTESTANTS. American, English, Scotch or German; one as cook only, thorough in her profession; the other as chambermaid and waitress. . . . (*NYT*, 16 March 1865, 8)

In it, Irish Catholics are doubly excluded through religion and ethnicity. Conversely, a search under "no negro" or "no colored"[2] in classified advertisements during the same period returns no records; positive queries for "Irish only" or "Catholics only" also return no records. From this information, it can be extrapolated that Poole's song is correct in claiming anti-Irish discrimination in help wanted newspaper advertising. NINA advertisements were only the observable tip of an iceberg of bias that sank the aspirations and endangered the livelihood of many within the community because Catholic Irish job applicants could simply be told their qualifications were insufficient or that a position was already filled.

The value of song lyrics in the study of New York Irish Catholic integration can be appreciated when Poole's text is examined alongside period newspaper advertisements and employed to test a claim made by Kerby Miller (1985, 324) that "rancorous bigotry" persisted during the Civil War era. Miller's assertion was opposed by Richard Jensen (2002, 405), who writes, "The Irish American community harbors a deeply held belief that it was the victim of systematic job discrimination in America, and that the discrimination was done publicly in highly humiliating fashion." The author claims no record of large-scale employment bias against Irish Catholics exists: "It is possible that handwritten No Irish Need Apply signs regarding maids did appear in a few American windows, though no one ever reported one. Apart from want ads for personal household workers, the NINA slogan has not turned up in newspapers." Here Jensen attempts to make his point by dismissing the most obvious means of hiring discrimination against Irish Catholics, a portion of which is immediately verifiable through highly visible help wanted advertising in mass circulation papers. The discrimination is undeniably systematic: potential employers used newspapers (which mitigated the immediate possibility of broken windows), and the advertisements, which contained discriminatory language, were accepted and published. Though not apparent in Jensen's title or stated in his opening paragraph, his main interest is in potential employment discrimination against males in window signage displayed in commercial and industrial settings. Why he should exclude service sector employment is difficult to comprehend, because mid-nineteenth-century New York was "a city of countless boardinghouses, large hotels and elegant mansions," and large numbers of household workers were required to staff these operations. In 1855, Irish-born servants amounted to 79.3 percent of the city's household and hospitality workers (Ernst 1965, 65–66). Service, therefore, was one of the largest sources of income for Manhattan's Catholic Irish, and, because supply and demand for labor are rarely perfectly matched, selection bias is always a possibility and needs to be fully considered in discrimination discourse, especially when a victimization "myth" theory is proposed.

Prejudice remained "blatant" in the United States even during the Civil War according to Miller (1985, 324), who cites, among other examples, "the mistreatment of Irish American conscripts and soldiers." During the Civil War, fearing unfair treatment from American officers, immigrant soldiers from various nations, the majority of whom were Catholic, used self-imposed segregation to avoid hostility and discrimination by enlisting in separate ethnic military units. Government encouraged the practice because fellowship in ethnicity increased enlistments in a war where recruits were in great demand. In addition to providing camaraderie and comfort, ethnic corps offered protection under the presumption that military justice would be applied equitably.

Ballad printers in Ireland followed events in the United States, so an Irishman, even before he crossed the Atlantic, might have heard the epic narrative "O'Brien of Tipperary" about the possible consequences of a "greenhorn" being swept into a native regiment:

In the Philadelphia regiment I mean to let you know,
O'Brien many a battle fought against the southern foe,
The Majors daughter fell in love with him you plainly see,
Her father then resolved to prove her destiny.

On March the fifth in New Orleans the major he did swear,
The[n] did insult that soldier brave all on the barrack square,
You may thank your daughter said O'Brien, or else I'll end your
    strife,
The major then his sword he drew and thought to take his life.
    (Wright 1975, 465)

Here, the protagonist makes the mistake of enlisting in a regiment centered on American geography, rather than Irish ethnicity. Soon, the attention of his commander's daughter becomes a source of contention.

The ethnic regiment of the Union army with the widest fame was the Sixty-Ninth New York State Militia, one of the few Northern units to comport itself well at the chaotic Battle of Bull Run. However, the bravery and steadfastness shown by the Sixty-Ninth during the first major engagement of the Civil War engendered another of the contemporary issues of prejudice, "the unnecessary, if not intentional, waste of Irish regiments in hopeless combat situations," mentioned both by Miller (1985, 324) and Susannah Ural Bruce (2006, 82–135).

Of the more than 2,000 Union army regiments active in the four-year conflict, New York's Sixty-Ninth suffered the sixth highest number of soldiers killed or mortally wounded in action—259; seventh highest at 250 was the Massachusetts Twenty-Eighth, another unit of the Irish Brigade (Fox 1889). Miller's observations vis-à-vis American Protestant discrimination toward Irish Catholics are indeed supported, and the first-person period detail of song offers a fuller appreciation of the resistance they faced in New York City during the Civil War years.

On 16 April 1861, when the tenor of the city was at fever pitch (the shelling of Fort Sumter had begun on the night of 12 April), the *New York Times* speculated whether the Sixty-Ninth would support the Union war effort. In an article pejoratively entitled "Loyalty of the Irish Element," it nervously tried to put down rumors that the Sixty-Ninth Regiment might jump to the Confederate cause en masse (Spann 2002, 22; McKay 1991, 57). They did not, and Irish group image improved dramatically after the Battle of Bull Run. However, the longer-term question was whether, as many nativists believed, the Irish were doing only what they were believed to do best—*fight*—and thus could never become true Americans. This chapter examines the continuing, progressive struggle of the New York Irish for *integration*, as opposed to *assimilation*. While nativism receded from its mid-1850s peak during the Civil War period, opposition to Irish Catholics did not disappear from New York City. Resentment was now expressed less openly and violently, but anti-Irish, anti-Catholic feeling was still obvious. In this penultimate chapter, the uneven, advance-retreat progress of Irish integration continues, while the hard-won respect earned by the Sixty-Ninth and other Irish American military units was compromised by hideously violent mob resistance to the blatantly inequitable Enrollment Act of 1863.

Colonel Corcoran and the Prince of Wales

On 11 October 1860, Prince Edward, son of Queen Victoria and heir to the British throne, arrived in New York, becoming the first member of the royal family ever to visit America's foremost city. An extensive article appearing in the *Times* of London (27 October 1860) called his public reception at the Battery "an ovation as has been seldom offered to any Monarch in ancient or modern times." As the prince disembarked near the Castle Garden, Mayor Fernando Wood greeted him with the words, "Your Royal Highness, as chief magistrate of the city, I welcome you here. In this welcome I represent the entire population, without exception." The *Times* (27 October 1860, 9) reporter observed

> Five brigades of the New York Militia—mustering in all some 6,000 or 7,000 men. . . . The 4th Brigade, to use Lord John Russell's simile, was "conspicuous for the absence" of the 69th Regiment. Colonel Corcoran and his men refused to turn out and welcome the Prince. No national slight is implied here. The 69th is composed almost entirely of Orangemen. . . . The insult, however, will not be passed over so lightly in New York. Colonel Corcoran will, it is said, be tried by court-martial and dismissed for refusing to obey orders, and the whole regiment itself may probably be disbanded, for the feeling is strong against it.

The description of the Sixty-Ninth in England's foremost newspaper was erroneous. The regiment was composed almost entirely of Fenians, Irish Republicans, who were the antithesis of Orangemen. Mayor Wood was likewise incorrect—duplicitous, actually—when he added the words "without exception," for he knew full well that Irish Catholics, who were somewhat more than one-quarter of New York's citizenry, strongly opposed the prince's visit. The Sixty-Ninth had met and voted to boycott the festivities specifically because Her Majesty's government had failed to support Ireland adequately during the potato blight (Bruce 2006, 43–48; Kenny 2000, 90–97).

There were additional ironies about the royal visit: during the American Revolution, eleven thousand American men and women had died from starvation, contaminated water, and disease while held prisoner aboard British hulks lying in New York harbor (Burrows and Wallace 1999, 253–54; Lankevich 1998, 47); within living memory, the Royal Navy had impressed and sorely misused American merchant seamen; and Castle Garden, the very place where the prince landed, was erected in 1811 as a gun battery intended to defend New York from an expected British invasion. Six months after Edward's visit, the Civil War began. Once the Union blockaded Confederate ports, English mills were deprived of Southern cotton, and British shipyards

Figure 18. Daniel J. Pound, *His Royal Highness the Prince of Wales, K. G. as Colonel in the Army.* Engraving. J. E. Mayall, photographer. New York Public Library.

Figure 19. Fernando Wood, Mayor of the City of New York. Print. Emmet Collection. New York Public Library.

began clandestine construction of sleek blockade runners to dash past cordons of Union ships (Anderson 1962, 215–22), and of commerce raiders that waged a war of attrition against the economy of the North (Anderson 1962, 196–214; Semmes 1996). These issues—past, present, and future—were brushed aside as Prince Edward landed in Manhattan.

Flowery praise in the *New York Times* (1 August 1860) heralded his impending arrival, including this dreamy description: "There is something in the youth of the Prince as contrasted with the antiquity of the crown he represents, which wears in itself a color of romance." But moonstruck hyperbole was a minor offense compared to what followed. Edward's officially private tour of the United States was an addendum to his state visit of Canada. The elite newspaper deigned to suggest the prince's presence in Canada would "bring the moral weight of institutions that have stood the test of centuries, upon colonies which, geographically at least, may be said to be exposed to the freaks and passions of our restless, wild and eccentric Republic." So frenetic was New York's fascination with the future king that the pandering newspaper felt free to belittle America's treasured tradition of democratic republicanism. One-quarter of New York may have despised England, but much of the remaining three-quarters felt deep kinship with it. Ignoring a litany of errors and incongruities, most American Protestant New Yorkers reveled in royalty (at least as long as they did not have to pay its bills). Still, there were some dissenters, as evidenced by "The Prince of Whales, No. 2," a popular song sheet printed by H. De Marsan:

> The Prince of Whales will soon be here.
>   Ye codfish all, I pray draw near;
> His Grace, my Lord, the Prince you'll meet
> To pay your homage at his feet;
> Let ev'ry boson heave with joy,
>   For soon you'll greet the Princely boy;
> What though it cost you many dimes,
>   You will no doubt have glorious times.
>
> · · · · · · · · · ·
>
> This liberty we will maintain
>   Till Kings and monarchs cease to reign;
> To Prince or king we'll not bow down,
>   Nor homage pay to earthly crown.

Persecution drove our fathers here,
> With their lov'd wives and children dear,
To find that calm, sweet peace of mind,
> Which they in England could not find.
>   (NYSL BD SCO1053)

Edward left New York after a three-day stay, though memory of his visit remained with the Hibernian community. New York, their adopted home, had trampled on them in its haste to celebrate the arrival of a symbol of their oppression in Ireland. Four years later, New York Irish music hall performer Joe English sang,

When the Prince of Wales came over here, and made a hubbaboo,
Oh, everybody turned out, you know, in gold and tinsel too;
But then the good old Sixty-ninth didn't like these lords or peers—
They wouldn't give a d—m for kings, the Irish volunteers!
We love the land of Liberty, its laws we will revere,
"But the divil take nobility!" says the Irish volunteer.
>   (English 1864, 17)

The author-singer's curious surname derived from the fact that his forbearers were among the first people in their Irish-speaking area to adopt the English language; and his song mocked the city's upper classes, who connived for tickets to receptions honoring the prince, reminding them America was founded on the principle of equality. In the eyes of Irish Americans, *they* were true patriot defenders of the Republic. Even before Joe English took up his pen, this charge was corroborated when British shipbuilders manufactured the first commerce raiders for the Confederacy (Anderson 1962).

The *Times'* suggestion that Colonel Michael Corcoran would be tried by court-martial proved true. Anglo-American loyalty to England as the ancestral homeland of the United States demanded recompense for what was roundly perceived as an embarrassing, disloyal act. On 17 November 1860, the *New York Times* carried the report that Corcoran, "having been arrested on a charge and specification for disobedience of orders," was relieved of duty. This action had highly serious potential consequences, for it was a figurative line drawn in the sand between American Protestant and Irish Catholic Manhattan. In the opinion of the former, the Gaels had gone too far in snubbing the prince. But New York's Catholic Irish were only just emerging from a fiery passage through the gauntlet of extreme nativist oppression, and, in the eyes of Great Hunger refugees, it was the British government that had consigned and compelled them to New York.

Regardless of risk, the Catholic Irish of America immediately circled around Colonel Corcoran. Boston's Irish community invited him to be feted by the banks of the Charles River (*NYT*, 19 November 1860). Gifts arrived. From "South Carolina, there came a gold-headed palmetto cane; from San Francisco, a one-pound gold medal for the regiment, to be worn by the colonel on public occasions; from fellow New Yorkers, an elegant, gold-ornamented sword" (Lane 1997, 21). Thus, a man who was seen by the city at large as an ingrate, an embarrassment, and a potential traitor was viewed by his own outsider group as a man of chivalry, an elite of the famine-era immigrant horde.

Michael Corcoran's civilian occupation was manager of Hibernian Hall (located directly across Prince Street from Saint Patrick's Cathedral), so he was a highly visible, respected, and well connected member of Manhattan's Irish society: even more so because he was an officer of the American Fenian Brotherhood, which advocated Irish independence by direct force. Corcoran's importance was well known to the coalition-building Democratic Party, whose support did not waiver despite the colonel's difficulties. Even when he was in the throes of court-martial, Tammany Hall proposed him for party positions and political office (*NYT*, 26 November 1860). That December, he was elected as a school inspector for the Sixth Ward (*NYT*, 23 December 1860). His Irish credentials were impeccable and his lineage was actually no less stellar than Prince Edward's—*plus* he had real-life experience to add to his DNA. Descended from Patrick Sarsfield, one of Ireland's greatest warrior-heroes, Corcoran had served as a revenue policeman in northwest County Donegal before immigrating to New York. Closely viewing Britain's inadequate response to Ireland's hunger by day, he rode at night with the vigilante Ribbonmen. After his double life fell under suspicion, Corcoran left Ireland quickly and made for New York, where he found friendship and respect among his émigré countrymen (Lane 1997, 14–15).

During his trial, the colonel's defense maintained that the regiment, a part-time militia unit, whose members paid for their own uniforms and held civilian jobs, had already completed its legally mandated parade requirement for the year and could not be further compelled. Though Corcoran may have been within his rights, popular perception cast the Sixty-Ninth and, through loose connection, *all* Irish immigrants as ungrateful (*NYT*, 23 October 1860, 4), thereby threatening to set back community prospects for integration.

While most of the mainstream press vilified Corcoran, his case proceeded slowly and was still undecided, when the city's attention turned swiftly away from the Prince of Wales incident. Fort Sumter was bombarded on 12 April 1861. The Civil War was at hand, and the overwhelming issue now became how to fight the conflict that virtually no one in New York either desired or expected. The Irish, unwanted in time of peace, became necessary in time of conflict.

Broadway to Bull Run and Beyond

On 20 April 1861, charges against Michael Corcoran were dropped and his court-martial dissolved (Conyngham 1867, 20; McKay 1991, 61–62). Three days later, 1,130 officers and men of the Sixty-Ninth embarked by steamer for Washington and war (fig. 20).

Figure 20. Departure of the Sixty-Ninth Regiment, N.Y.S.M., Tuesday April 23rd 1861. New York Public Library.

The Americanization that might come with Irish support during the Civil War was not necessarily what *all* Irish Catholics wanted most. Choice of domicile was a decision contingent on the obligations and opportunities of each individual. But at least until Ireland became open and autonomous, each year they stayed on in New York, they became more rooted, realizing that as citizens they should enjoy the guarantees of the Constitution. However, those civil liberties in turn carried the responsibilities of citizenship, including military service to the nation. That was made clear by Tammany lawyer-politician Richard O'Gorman speaking at the Union Square mass war rally on 20 April 1861 (*NYT*, 21 April 1861, 1). Though Irish Catholics had a great deal to lose—not only the lives of combatants but the livelihood of dependents in an era long before the existence of governmental social welfare plans—they, along with their church, subordinated their duty to Ireland by supporting the nation that had sheltered, if not actually welcomed, them (McKay 1991, 59–60). As a result, the Civil War became a powerful opportunity for Irish societal incorporation. If they performed well on the battlefield, mainstream New Yorkers would be forced to credit and accept them on their merits, an essential stage in the process of integration. This reassessment of divided loyalties between Ireland and the United States was ongoing—not spontaneous but gradual. It was a philosophical process carried out on both individual and group levels.

In addition to his responsibilities at Tammany, Hibernian Hall, and the Sixty-Ninth, Michael Corcoran was also chief officer pro tem of the American Fenian Brotherhood. On the day before leaving New York for Washington, he wrote an official communiqué transmitted to all Fenian cells. In doing so, he sought to shore up the argument for Irish involvement in an American Civil War based on the future promise it held for freedom in Ireland: "I am leaving in great spirits and hope. My last wish and most ardent desire is that the organization should be preserved in its strength and efficiency, and that every man will do his whole duty. We will not be the worse for a little practice, which we engage in, with the more heart because we feel it will be serviceable on other fields" (Cavanagh 1892, 371).

While writing about the necessity of a military solution for the woes of his Irish homeland, the colonel was simultaneously moving farther from the land of his birth and placing in mortal jeopardy the lives of more than 1,100 committed patriots. In April 1861, focusing on preparation for the liberation of Ireland helped ease the hardship placed on the community, while the Sixty-Ninth's early departure for the front underscored to the city at large the patriotism of the Catholic Irish. Little more thought was given to this, because it was widely believed the war would last only a few months.

Following the capture of Fort Sumter, Irish New Yorkers coalesced quickly around the preservation of the Union. Strongly pro-South Thomas Francis Meagher did a quick about-face after learning of the attack (Cavanagh 1892, 369–70), forming a company of Zouaves that would be incorporated into the Sixty-Ninth Regiment before the first land battle of the Civil War.[3]

New York broadside printer Henry De Masan's "Glorious 69th" (Duke ID bsvg100279) is a song from the initial days of the conflict. In twelve verses—long for the period—it recalls the parade down Broadway, the departure from Manhattan, the voyage to Annapolis (avoiding Baltimore, where Confederate sympathizers were believed to wait in ambush), and the arrival in Washington. Its depiction of the departure scene is upbeat and conveys expectations that the rebellion will be quickly quelled. There is no indication that Corcoran, who had taken ill during his trial and was still unwell, sat in a carriage en route to the transport ship, too weak to ride on horseback; such news might have deflated the buoyant mood. Therefore, "Glorious 69th" promotes celebration, community pride, and patriotism. Purposely, the song does not mention the concerns held by the crowds, who throng to see off the Sixty-Ninth and recognize the clear danger both to individual life ("God bless ye, boys, and send ye safe home!") and group reputation ("Remember your country, and keep up its credit, boy!") (Cavanagh 1892, 375). But these ominous fears expressed as on-street outbursts were later recalled as ethereal echoes in another, quite different, yet similarly titled song, "To the Glorious 69th," a brooding parlor ballad:

I never shall forget that look, when last he said: good-bye!
He gave my hand a friendly shake, a tear was in his eye;
His chin began to quiver, the bitter cup he drank,
And then away, with soldiers to march in the front flank.

I had a premonition dream, which I forgot to tell;
I dreamed my loving husband fell backward in a well;
In vain I tried to raise him, the vital spark hath fled,
And in the morn when I awoke, we were both safe in bed.

(Wright 1975, 450)

These two songs tell us that the days spent by the Irish community in New York awaiting the return of loved ones were long and filled with continuously varying emotions, that martial songs served to justify the parting, and that melancholy songs helped the community cope with the long ordeal of fearful separation.

The first test of both armies occurred on 21 July 1861, on a section of rolling countryside south of Centreville, Virginia, below which ran a sluggish stream named Bull Run. Northern forces gained an early upper hand, with Corcoran's men "first capturing three Confederate artillery batteries" (Spann 2002, 27), but a Confederate counterattack precipitated a Union rout (fig. 21). The Sixty-Ninth withdrew as "an intact unit in the midst of the increasing chaos"; however, "as Colonel Corcoran changed formation from square to column to negotiate some difficult terrain, the 69th was overrun by two fleeing Union regiments" (Bilby 1998, 13). Drawn into the muddled mess, the Sixty-Ninth retreated, while Corcoran, who was wounded, and seven men who stayed with him were captured (Daly 1962, 100–101). Though the unit's US flag was taken, its regimental colors, sarcastically known as "the Prince of Wales flag," were saved. On 24 July, the *Sun* carried news that "above our shame and sorrow, the wonderful endurance of our New York regiments, shines like a hale of glory. The Sixty-ninth (Irish) led the advance, and a valor and persistence superior to theirs is not on record in history, ancient or modern."

Prior to the battle, the expectation had been that the insurrection—it was not yet spoken of in the North as a civil war—would be put down quickly. With their initial enlistment period expiring, the regiment returned to New York as soon as possible after Bull Run, arriving on 27 July 1861. De Marsan had the song sheet "Long Live the Sixty-Ninth!" waiting:

Hail to the men now in triumph returning,
Black with the battle smoke, radiant with fame!

Figure 21. Col. Michael Corcoran, at the Battle of Bull Run, 1861. Lithograph.
Currier and Ives. Collection of author.

Ireland is proud, and America is grateful:
The heart of each Irish girl bounds at their name!
    Caed millea failtha, men!
    Out on the air again
Rings the clear sound of the Irish hurrah,
    As up from the surging crowd,
    Bursts the shout, deep and loud:
Long live the Sixty-Ninth! Erin go Bragh!

. . . .

The honor of Ireland was safe in their keeping;
The Sunburst and Stars and Stripes safe in their hands;
No marvel, they fought with a strength superhuman:
For, each man, in the Sixty-Ninth, struck for two lands!
    Hail to the true and tried!
    Shout their praise far and wide!
Greet them at once with an Irish hurrah!
    Swift to charge, firm to stand,
    Brave heart and steady hand;
Long live the Sixty-Ninth! Erin go Bragh!
                (LC amss.cw103370)

The tribute was composed by two members of the Irish community ("Words by Mr. Mullaly—Music by John J. Daly") and stresses the dual nationality of most soldiers of the Sixty-Ninth, as well as the city's Irish en masse. It presupposes that the regiment's brave behavior would inspire the city as a whole to take to the streets to welcome their return. Perhaps many Anglo-Americans did, but far from all were ready to fete the Sixty-Ninth, which only eight months earlier had snubbed the heir to the British throne. The following day, the *New York Times* (28 July 1861, 1) ran the page 1 headline, "Our War-Worn Heroes—Return of the 69th Regiment"; but the article beneath it, while congratulatory, bore the weight of condescension in such passages as "the aspect present on our streets yesterday was eminently flattering to our mobocracy" and "it seemed as if every Biddy [the Irish working-class everywoman] in the land had suddenly and mysteriously burst into sight for the express gratification of the gallant Sixty-ninth." It continues by dwelling unnecessarily on Irish women as domestic servants, as though all were and fit for nothing else. While the *New York Times* acclaim for the Sixty-Ninth's bravery is strong in places, also woven inappropriately into the article is an account of a soldier who was killed on the train journey north, when he reached out to view the surrounding countryside. Were readers meant to conclude that the men of the Sixty-Ninth were courageous because they lacked the sense to recognize danger? The report continued that on the battlefield, "those who were nearest the gallant fellows, and saw them toiling and fighting as if to toil and to fight were but pleasant pastimes, are loudest in their praise." Was it to be inferred that the Irish fight because fighting is their second nature? The combination of these and other slights makes the article at once both complimentary and demeaning. More importantly, what the newspaper does not do in its lengthy coverage is to position the Sixty-Ninth *within* the American populace, unless one considers the following inclusionary: "In that green and lovely island where all the women are virtuous, and all the men are brave, they don't stand on ceremony, and we have Irish hearts here as true and impulsive as any that beat in Erin." Nativism still prevailed at the *New York Times* and among its elite readers, proclaimed not with a club but with a snub, perhaps to compensate for the Prince of Wales incident.

Conversely, the likewise conservative and elite *Sun* (28 July 1861) provided the missing references: "Immense was the crowd all along the way. At Fourteenth street, they marched past the statue of WASH-INGTON" and made clear their humanity and sacrifice. It continued, "So fatigued, however, were the men, that several lay down on the floor and, amid all the crowd, slept soundly. Poor fellows, for two days they had had neither rest or slumber." On page 1 of its 28 July issue, the abolitionist-minded *New York Daily Tribune* made the same connections resoundingly:

> [The] Irish national banner, emblem of a great, chivalrous and brave people, was borne through the streets by the brave 69th. The greeting to the Prince of Wales did not compare in heartiness or significance with that which our city *en masse* gave to the battle-stained heroes whose deeds at Bull Run are the theme of national praise, and whose toil-worn appearance, tattered uniforms and bronzed faces are tangible proofs of a hard-fought and glorious field. . . . It was a splendid demonstration of the gratitude of the metropolis for the Irish Americans who have gone forth to strike in its defense, and showed that they did not love Ireland less, but America more.

Clearly, the Sixty-Ninth's performance was effecting a softening of position among *some* in Gotham's "better" classes; however, it was the others, those who accepted the blood sacrifice of the Irish in support of the Union, yet would not grant them equal opportunity, who had to be confronted. It was they whom John F. Poole addressed the following year with "No Irish Need Apply" (begun above and continued here), reminding them of the founding documents of the nation and the daily sacrifices made by Irish Americans on behalf of the Union:

> Sure, I've heard that in America it always is the plan
> That an Irishman is just as good as any other man;
> A home and hospitality they never will deny
> The stranger here, or ever say: No Irish need apply.
> But some black sheep are in the flock: a dirty lot, say I;
> A dacint man will never write: No Irish need apply!
>
> Sure, Paddy's heart is in his hand, as all the world does know,
> His praties and his whiskey he will share with friend or foe;

His door is always open to the stranger passing by;
He never thinks of saying: None but Irish may apply.
And, in Columbia's history, his name is ranking high;
Thin, the Divil take the knaves that write: No Irish need apply!

Ould Ireland on the battle-field a lasting fame has made;
We all have heard of Meagher's men, and Corcoran's brigade.
Though fools may flout and bigots rave, and fanatics may cry,
Yet when they want good fighting-men, the Irish may apply,
And when for freedom and the right they raise the battle-cry,
Then the Rebel ranks begin to think: No Irish need apply.

It is hardly surprising that a vast number of Irish American songs first published during the Civil War focused on the military and, whether journalistic, poignant, or humorous, were serious in nature. Early on, they were highly optimistic, centered on praising bravery and encouraging recruitment, and almost always played up the dual loyalties of recruits as both American and Irish. "The Gallant 69th, No. 8," written before the first battle, is an example:

The sons of old Granua are arming
    In defense of the Stripes and the Stars,
Defenders of their land of adoption,
    And help her to fight all her wars.
Then woe to the foemen who meet them!
    They'll teach them a lesson so true,
That they'll remember the Sixty-Ninth Regiment,
    That fought 'neath the Red, White, and Blue.

Although in the land of the stranger,
    Let the old Irish Flag wave on high,
And ere that old Flag shall be trampled,
    We'll show them how Irishmen can die.
As our fathers marched to honor and glory,
    Bearing that old Flag so true,
We will show them how their sons, in Columbia,
    Can fight 'neath the Red, White, and Blue.
                                   (Milner collection)

Though available for purchase by anyone in the city, this song sheet was intended for an Irish audience, as evidenced by its use of typical immigrant references to "Granua" (Granuaille, the legendary Irish warrior queen) and "the land of the stranger." While the latter phrase might be misconstrued as hostile by a non-Irish audience, to Irish people, every country other than Ireland was the "land of the stranger." There is also a direct link to Catholicism in the fourth verse: "With Father Mooney marching before them." As it happened, the popular yet impulsive chaplain Thomas Mooney of St. Brigid's Parish on Tompkins Square did not march with the Sixty-Ninth for long. He was recalled to New York before the Sixty-Ninth saw action because of, as Archbishop John J. Hughes put it, his "inauguration of a ceremony unknown to the Church"—specifically, the blessing of a cannon (Shaw 1977, 326, 341). Without a doubt, the New York Irish, even their clergy, were highly enthusiastic in defense of the Union. Archbishop Hughes had ordered the Union flag to be flown above every church as soon as war was declared.

Beyond their usefulness for recruitment and esprit de corps, military songs also distracted soldiers from the fear of death, injury, and capture. Resolve, rather than despair, is accented after Michael Corcoran's capture in "The Battle of Bull Run," printed by both Henry De Marsan and James Wrigley:

> When the gallant Colonel Corcoran lay prostrate on the ground,
> Weary, and fatigued, and exhausted from his wound,
> He cried unto his gallant men: Brave Boys, I'm not undone,
> We'll make them pay some other day for the Battle of Bull-Run!
> (LC amss.as200270)

Composed and printed immediately after Bull Run, "Free & Easy of Our Union" by John C. Cross is noteworthy in that it is a mainstream, rather than ethnic, production. It is a precursor to Irish integration, evidenced by the way the Sixty-Ninth Regiment is incorporated into the Union army, rather than extracted for separate treatment. Its members are mentioned not because they are Irish but because their ranks are filled with brave Union soldiers, who like the New York Fire Zouaves (recruited from New York City's fire companies) fought fearlessly during the first major engagement of the Civil

War; likewise, their commanders, the missing-in-action Colonel Michael Corcoran and killed-in-action Colonel Elmer Ellsworth of the Zouaves, receive equal mention:

> Patriot's to the war are going,
> Leaving happy homes behind;
> Fighting for our glorious Banner,
> Which by Liberty is entwined.
>
> Glory to those sons of Erin,
> Who fought with an Iron will;
> Told the Southrons what may happen
> They were for the Union still.
>
> Fire Zouaves immortal heroes,
> Avenge brave Ellsworth every one:
> You have now a crown of glory,
> Brighter than the blazing sun.
>
> Brave CORCORAN now is missing,
> And his life hangs on a thread;
> Irish men rescue him if living,
> Or avenge him if he's dead.
>   (LC amss.cw101840)

Michael Corcoran's capture at Bull Run, and his subsequent imprisonment, kept the city and much of the nation focused on the Sixty-Ninth Regiment for more than a year; and, as seen here, songs contributed importantly to that. Rather than being the opposite of soldiers killed in action, prisoners of war were their counterpoint because of the ever-present specter of maltreatment. This was very much the case for the Irish colonel, whose conditions in detainment were pathetic. Though offered "parole" on numerous occasions, he refused as a point of honor because it was predicated on his never again taking up arms against the Confederacy (Corcoran 1864, 61; fig. 22). Corcoran's Southern captors moved him often. He escaped a prison fire, contracted typhoid fever, and was chosen by lot to be a hostage held in solitary confinement and hanged if the Union executed a Confederate

Figure 22. Corcoran in a Southern Prison. Does He Look in Vain for the Expected Aid and Comfort from the North?, 1861. New York Public Library.

privateer, whom it regarded as a pirate (Corcoran 1864). Each of these perils was circulated through New York newspapers and raised Corcoran's image and group esteem. The broadside press likewise kept public attention focused on the colonel. Henry De Marsan published "Corcoran to His Regiment, or I Would Not Take Parole," written by "an Irishman." It is a call to New York's Hibernians to remember his sacrifices. Likening his courageous behavior to that of Ireland's greatest military heroes—Patrick Sarsfield (circa 1655–93) and Owen Roe O'Neill (circa 1582–1649)—it not only mythologized Corcoran but immortalized a hero who daily lived close to death. Such references stressed Irishness and aided recruitment, while the song as a whole demonstrated that there was no contradiction in the Catholic Irish claim that they could be loyal Americans every bit as much as steadfast Irish:

Raise that green Flag proudly, let it wave, on high,
"Liberty and Union" be your battle-cry;
FAUGH-A-BALLAGH shout from your centre to your flanks,
And carry death and terror wild, into the foeman's ranks.

Think how your brave fathers for your freedom fought;
Think of those bright deeds that Irishmen have wrought;
Meet advancing hosts, boys, let them feel your steel,
And prove you're worthy of the land of Sarsfield and O'Neill.

(LC amss.sb10049a)

A song like this was particularly useful for recruiting drives and patriotic tableaux in variety theaters.

By 14 August 1862, when Michael Corcoran was freed in a prisoner exchange, enlistments had declined drastically; however, on his return to Manhattan, a major city celebration produced a temporary trend reversal (Bruce 2006, 110–12; Spann 2002, 115–17). The *New York Times* (23 August 1862, 4) gushed over the demonstration:

> The outpouring was immense, and it embraced every rank and condition of life. Many places of business were closed, and entire classes of our laboring population left their work *en masse* to join in the ovation. The multitude on foot, pressing on the line of procession and the point of reception, was numbered truly by the hundred thousand, and the sentiment pervading all was that of exultant pride in the man they had met to honor. . . .
>
> Yesterday was a day peculiarly one of exultation to the Irish. Because . . . it was one of themselves wrestling with hard fortune in this City, who had now grown so famous as to enforce a popular homage here which himself had been foremost to deny to a Prince of the purest blood and of the Royal line. But never were nationalities more entirely forgotten than in New York's reception of Col. Corcoran. The spontaneous enthusiasm of the masses fused all hearts and united them in one glowing expression of honor. . . .
>
> But if any class of our population who yesterday so grandly received and honored Col. Corcoran had a special appreciation of the occasion, we hold that it was the native-born Americans. And the reason is this: that Col. Corcoran, in all his military career, marked as it has been by the vicissitudes unequaled in the war, has on all occasions exhibited a devotion to the American Government and to republican principles that proves him a pattern of faultless intelligence and perfect mold.

The article ends with a recruiting call:

> Who will now to revisit and smite the prison bars that held him so
> long and so cruelly? . . . The hero of yesterday's ovation is now a
> *General of the Republic*, commissioned to organize and lead fresh
> thousands to the field where his laurels grew.

Descriptions by the *New York Times* and the *New York Herald*
of Corcoran's reception provide an illuminating contrast. While the
Republican standard-bearer heaps praise on one exemplary Irishman —
and, astoundingly, local American natives who had earlier hoped to
imprison him — the *New York Herald* (23 August 1862) credits both
Corcoran *and* the Irish community: "[To General Corcoran] we unquestionably owe much of the enthusiasm with which our fellow Irish
citizens took up arms to assist in putting down the rebellion. His personal gallantry in the face of the enemy had also its effect in stimulat-
ing his countrymen to deeds of bravery."

Group recognition of the Irish in a general circulation newspaper — not just praise accorded to an exceptional military leader —
is an advanced indicator of acceptance and integration. While the
New York Times was an organ of the Republican upper crust and
the bourgeoisie, the *New York Herald* was generally oriented toward
the Democratic Party. The latter was nevertheless often remarkably
independent. That a dual debt is owed Corcoran *and* his men is notably visible in the contemporaneous De Marsan song sheet, "The
Return of Gen. Corcoran of the Glorious 69th." Here, the value of
song as historical testimony can be seen again as it reflects the beliefs
of the people rather than the bias of the press:

> God bless the noble CORCORAN, who led them on the field!
> Against the odds of two to one, he fought, but could not yield:
> For, CORCORAN, valiant CORCORAN, the bravest of the brave,
> Would fight to death, but ne'er retreat before a rebel knave.
>
> God bless the Gallant Sixty-Ninth! God bless each manly heart!
> They've done their duty faithfully, they acted well their part:
> For, on the bloody battle-field, where lay their martyrs dead,
> Was heard their wild and fierce hurrah, when Southern traitors fled.
>
> (LC amss.sb40538a)

While returning to New York, Corcoran stopped at the White House, where President Abraham Lincoln elevated him to the rank of brigadier general, retroactive to the Battle of Bull Run (*NYT*, 19 August 1862). Secretary of War Edwin Stanton next offered him a "bittersweet choice: the command of an existing but leaderless brigade or the opportunity to recruit and command his own" (Lane 1997, 26). Unfortunately, because the Sixty-Ninth was now part of the Irish Brigade commanded by Brigadier General Thomas Francis Meagher (fig. 23), neither choice could include Corcoran's being reunited with his former command. Retirement was another honorable option, but instead he chose to form a new ethnic unit, which became known as Corcoran's Irish Legion. On 27 August 1862, the general appeared at a City Hall Park reception held in his honor that was attended by the mayor and remaining members of the Sixty-Ninth, which was only then returning from the fiercely fought Peninsula Campaign (*NYT*, 28 August 1862). Before he addressed an immense crowd, a resolution was read urging "the President to authorize Gen. Michael Corcoran to recruit a legion of twenty thousand men to be under his command and to fight with him for the land of our adoption or birth" (*NYT*, 28 August 1862). Surely, this was a guarded preannouncement of an existing agreement with the War Department; and because Colonel Robert Nugent of the Sixty-Ninth was recruiting for his unit at the same affair, the loyal and proper Corcoran wisely decided not to interfere with his efforts to raise the reinforcements the Sixty-Ninth desperately needed.

Lyricist Eugene Johnston's "Corcoran's Irish Legion" appeared shortly afterward to support the general's new initiative:

A song for our Flag proudly waving on high,
The Emblem of the old Irish Nation;
Its Glorious Sunburst over shall fly
With the Pennant of the Eagle in station!
It's the Flag that we love, and by it we'll stand,
Till the bonds of Rebellion we'll sever
And peace is restored to our dear adopted land,
And Traitors are crushed forever and ever . . .
And Traitors are crushed forever!

Figure 23. Gen. T. F. Meagher, U.S.A. Civil War Photographs, 1861–1865. Prints and Photographic Division. Library of Congress.

When Treason's black Flag was raised in the land
By a ruthless foe that did hate it,
And the Capitol threatened by a dastardly band
Who would have Washington's tomb desecrated,
The President called: and we rushed, hand in hand,
The bonds of Rebellion to sever,
And to fight for our home, our dear adopted land,
And to crush out the Traitors forever and ever . . .
And to crush out the Traitors forever!

Brave Corcoran, our Leader, is again to take Command;
To a Traitor he never shall yield;
As a patriot he's loved and honored throughout the land,
As he's hated by his enemies on the field;
With a legion of Irishmen he'll bravely lead the van,

And give old Stone-wall Irish thunder;
He never yet did fail; he is the very man
To crush the Traitors asunder, asunder . . .
To crush the Traitors asunder!

(LC amss.sb10049b)

"Corcoran's Irish Legion" is not a lyric that seizes an audience by
the ears and demands attention, and it is possible the song was never
sung anywhere beyond recruiting drives. But it does present a proud
account of Irish activities in the Civil War to that point, providing
inspiration for potential new recruits; and it also reminds American
natives within earshot that Irish New Yorkers have not been reticent
about placing themselves in harm's way to preserve the Union. The
first verse makes clear that they are no less American because they
were born in Ireland. The second returns the listener to the early days
of the war, when the Sixty-Ninth was among the first Union units to
respond in the defense of the nation's capital. So quick was their departure, they hardly had time to prepare. On that day, conservative
Wall Street lawyer George Templeton Strong walked along Broadway
as the Sixty-Ninth headed to their transport ship. He later wrote in his
diary that [they] "marched down about four [p.m.] . . . and there were
a large infusion of Biddies in the crowd 'sobbing and sighing.' [The
Sixty-Ninth] looked as well as one has a right to expect of levies raised
on such short notice." He noted a large number were dressed in civilian clothing and without arms (Strong 1952, 132), indicating the haste
with which they mustered.

The third verse of "Corcoran's Legion" seizes on the high regard
for the commander, whose return from captivity "attracted almost
as much attention as any event in the war" (McKay 1991, 151). The
praise-in-song accorded General Corcoran is in some ways an echo
oddly reminiscent of the tribute paid Lord Rawdon in "Patrick's
Hearty Invitation to His Countrymen" (chapter 1). However, in contrast to Rawdon, Corcoran's ability to lead, his demonstrated fairness
in command, and his personal sacrifice in the national interest were
documented facts rather than paid hyperbole. Moreover, enlistment
in the Irish Legion was effected without the lure of alcohol and the
promise of fawning women. Rather than an antidote for boredom, en-

listment was regarded as a cure for the sufferings of Ireland and, by extension, of Irish America.

By summer 1862, the illusion of a quick war had completely disappeared and the Union cause was in trouble both in the field and at home. On 8 July, President Lincoln visited General McClellan and his staff at Harrison's Landing, Virginia. A lieutenant of the Irish Brigade passing the Sixty-Ninth's camp saw the president lift a corner of the its colors and kiss it, exclaiming, "God Bless the Irish Flag" (Bilby 1998, 49; *New York Herald*, 10 February 1917). By that time, the Sixty-Ninth, which began the Peninsula Campaign in Virginia with 750 officers and men had been reduced to 295 (Bilby 1998, 49). The two Irish brigadiers were now effectively competing for recruits, and Corcoran was winning by a large margin, partly because of the sensation brought by his release—effectively proclaimed to the masses by the immensely popular songs written in his honor—and partly because the community placed greater faith in his ability to return soldiers home safely (Bruce 2006, 112). Those who signed on with Corcoran rather than Meagher were lucky at first, for the Irish Legion saw comparatively limited action through 1863; however, that relative calm changed the following year, when the regiment was "thrown into the bloody conflicts in Virginia under Ulysses Grant and was decimated along with the remnants of the Irish Brigade" (Spann 2002, 117). In the field of war, no place is entirely safe, but the Irish too frequently received the worst assignments, suffering staggering losses when ordered to mount impossible charges into heavily fortified positions, the very point made by Miller (1985, 324). Colonel St. Clair Mulholland (1903, 44) described the feeling within Meagher's Irish Brigade as they prepared to take the field at the Battle of Fredericksburg: "To charge an enemy or enter a battle when one knows there is no chance of success, requires courage of a higher order than when a soldier is sustained by the enthusiasm born of hope. . . . When our troops debouching from the town, deployed upon the plain in front of Mary's Heights [*sic*], every man in the ranks knew that it was not to fight they were ordered; it was to die." Their assignment was to charge a half mile uphill toward two Confederate brigades sheltered behind a stone wall. Chaplain William Corby (1992, 131–32), who would become the third president of the University of Notre Dame, wrote, "As we advanced, our men simply melted away before the grape and canister, and the tens of thousands of muskets, well protected behind the carefully constructed breastworks. . . . [The] place into which Meagher's brigade was sent was simply a slaughter-pen." The diary of Private William McCarter also gives a lengthy first-hand account of the charge up Marye's Heights that day (O'Brien 1996).

Florence Gibson (1951, 128) provides sickening statistics for the Sixty-Ninth Regiment's casualties at Antietam, Fredericksburg, and Gettysburg: "At Antietam they lost 196 of 317 men. . . . They filled their ranks with recruits again only to lose 128 of 238 leading the charge at Fredericksburg. By the time of Gettysburg, their numbers were down to 75, of whom they lost 25." "Pat Murphy of Meagher's Brigade," which appeared on broadsides printed by De Marsan and Wrigley, was composed during this period. Murphy represents the Irish everyman soldier, but as the war entered a killing-field stage, he might have been any combatant in the Union army, as what happens to him could happen to anyone. A far, melancholy cry from upbeat recruiting anthems, the song is still neither morose nor ethereal. It is instead realistic, mentioning "bleeding and gory" dead lying "in heaps," effectively an indication it was sung during patriotic scenes in theaters and variety houses—in fact, Wrigley associates it with the important New York impresario and singer Tony Pastor. England, the Confederacy, and abolitionists are identified as the cause of America's troubles. Noteworthy by its absence is any mention of enlistment; but apparent in the last verse is the expectation of Irish Americans that the United States will aid Ireland's struggle for freedom once the Civil War is concluded:

'Twas the night before battle: and, gathered in groups,
The soldiers lay close in their quarters;
They were thinking, no doubt, of the dear ones at home..
Of mothers, wives, sisters, and daughters..
With his pipe in his mouth, sat a dashing young blade,
And a song he was lilting quite gaily:
It was honest Pat Murphy, of Meagher's Brigade,
And he sang of the Sprig of Shillaly.

Och, murdher! says Pat, it's a shame for to see
Brothers fighting in such a quare manner:
But I'll fight till I die, (if I shouldn't be kilt)
For America's bright Starry Banner.
Now, if it was only John Bull to the fore,
I'd rush into battle quite gaily;
For the spalpeen I'd rap with a heart an' a half,
With my illigant Sprig of Shillaly!

Jeff. Davis, you thief! if I had you but here,
Your beautiful plans I'd be ruinin:
Faix! I'd give ye a taste of me bayonet, bedad!
For thrying to burst up the Union:
There's a crowd in the North, too, an' theyre just as bad:
Abolitionist spouters so scaly —
For throubling the naigers I think they desarve
A Whack from a Sprig of Shillaly!

The morning soon came, and poor Paddy awoke,
On the Rebels to have satisfaction:
The drummers were beating the divil's tattoo,
Calling the boys into action.
Then, the Irish Brigade in the battle was seen,
Their blood, in our cause, shedding freely;
With their bayonet-charges they rushed on the foe,
With a shout for the Land of Shillaly!

The battle was over.. the dead lay in heaps:
Pat Murphy lay bleeding and gory:
A hole through his head, from rifleman's shot,
Had finished his passion for glory;
No more in the camp shall his laughter be heard,
Or his voice singing ditties so gaily;
Like a hero he died.. for the Land of the Free.
Far away from the Land of Shillaly!

Then, surely, Columbia can never forget,
While valor and fame hold communion,
How nobly the brave Irish Volunteers fought
In defense of the Flag of our Union;
And, if ever Old Ireland for Freedom should strike,
We'll a helping hand offer quite freely:
And the Stars an the Stripes shall be seen along-side
Of the Flag of the Land of Shillaly!
(LC amss.sb30412b)

"Shillaly" (more commonly spelled shillelagh) refers to the wooden (oak or blackthorn) cudgel, whose manly application often settled serious disputes in the Irish countryside. Ironic here is that its use in Ireland was generally nonlethal. References to "abolitionist spouters" and "naigers" are typical expressions of hostile attitudes prevalent in New York at the time.

After the Peninsula Campaign (March–July 1862), John F. Poole's "No Irish Need Apply" was parodied by "What Irish Boys Can Do." The song is a list of positive characteristics and accomplishments made by the Irish. It speaks from high ground, using direct humor to make its point, while the bitter sarcasm at the close of the sixth verse is particularly poignant:

And then, too, in the present war between the North and South,
Let no dirty slur on Irish ever escape your mouth;
Sure, did you ne'er hear tell of the 69th, who bravely fought at
    Bull-Run!
And Meagher, of the seven days fight, that was in front, of
    Richmond,
With General Shields, who fought so brave for the Flag Red, White,
    and Blue?
And anything like a bayonet-charge the Irish boys can do.

The seventh and last verse asks for the just reward of respect that service to the American nation deserves:

Then, why slur upon the Irish? Why are they treated so?
What is it you have against them? is what I want to know.

Sure, they work for all they get, and that you can't deny!
Then, why insult them with the words: No Irish need apply?
If you want to find their principles, go search the wide world
    through,
And you'll find all things that's noble the Irish folks can do.

(LC amss.sb40589b)

Though it relies on biting wit, "What Irish Boys Can Do" stops short of scathing acrimony. In New York, that guarded, more patient approach disappeared once African Americans were admitted into the army.

Before the huge influx during the Great Hunger, African American men and women predominated in many servile occupations within the city. But the large numbers and poverty of famine refugees allowed employers to use them to undercut the wages of African Americans, breaking their lock on a variety of low-skilled occupations (Man 1951, 376–77). "One of the most dramatic developments was the supplanting of African American women by Irish domestics in the 1840s and 1850s," writes Hodges (1999, 232). Irish longshoremen had attempted to excise African Americans from the New York docks during the 1840s and had achieved hegemony by the Civil War (Winslow 1998, 10, 75). In theory, this excision should have provided the Irish good incomes, but dock work was unsteady; at the same time, inflation ran rampant while wages were stagnant (Man 1951, 392–93, 395). Wages were still under pressure during the war. In 1863, Irish longshoremen engaged in a series of strikes enforced by violence against nonunion workers. On 13 April, longshoremen attacked African Americans unloading barges at Pier 4 on the East River. "Stones and other missiles were freely used for a short time until the interference of the police put an end to the affray" (*NYT*, 14 April 1863). The antislavery *New York Tribune* (14 April 1863) wrote that the attackers were "two or three hundred vagabond Irishmen" and blamed "the persistent effort of the Pro-Slavery press of [New York] to strengthen the prejudice, and embitter the hate of its readers, and the rest of the most ignorant part of the populace against the negro." Though ethnicity was not specified, on 8 June about five hundred dockworkers chased nonunion laborers unloading cargo from a ship. At that time, a strike by the Longshore-men's Association encompassed the southern extent of Manhattan's waterfront from Pier 8 on the East River to Pier 11 on the Hudson (*NYT*, 9 June 1863). Six days later, imprisoned deserters from Gover-nor's Island were loading government cargoes bound for captured ports in the South. Longshoremen looked on anxiously while army regulars with fixed bayonets provided security. Three thousand dock-workers were estimated to be out of work by then (*Tribune*, 15 June 1863). On 16 June, the *New York Times* reported, "Between 3 and 4 o'clock yesterday afternoon, notice was received at the First Ward Station-house that the white laborers had again made an attack upon the colored men who were employed in discharging freight in the neighborhood of Coenties-slip. A platoon of officers was immediately dispatched to the scene of the disturbance, and quiet was soon re-stored. The Police arrested a colored man named McHeney, who is charged with having struck a 'longshoreman, during the *melee*, upon the head with a hook. The injury, it is believed, will prove fatal."

While the root cause of Irish opposition to African Americans was economic competition and the flashpoint was the changing basis be-hind the Civil War, its form was also tied to the "party fights" and rec-reational violence of Ireland (Barrett 2012, 113–22; O'Rourke 2000; Zimmermann 2002, 19). There was another factor also. John Kuo Wei Tchen (1999, 221) provides what may be the most concise and cogent appraisal of the more general relationship between African and Irish American men:

American social identities have been inextricably tied into a hier-archy of race—a hierarchy quickly complicated by other migrants and immigrants variously defined as "ethnic" or "racial" groups. Within the discourse of Irish British relations, colonized Irish Catholics were de facto cast as an inferior race. Yet when the Irish entered the black/white discourse of the United States, they could occupy a more ambiguous position in the social hierarchy. Irish Catholics were despised by Protestant patricians yet privileged over African slaves and freed men. In the face of mainstream antipathy, a positive Irish American identity was being forged within the existing (Protestant) pro-white/anti-black discourse. The classic means for Irish Catholics to defuse the longstanding Anglo-American and European-Protestant hatred toward them was to symbolically displace this valuation onto an even lower group.

To this adverse relationship can be added the strange, uneasy commonality shared by Irish and African Americans: at the lowest level, each group spoke in a nonstandard dialect and dressed unconventionally. Both groups were depicted at various times by American bigots as subhuman — Africans primarily for their skin color and Irish for their perceived backward culture and foreign religion. Both groups wished to escape stigmatization, while in general neither was broadly comfortable being associated with the other in this context.

But war on the waterfront was not the entire story. America's Empire City was by now huge, and physical location and its human properties mattered immensely. Graham Russell Hodges (1999, 235) points out, "Tolerance in [one Sixth Ward neighborhood] was so great that while a hint of interracial love might spark riots in other wards, Five Points was home to married couples of African and Irish descent."

Human geography in the megacity and the diversity of lifestyles it might engender are also apparent in a recent article by Virginia Ferris (2012, 152–77). A few miles to the north of Five Points and seven years later, the 1870 US Census recorded "a much greater level of interracial stability and intimacy than has been presumed in discourses about Irish and black relations during this period in New York," specifically eighty Irish African families totaling 273 persons within an area that today makes up southernmost Greenwich Village and SoHo (152). The pairings were mainly between black men and green women. A key to understanding this settlement pattern can be seen in group gender imbalances within the 4th Election District where Irish-born women (378) outnumbered Irish men (243), while the number of black men (219) exceeded that of black women (180); a second likely catalyst was that Irish women and African men both worked as servants for the "Washington Square gentry" (Burrows and Wallace 1999, 854; Ferris 2012, 154). Thus, this mixed group of servants interacted amicably on a daily basis and could choose mates from an informed, humane perspective.

As the Civil War progressed ever so slowly, many Irish laborers grew concerned about their chances for employment in the postbellum era. During the 1860 election campaign, in an effort to steer votes toward the Democratic Party, *New York Herald* editor James Gordon Bennett "warned workingmen that 'if Lincoln is elected you will have to compete with the labor of four million emancipated negroes'" (Burrows and Wallace 1999, 865). While most Manhattan Irish had heartily supported the war effort, memory of Bennett's words lingered. Declining enlistments, casualties, and desertions within the Union army resulted in a net loss of combat personnel, prompting policy changes that allowed African Americans to enlist, first as laborers, in mid-1862, and then as combatants, beginning in 1863. The loss of Union morale and men, and the measures taken to recoup manpower, set in motion a series of events that, apart from the Civil War itself, produced the "largest civil insurrection in American history" (Foner 1988, 32).

The New York Draft Riots of 1863

On 29 August 1862, Brigadier General Michael Corcoran addressed "an immense multitude" gathered on the Common in Boston, Massachusetts. The following day, an account in the *New York Times* (30 August 1862) reported, "Nearly all the stores in the city were closed, and the reception was one of the greatest ovations ever witnessed in Boston." Freed from imprisonment only fifteen days earlier, Corcoran was in the Bay State recruiting for the Irish Legion. In his closing comments, he informed the crowd, many of whom he hoped to enlist, that "[the] President of the United States intends to follow up this war for the restoration of the Union, nothing more, nor nothing less. We have nothing to do with the Slavery question. As a matter of course, it will settle itself as we march along. The Government is not going to make war for it. We are fighting for the Constitution and the Union and nothing else."

Ten days earlier, Corcoran had dined with President Abraham Lincoln at the White House and also met with Secretary of War Edwin Stanton, so it may be assumed that the general's guarantee to the Boston crowd was based on guidance that came from the highest levels of government and had been cleared for use in his recruiting oratory.

However, the promise to prosecute the war solely for the preservation of the Union evaporated in a little more than three weeks. Once the Emancipation Proclamation was declared on 22 September 1862, New York's Irish adopted a mood expressed in part by "Parody on When This Cruel War Is Over":

> Och, Biddy dear, do you remember
> Whin last we did meet?
> 'Twas at Paddy Murphy's party,
> Down in Baxter street;
> And there, all the boys did envy me;
> And the girls envy'd you—
> When they saw my great big bounty
> In Green-Backs, all new?
>
> Next day, I shouldered my ould musket,
> Braver than Ould Mars;
> And, with spirits bright and airy,
> Marched off to the wars;
> But now me drame of glory's over;
> I'm home-sick, I fear;
> I'd give this world for a substitute,
> To take my place here.
>   (NYSL Broadside Ballads SCO BD0987)

This song expresses the sentiment that enlistment seemed like a good idea at first because it provided a significant reward, but proved otherwise once harsh reality set in. Certainly, this was due in part to the very nature of war, filled far more with horror than glory, but also owing to the changing rationale propelling it. A bonus or bounty might have provided the economic basis for a better future in the postwar era; however, if a Union victory implied the reconstruction of New York in a Republican vision broadly detrimental to most Irish residents, then the reward certainly would not warrant the risk.

The Emancipation Proclamation reaffirmed the ideal of human equality expressed in the Declaration of Independence and initiated the policy of Reconstruction by "thoroughly revolutionizing American race relations," including demolishing the "caste system and racial bigotry in the North" (Schecter 2009, 62). But New York, which had been antiblack at least since 1800 (Ernst 1965, 40–41), was still a "profoundly racist city" in 1863 (Spann 2002, 170), and opposition to emancipation within the majority Democratic Party was nearly unanimous. In February of that year, New York State governor Horatio Seymour affirmed his "opposition to emancipation and the enlistment of black troops" (Schecter 2009, 64). Manhattan Democrats were opposed to African Americans in part because they were clients of the Republican Party, and the federal government was simultaneously curtailing civil liberties through the suspension of habeas corpus, not just to augment the war effort but also to support its political agenda (McKay 1991, 161–62). Objection to national government heavy-handedness can be seen in the sixth verse of the enraged, mean-spirited, and basely bitter "I Am Fighting for the Nigger," a wildly racist song full of the sarcasm of men who believe they have been tricked into enlistment, only to be betrayed by what they believe to be the unfair preferment of others. Though its author, William Kiernan, bears an Irish name, there is nothing in the lyric that specifically identifies its message as intended *only* for Irish Americans. It is rather an incitement to all whites to resist draft and emancipation with force:

> Each soldier must be loyal, and his officers obey,
> Though he lives on mouldy biscuit, and fights without his pay;
> If his wife at home is starving, he must be content,
> Though he waits six months for Green-Backs, worth forty-five
>   per cent.
>
> If ordered into battle, go in without delay;
> Though slaughtered just like cattle, it is your duty to obey;
> And, when old Jeff Davis is captured, paid up you may be:
> If you do not mind the money, don't you set the nigger free.
>
> Moreover, if you're drafted, don't refuse to go,
> You are equal to the nigger and can make as good show:
> And when in the battle. to the Union prove true:
> But don't, the nigger is as good a man as you.
>
> (LC amss.sb20221a)

The song was probably performed in some minstrel shows, but because it contains little humor, its angry, sarcastic lyric seems more appropriate for workingmen's concert saloons.

General Corcoran wrote to Judge Charles P. Daly at the end of November 1862 concerning the great difficulty he encountered obtaining recruits to reinforce the Irish Legion. Horrendous casualties and overall "war fatigue" had sapped the flow of recruits into the US Army, but emancipation, confirming the worst fears of many who viewed it as a total change of purpose and one with calamitous economic consequences for lower-class whites, virtually cut off volunteerism. By then, the outflow of deserters across the entire Union army exceeded the inflow of enlistees (Hammond 1954, 167). Simple arithmetic made it evident the Union would lose the war unless a new means was devised for bolstering the military. The government then began to consider a national conscription program to sustain its forces.

In a short summation of Senate activity published on 15 February 1863, the *New York Times* reported on a proposed bill that contained a section allowing a drafted man to pay the government a sum of money ($250 at the time), which would then be offered as a bounty for a substitute. The newspaper offered the opinion that the exemption was "closely modeled after the French Conscription law," which it termed "eminently wise and just," continuing, "For some unknown reason, it was stricken out in Committee, but it is hoped that it may be restored before the bill is passed." The (supposedly) unknown reason was, of course, political opposition, mainly from the Democratic Party. Officially termed the Enrollment Act, the final legislation became law in early March. In short, it sought to provide the army with men, if not by enlistment, then through a draft. There were also clauses meant to discourage opposition to the conscription process by the levying of fines and jail sentences. A subsequent report in the *New York Times* on 10 March 1863 voiced criticism of Peace Democrat and activist Clement C. Vallandigham's call for "resistance" to conscription and demanded federal government action to "meet these sedition mongers promptly, the first instant they trench upon the law." The new law provided for a draft pool of all able-bodied men from the ages of twenty to thirty-five and all single men from thirty-six to forty-four inclusive. Certain expected exemptions were allowed, such as those for high government officials, only sons of elderly parents, fathers of motherless children, felons, and so on. However, the exemption most commonly granted was for citizens and resident aliens, who either found a replacement willing to serve in their steads or who paid the government $300 (inflation adjusted to $5,430 in 2018) to compensate a volunteer. A defined monetary payment without consideration of extenuating circumstances was thus the basis of the most used exclusion from national military service. Greatly disadvantaging the working-class—a longshoreman at this time made $1.50 per day (inflation adjusted to $27.15 in 2018) and only infrequently worked a full week—the Enrollment Act brought the will of the Republican-led "Federal Government into the community, into the waged workplace, and into the household—into nearly every corner of working-class life" in Democratic-led New York City (Bernstein 1990, 8).

Such blatant inequality further inflamed the already-ignited city, and broadside scribes quickly picked up their pens. The new law provided for federal agents to canvass house-to-house, enrolling eligible men and then drafting the required number by lottery. Henry De Marsan seized on that highly unpopular protocol when he published the minstrel-inspired "The Draft Is a Coming":

Say Gents, hab yon seen de enrolling officer,
Wid de muff tach on his face,
Go long dis block sometime dis morning,
Like he gwine to leab de place?
He seen de smoke way up in Harlem,
Whar de anti-draft-men lay:
An he took his books, an left berry sudden:
So I spec he's run away!

. . . .

Every body's feeling berry lonesome:
For, dey spec' de draft to cum;
For, when de draft goes in operation,
Dey'll call on ebery one;
But rec'lect some had t'ree hundred,
An' dey're exempt, you know—

An' those dat hab got to do de fighting,
Are de poor dat hab to go.

Congress makes us a good-deal ob trouble:
For the Union dey don't care:
Mixed up in some money spec'lation,
Dey all hab a very good share;
Dey hab seen our men killed by de t'ousand,
Dere's no use for to laugh:
Dey still tink to carry on dis impartial,
An' now dey gwine to draft.
    (Duke Digital Collections bsvg 100193)

Class, wealth, race, injustice, official impropriety, irony, and fear mix wildly in this blackface minstrel satire. The commentator is a Caucasian, who poses as an "Ethiopian," disguising his identity by hiding behind a mask of burnt cork, a peculiar "in-your-face" reinterpretation of speaking from behind a stage curtain. Commonplace in the North beginning in the late 1820s (J. Cullen 1996, 65), minstrelsy merged melodic components that originated in Britain and Ireland with rhythm and dialect drawn from African American sources, notably street singers who busked New York, Philadelphia, and other cities at this time (Wittke 1930, 9). In racist Manhattan, black dialect heightened an affront directed at enrolling officers, and the insult was made even worse because it came from the mouth of a supposedly ignorant man. White objection to the performance of military service by African Americans was based on the idea that, even if the conflict were popularly perceived in New York as a rich Republican's battle fought by poor Democrats, war was still considered white man's work. If black Americans could prove themselves capable in combat (as the green Irish were now doing), the possibility of their being rewarded with civilian employment after the war in areas currently reserved for working-class whites could be increased. Should this occur, unskilled white workers would be heavily affected, with Irish laborers likely to be the largest losers because they were overwhelmingly engaged in the least-skilled occupations. The greatest fear was of military service by blacks freed from Confederate slavery (so-called contrabands) because, following James Gordon Bennett's prewar warning, it had long been assumed former slaves would relocate to the North in massive numbers if the South were defeated.

The present combination of issues—the apparent change in motivation behind the war, a repeated pattern of misuse of Irish soldiers in hopeless military assaults, unprecedented interference by national politicians in local affairs, disastrous economic conditions for wage earners in New York, fear of a postwar mass inflow of low-cost laborers, and most of all the blatantly unfair draft exemption clause—galvanized, enflamed, and emboldened the city's antidraft laboring class (Bernstein 1990, 7–11; McKay 1991, 208). The highly popular Tony Pastor, always a supporter of the common man, gained firsthand knowledge of how extreme popular ill will had become when he premiered a new composition, "The Draft," after the 3 March passage of the Enrollment Act. Pastor was always quick to market with topical songs, but on this occasion he was too fast and too rash to escape negative consequences. Several firm-minded and stout-hearted patrons of the "444" concert saloon took exception to Pastor's opinionated lyric, which he intended as purely patriotic:

> The draft, the draft, is the subject now
>   That causes agitation;
> You hear the which, the why, the how,
>   Discussed throughout the nation.
> We'll have at length, the people's strength,
>   That rebels long have laughed at;
> Our land to save, no man that's brave
>   Objects to being drafted.
>
> A dandy beau among the girls
>   Has passed for eight-and-twenty,
> His whiskers black and jetty curls,
>   From hair-dye used in plenty.
> But suddenly white locks appear,
>   Black hairs away are wafting;
> He owns at last he's fifty near,
>   For to avoid the drafting.

A gay young chap he falls in love,
    Among the belles he dashes;
Declares he's twenty-five by Jove!
    And twirls his young mustaches.
They talk of draft—he shaves it clean,
    And though he's jeered and chaffed at,
He wants a month of being eighteen,
    For to avoid being drafted!
                    (Pastor 1864, 22)

The suggestion that avoiding the draft was unmanly enraged the laborers. More than two years into a war that virtually no New Yorker had wanted, and one that was apparently being prosecuted for a different cause than originally announced, the alcohol-fueled men began to steam. Parker Zellers (1971, 19), a Pastor biographer, describes their reaction: "The toughs gave out with a continuous round of jeers and cat-calls. When the singer paid them little heed, they threw down their beer mugs and made for the stage. A number of hefty bartenders intercepted the crew and managed, with no small difficulty, to hustle them out of the hall. Pastor was unruffled by the demonstration. In the midst of it all, he coolly unfurled an American flag, held it aloft, and sang 'The Star Spangled Banner.'" This vignette characterizes the deep animosity prevalent in the city, a point Pastor, an otherwise keen observer of New York working-class life, missed until it was brought to his attention perforce. If Pastor could get it wrong, anyone could. Conscription was a wholly polarizing and highly explosive issue.

Enrollment progressed into the summer without institution of a draft. After Union military victories at Vicksburg (19 May–4 July 1863) and Gettysburg (1–3 July 1863), authorities believed it safe to proceed, even though the casualties of Irish combatants at Gettysburg had been very high. The actual lottery began on Saturday, 11 July, in an uptown district, a location chosen in the hope of testing popular reaction away from the core of the city before extending the process to presumably more volatile downtown neighborhoods; 1,236 names were drawn on the first day alone. On 12 July (coincidentally the anniversary of William of Orange's victory at the Boyne), working-class

New Yorkers read the names of those selected and mulled their response, which was demonstrated the following morning. Monday,
13 July, began with parades of skilled workers walking between industrial sites, their ranks swelling as they eventually reached the Ninth
District office at Third Avenue and 46th Street. As the lottery process
resumed, a volunteer fire brigade, known ominously as the Black Joke
company, arrived, commenced stoning the office, and set it afire. After
the police retreated, the violent demonstration turned into a riot, as
neighboring buildings were looted and set ablaze. Telegraph poles
were cut to block the tracks of street cars. Thirty-two invalid soldiers
on light duty were underway to the site when they were stopped by a
mob; two were killed and others injured. Police superintendent John
Kennedy was battered senseless with a club as he rushed uptown to
survey the scene. Gangs split off as the day progressed, their momen-
tum and boldness growing. Mayor Opdyke's house was threatened,
while highly visible Republican figures were sought out by mobs. An
armory at Second Avenue and 21st Street was raided, and carbines
were taken. About four in the afternoon, the Colored Orphan Asylum
was pillaged and burnt, fortunately with no loss of life.

At this time, African Americans lived in clusters spread throughout the city. That night, as reports of extreme violence—including
lynchings and fatal beatings—increased against blacks, many African
Americans fled Manhattan. On this first of four riotous days, the total
complement of federal and state troops on hand was about a thousand,
and their primary function was to defend New York City against a
possible Confederate attack (Bernstein 1990, 8–13; Bruce 2006, 178–
79; Burrows and Wallace 1999, 888–90; Cook 1974, 54–74). On Tuesday, the more diverse crowds of Monday receded, giving way to the
criminal element and, in certain neighborhoods, largely Irish mobs,
who began barricading their bailiwicks and roaming beyond them to
wreak havoc on their perceived enemies—poor blacks and rich, white
abolitionist Republicans. Irish peacekeepers also caught the wrath of
these rioters. After Colonel Henry O'Brien ordered that a howitzer
be fired into a mob, his house was burned; when he was caught by a
crowd, he was beaten, mutilated, killed, and hanged from a lamppost
(*Herald*, 15 July 1863, 1; fig. 24). The 86th Street home of Colonel
Robert Nugent of the Sixty-Ninth was invaded (*Tribune*, 15 July

Figure 24. New York—The Rioters Dragging Col. O'Brien's Body through the Street, [1888?]. Print. Mid-Manhattan Picture Collection. New York Public Library.

1863, 8). Nugent, who was in New York recuperating from wounds received in battle, had accepted the position of acting assistant provost marshal general supervising the draft. Before setting a blaze, rioters threw out the "torn and tattered battle flag of the Sixty-Ninth regiment," presumably there for safe-keeping, from a window of the dwelling. Portraits of Nugent and Meagher "were broken in pieces . . . but Corcoran's was untouched," suggesting the mob regarded Nugent and Meagher as turncoats but considered Corcoran to be one of their own (*NYT*, 29 July 1863, 2).

The murder of black men ratcheted wildly upward as savage torture and ghastly mutilation added elements of sexual jealousy and ritualistic punishment (fig. 25); however, this was far less the case in areas where African Americans and Irish mixed harmoniously. In the

Figure 25. New York—Hanging and Burning a Negro in Clarkson Street. Print.
Art and Picture Collection. New York Public Library.

humble Five Points area of the Sixth Ward, where interracial mixing
was not uncommon, riotous acts were far more subdued than those
uptown (Anbinder 2001, 314–16). The first federal troops arrived on
Wednesday and commenced clearing centers of resistance with the
same strong force shown in cities of the Confederacy. Manhattan had
been retaken by Thursday night, and many laborers returned to work
the following day (Bilby 1998, 92; Bruce 2006, 180; Burrows and Wallace 1999, 895).

The brutality meted out to African Americans during the draft
riots by largely Irish mobs was partly rooted in the long-held disdain
with which most white workers in New York regarded blacks. A
French visitor had reported in 1833 that "there was not one trade in
the city where colored persons were allowed to work with white"
(Ernst 1965, 40–41). Even more telling are the words of an English observer in 1844:

Ten or twelve years ago, the most menial employments, such as scavengers, porters, dock-labourers, waiters at hotels, ostlers, boot-cleaners, barbers, etc. were all, or nearly all, black men, and nearly all the maid servants, cooks, scullions, washerwomen, etc., were black women, and they used to obtain very good wages for these employments; but so great has been the influx of unskilled labourers from Ireland, England, and other countries within the last few years, into New York, Boston, Philadelphia . . . that it has reduced the wages of blacks, and deprived great numbers of them of employment, hence there is a deadly hatred engendered between them, and quarrels and fights among them are daily occurring. . . . But if the blacks were to be emancipated, probably hundreds of thousands of them would migrate to these northern States, and the competition for employment would be so much increased, that . . . better, therefore, for us, that they remain slaves as they are. (Finch 1844, quoted in Ignatiev 1995, 97–99)

The decision to diminish the status of black Americans was clearly made by white Americans and later embraced by the Irish. The antagonism that reached its zenith during the draft riots was particularly savage. The reasons included hard economic conditions, war weariness, and the intrusion of the federal government into local affairs. Politics in New York provided an additional dimension. The Catholic Irish were overwhelmingly Democrats, a "deeply racist, openly white man's party hostile to freedom for black people in general" (Spann 2002, 2–3), who viewed the revised Civil War rationale as promulgated by Republicans, many of whom were former Know-Nothings. Irish immigrants adopted the platform and prejudices of their own Democratic sponsors, which aligned well with their own needs and were consistent with their ancient history of violent opposition in Ireland.

If the draft riots of 1863 generated no great song legacy, it is because riot is anarchical and opportunistic, and its participants are primarily focused on ranting, looting, and inflicting damage (McKay 1991, 203). Far from providing a musical position statement, the focus is on exacting retribution, acting randy and wrong, defiling space and place, and leaving others to clean up afterward.

Conversely, newspapers had much to say about the insurrection, typically adopting positions consistent with the inclinations of their readers. The *New York Herald* assumed a balanced stance, headlining the "Fierce Hostility of the People" (15 July 1863), "Positive Suspension of the Draft," "More Persecution of Colored Population," and "Conflicting Rumors as to the Hanging of Col. O'Brien" (16 July 1863). Though the initial outburst was propelled by an ethnic spectrum that included many Irish, conservative newspapers such as the *New York Times* and *New York Tribune* saw *only* Irish rioters in the mob (Bernstein 1990, 23; *NYT*, 16 July 1863, 1). The *Tribune* (14 July 1863) wrote, "The real ground of hostility to the draft is sympathy with Jeff. Davis and his minions. Those who fomented and hounded on the riots of yesterday would have split their throats cheering had Lee's army been making a victorious promenade up Broadway." The *New York Times* (16 July 1863) chimed in wholeheartedly: "The *Tribune* of yesterday morning has the following, 'It is a curious fact, that of all the arrests made, every one is Irish.' However this may be, it is a fact, patent to everyone who has seen anything of the mob, that it is composed almost exclusively of Irishmen and boys." In actuality, "Out of 184 whose country of birth can be determined, 117 were born in Ireland, 40 in the United States, 16 in Germany, seven in England, and one each in France, Canada, Denmark, and Switzerland"; of these, "most had led quiet, respectable lives" and "few had any records of involvement with the law" (Cook 1974, 196–97).

The draft riots represented a serious setback for Manhattan's Catholic Irish, but suggestions of an immediate return to nativist days were set aside (Cook 1974, 189) as the city at large developed a collective amnesia that clouded memory of the insurrection (Bernstein 1990, 4). Indeed, there was plenty of blame to go around: while attempting to preserve the Union and establish racial equality, the federal government had affirmed the privileged status of wealthy citizens through law; the city and state had failed to provide adequate protection for the populace; and elements of the public had foregone peaceful protest for destructive violence. Eight days after the rioting and following some reflection, *Harper's Weekly* (25 July 1863, 466) determined that "there was nothing peculiar to New York, or to the Irish race in this riot. . . . Precisely similar mobs have been seen in Paris, London, Vienna." On 1 August 1863, *Harper's* (482) concluded that "in many wards of the city, the Irish were during the late riot staunch friends of law and order; that Irishmen helped to rescue the colored orphans in the asylum from the hands of the rioters; that a large proportion of the police, who behaved throughout the riot with the most exemplary gallantry, are Irishmen; that the Roman Catholic priesthood to a man used their influence on the side of the law. . . . It is important that this riot should teach us something more useful than a revival of Know-Nothing prejudices."

That *Harper's* assumed the mantle of peacemaker is particularly important, for it employed the cartoonist Thomas Nast, famous for his depiction of New York's Irish and Africans as apes, and its parent company had earlier published the false and inflammatory *Awful Disclosures of the Hotel Dieu Nunnery* (1836) by Maria Monk. In 1844, James Harper, eldest of the Harper Brothers publishing family, met with Bishop Hughes as nativist mobs gathered in Manhattan to purge the city of Catholics. He was then the American Republican Party mayor, and he asked Hughes whether he was afraid his churches might be burned. Hughes's steely and famous reply was, "No, sir, but I am afraid some of *yours* will be burned." Mayor Harper then used his personal connections to have the explosive rally cancelled (Burrows and Wallace 1999, 633). Harper clearly remembered the aversion of a near catastrophe years earlier and recognized that New York, while far from perfect, had changed for the better. He also desired that the war should be concluded successfully, acknowledging that Irish Americans had contributed a valiant share in its prosecution and Catholic police, priests, and military veterans had worked tirelessly to contain disorder.

The draft riots thus presented a blurring of the Catholic Irish image. One side of the stereograph displayed a picture of dutiful, community-minded Americans performing difficult, dangerous, and noble acts, while the other showed subhuman monsters tearing the city apart and setting it ablaze. This strange, too-broad contrast needed to be resolved and brought into focus, something that would require further reflection. The main conflict of the period was not in New York City but on the borders of two warring nations, whose constituents killed each other daily. Irishmen were still greatly needed to fight in the Union cause, so the status of the Manhattan's Irish Catholics would not be resolved until the cruel war was over.

Songs of the Home Front

Paradoxically, while the City of New York was absorbed with the uncertainty and horror of war, it further expanded as a bustling pleasure center. An 1864 police census indicated the city contained 599 bordellos and 72 lewd entertainment emporiums (McKay 1991, 141). The latter were the bawdiest of a New York institution known as the concert saloon. At the height of the Civil War, somewhere between 300 and 600 concert saloons—bars featuring variety entertainment—were open for business in Manhattan (Browne 1868, 327; McNamara 2002, xi). In practice, most concert saloons were places where "Venus sported with Bacchus" (O Lochlainn 1960, 85)—a "combination of the theater and the brothel in the atmosphere of a saloon" (Crawford 2001, 475), as well as a place where middle- and upper-class men "slummed," workmen "blew off steam," and war-weary soldiers attempted to diminish the pain of battle. At the same time, a veritable flood of song sheets flowed from the presses of printers located on Chatham Street and other downtown locations, thereafter to be hawked on crowded city thoroughfares. Contemporaneously, successful performers had inexpensive songbooks made so patrons of concert saloons and lower-class musical theaters could join in choruses during performances and return home with the words of songs they enjoyed. Thus, the city portrayed dual personalities, contrasting the gloom emanating from protracted conflict, including fear for endangered combatants and the economic hardship borne by their families (*NYT*, 16 July 1862), with the gaiety of transient escape embodied in humor-filled variety entertainment, heavy drinking, and risky sexual behavior. Irish Americans (and their imitators) were players in these contrasting scenes of New York's Civil War drama.

Three decades after the war, Alfred M. Williams (1892, 267) reflected in the *Journal of American Folklore* that "there was an immense amount of song-writing as well as song-singing during the war. . . . The illiterate poets were as busy as those of higher education; and those . . . [who sought their public] through the badly printed sheet of the penny street ballad, or through the mouth of the negro minstrel, contributed almost as much to the poetry of war as their brothers. Dime songbooks containing a curious admixture of the common and the polite, the appropriate and the incongruous, were innumerable."

The Irish song tradition influenced period American popular music greatly. Hibernian immigrants were numerous and largely fluent in English. As a result of their substantial oral culture, they regarded singing highly and had much about which to sing. Wolf (1963, v) comments on this point with respect to Irish American song production: "This brings us to a phenomenon, not sufficiently recognized, the tremendous influence of the Irish upon American songs and ballads during the period. For two decades before 1860 the immigration of Irishmen into the United States was of vast proportions. . . . But, there were growing pains that a foreign-born group had to suffer. . . . The Irish were mocked by their enemies and praised by their friends. And the sweet body of Irish songs was added to the voice of the nation." In this regard (and certain others), America's Empire City emulated Ireland, which Williams (1892, 267) identified as virtually the only country where song sheet production and sale lingered in quantity and force at the close of the nineteenth century. The phenomenon was actually logical because on the eve of war the Irish represented in excess of one-quarter of the city's total population of 813,669 (Rosenwaike 1972, 42), plus an undeterminable number of second- and third-generation Americans who also identified as Irish.

Henry De Marsan acquired John Andrews's broadside publishing enterprise at 38 Chatham Street in 1859 (Charosh 1997, 469) and immediately instituted changes bringing it into accord with the milieu and tastes of the postnativist era. Andrews had printed a variety of song types, including violent Know-Nothing rants and sentimental Irish pieces, such as "Pat's Farewell to His Sweetheart" and "My Good Old Irish Home" (to the tune of "My Old Kentucky Home"); but he also printed the angry, churning departure song "The Emigrant's Farewell," the outpouring of a man who views himself as an exile, and is hostile toward England, but fortunate to be headed to America. Adding to his pain, he doubts he will ever see his loved one again:

> I would not live in Ireland now for she's a fallen land,
> And the tyrant's heel is on her neck, with her reeking blood-stained
>   hand.

There's not a foot of Irish ground, but's trodden down by slaves,
Who die unwept, and then are flung, like dogs, into their graves.

My troubles make me grieve, Mary, and I often wish to die,
And I long to find the green churchyard where all my kindred lie.
'Tis pleasant when the heart is broke, to sleep beneath the dust
But still I hope for better days, and place in God my trust.

I'm leaving you, my Mary dear, they're painful words to speak,
My last embrace I'm taking now, and my lips are on your cheek.
The parting hour is drawing near, and the sails wave in the wind,
Oh, fold me closer to your breast, I'll leave you soon behind.
(NYSL Broadside Ballads SCO BD0250)

De Marsan reorganized the Andrews enterprise, maintaining everything that was singable and saleable regardless of age or origin (Williams 1892, 268) and discarding only the most offensive lyrics. Recognizing the huge Hibernian presence in Manhattan, he then marshaled the talents of Irish ballad lyricists and catered heavily to their countrymen. The mark of their pens is evident in "The Jolly 69th" (fig. 26):

It happened one fine day,
Down by the raging say,
Quite convanient to the boilin' Gulf of Mexico
That some fine chaps hauled down our flag,
And through the dust did drag,
Saying it should never float on Fort-Sumter, O

All very well says we;
But, Boys we're goin to see
If the proud Flag of Liberty is to be treated so:
Then up rose every man,
With his sword and gun in hand,
For, the Sixty-Ninth for fightin' are the haroes, O.
(Milner collection)

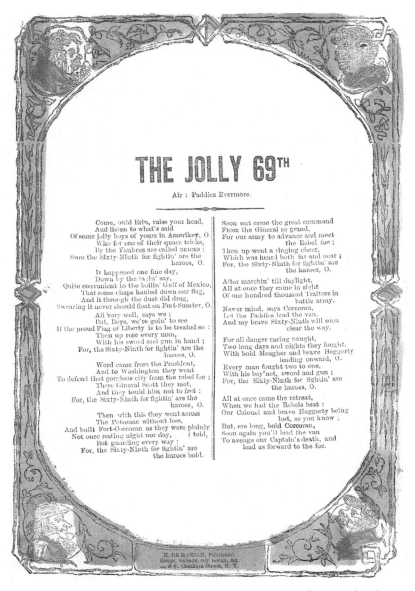

Figure 26. The Jolly 69th. Published by H. De Marsan. Collection of author.

With cocky naïveté, the narrator sings of the Sixty-Ninth Regiment as though its members were a champion football team. Rather than the denigrating "Paddy-the-Irishman" portrayals of earlier decades, he presents in "The Jolly 69th" the image of committed, confident Irish *Americans* on their way to preserve the national integrity of the United States. The Sixty-Ninth's volunteers are pictured as buoyant and brave. American Protestants, even those with nativist inclinations, could make little argument with the image of these valiant volunteers in service to the nation. The same, jocular juxtaposition of gravity and light-heartedness in addressing matters of considerable consequence was characteristic of urban working-class humor in Ireland. "The Finding of Moses," composed in Dublin twenty or more years before America's Civil War by ballad lyricist and hawker Thomas "Zozimus" Moran (1794–1846), conveys a similar feeling about a classic biblical story of epic proportion:

> On Egypt's banks, contagious to the Nile.
> Ould Pharoah's daughter, she went to bathe in style.
> She took her dip and then she came unto the land,
> And to dry her royal pelt she ran along the strand,
> A bullrush tripped her whereupon she saw
> A smiling baby in a wad of straw;
> She took him up and she says in accents mild
> "Oh tear-an-ages, girls, now, which of yis owns the child?"
>   (Harte 1993, 26–27)

If Wolf believed that "the sweet body of Irish songs was added to the voice of the nation" only from 1845 onward, he was literally incorrect. As seen previously, Irish songs were circulated in Manhattan in the early nineteenth century. Indeed, Thomas Moore's popular *Irish Melodies* was published there in 1818 and had a special character that struck a harmonious note with many Americans. But Wolf is quite right about broadside ballads. During the war, when a sailor who took part in the Battle of Mobile Bay wanted to versify his observations of the great naval conflict, he produced "Farragut's Ball" (LC Digital ID sb10130b), a parody of the Irish song "Lanigan's Ball" (O Lochlainn 1960, 104–5, 211), in which a minor accident at a dance results in a major altercation. The reference was clearly stated on the song sheet, an indication that most prospective purchasers were familiar with "Lanigan's Ball." In this simple, commercial procedure, a fully American experience was set to an Irish song framework, the implication being that Irish American song, driven by the vast increase in the Irish-born population and helped by a process of class division that separated bourgeois from working-class performance art during the 1850s (Allen 1991, 73–74), was by now endemic in the mainstream of working-class music in the nation's most trendsetting city.

At approximately the same time, something quite different and nearly as noteworthy occurred — songs easily recognizable as Irish but made in New York were brought to and circulated in Ireland, meaning that Irish American culture, which had gained credibility in New York, was now achieving success in the homeland. Such a lyric was "Tim Finigan's Wake" (Pastor 1864, 19–20), a song that ultimately would be regarded as one of the most quintessential of all Dublin ditties because of its welded connection to James Joyce. The adoption by Ireland's capital of a song composed in America's foremost city supports the proposition that the New York Irish community had strongly coalesced by the Civil War, because its entertainments had been developed to the point that their plebian artwork was being adopted not just by consumers in America but also in the center of mass culture in Ireland. The "Finigan" revelation was made by Jane S. Meehan (1976, 69–73). A composition of playwright, theater manager, and songwriter John F. Poole, "Tim Finigan's Wake" probably premiered during 1861 or 1862 while Poole and comic singer Tony Pastor worked together at the American Theatre, 444 Broadway, New York. In 1864, it appeared in *Tony Pastor's "444" Combination Songster*, one of a number of song collections Poole compiled for the star during their long association:

Tim Finigan lived in Walker Street
    A gentleman Irishman — mighty odd —
He'd a beautiful brogue, so rich and sweet,
    And to rise in the world he carried a hod.
But, you see, he'd a touch of the tippling way —
    With a love for the liquor poor Tim was born,

And to help him through his work each day,
    He'd a drop of the craythur' every morn.

    Whack, hurrah! blood and 'ounds, ye sowl ye!
       Welt the flure, yer trotters shake;
    Isn't it the truth I've tould ye
       Lots of fun at Finigan's wake!
           (Pastor 1864, 19–20)

Poole's text situates the Finigan residence on Walker Street, a narrow byway on the Lower Westside that intersects perpendicularly with Canal Street at Mulberry. Its meeting point with Broadway was a walk of only two-and-a-half blocks from the site of the American Theatre. The original text differs from later versions in a few ways but principally in the chorus. In 1864, William A. Pond published what was proclaimed as "the Only Correct Edition" of "Finigan's Wake," "the Popular Irish Song sung by Mr. Dan Bryant with Enthusiastic Applause," with no direct attribution to Poole. Copyright still meant little during the Civil War years. Popular songs were treated much as folk songs, from which they derived; though these songs were legally protected, the potentially small return from a lawsuit meant they were effectively free for the taking (*Sun*, 20 February 1876, 3). Publication of "Finigan's Wake" in multiple sheet music editions, as well as in songsters and broadsides, indicates it was extremely well liked, meaning its popularity certainly transcended ethno-religious boundaries, another leading indicator of de facto acceptance of the Irish. That the farce portrayed Irish as drunken, yet benign, battlers certainly increased its circulation, but "Finigan's" provenance indicates there was more to it than that. "Row and ruction" songs about staid social occasions gone awry had long been standard fare on New York stages, and "Tim Finigan's" last verse actually owes a direct debt to an older song, "The Fine Old Irish Gentleman," which is itself an alteration of the earlier "The Fine Old English Gentleman" (that relationship is particularly clear because John Andrews printed both songs on a single broadside). This linkage points out that excessive use of alcohol was not a trait possessed solely by the Irish; in Civil War New York, excessive drinking was almost universal.

Ethnic stereotypes were a large component of nineteenth-century variety entertainment. African American, Native American, German, Irish, Scots, and Yankee characterizations were all expected to follow set norms (Crawford 2001, 199; Snyder 2000, 5–6). That Italian American Antonio (Tony) Pastor adopted an Irish stage persona more often than all other ethnicities combined supports embryonic integration and acknowledges that Irish Catholics were not just a large numeric component of the New York City population but that their ethnic fabric was sewn into the tapestry of the metropolis by the Civil War. Other working-class Americans could see through song lyrics that the Irish contributed heartily to the broad cityscape by displaying lingering humanity in an increasingly commercial-industrial setting. Though Pastor's characterizations were often crude burlesque (Snyder 2000, 14), they were well within the bounds of period humor. His positive depiction of Irishmen as goodhearted and jolly rustic fellows at work finding their place in America's foremost city starkly contrasts with the ignorant plantation slave (Jim Crow) image of African Americans constructed by white minstrels—hardly surprising, as Pastor interacted with Irish people every day in Manhattan. Few minstrels, in contrast, seem to have had meaningful contact with the enslaved African Americans of the South they claimed to impersonate, principally because American blackface minstrelsy was a Northern phenomenon (J. Cullen 1996, 68).

The seminal Virginia Minstrels quartet, for example, were Northerners who had learned much of their purportedly black music from white men, such as the mysterious person known as "Ferguson" and Joel Walker Sweeney (Nathan 1962, 110–11, 114). Daniel Decatur Emmet certainly heard African Americans sing and play early on (Sacks and Sacks 1993), but that was near his home in Ohio. Emmet and Frank Brower toured in the South with the Cincinnati Circus Company in 1841 (Nathan 1962, 114), but there is no sure record of them visiting plantation slave quarters, though performer claims to that effect clearly enhanced credibility and box office allure. However, all four Virginia Minstrels did spend considerable time in Manhattan's Fourth, Sixth, and Seventh Wards, and had ample opportunity to soak up lower-class black culture within the earthy urban reaches around South Street, Catharine Market, and Five Points (Lott 1993, 94).

African American performers were not newcomers to New York. They had busked on the streets of Manhattan, probably to banjo accompaniment, as early as the American Revolution, and were well established by the early nineteenth century (Wittke 1930, 9).

It was the open frontier atmosphere of the Port of New York—an oceanic-continental point of exchange intensified by the city's significant coastal trade with the South, and through the Hudson River–Erie Canal waterway—that accelerated the coalescence of a musical form built from African, British, and Irish inputs (Smith 2011). The necessary ingredients for blackface minstrelsy existed in crowded Lower Manhattan. W. T. Lhamon's *Raising Cane* (1998, 23) reproduces an 1820 folk drawing of three blacks (a dancer accompanied by two rhythm accompanists) at Catharine Market in Manhattan. A diverse crowd watches from a distance, but close by, keenly involved and *almost* participating in the spectacle, are two stylish young white men in stovepipe hats and a capped workman playing the bones, any or all of whom might have been Irish. White theater audiences wanted black music interpreted for them by white performers, meaning spectacle was far more important than authenticity. The minstrel show, therefore, was a *show*, and minstrelsy a "confused" medium in the sense that, though its facade was black, its content was varied and included a slice of Irishness. Eric Lott (1993, 95) makes this point, writing that "minstrel characters were surely influenced by Irish low-comedy types from the British stage," and accounts for the ease with which "blackface songs and skits incorporated Irish brogues and other ethnic dialects, with absolutely no sense of contradiction; blackface, bizarrely enough, was actually used to represent all ethnicities." The young white singers who embraced black song and refashioned it into minstrelsy did so because they found it devilishly intoxicating. Minstrelsy further benefitted Irish singers by creating opportunities for them to extend their onstage functionality by adding blackface material to their repertoires.

The contrast between the classic stage personas of Irish and Africans makes for meaningful comparison. While both characterizations originated in Britain, the similarities end there. The image of Africans imported from Britain to the Northern states was at first positive and sympathetic but turned horrendously ugly as the debate over slavery intensified (Southern 1997, 88–90). In contrast, the Irish persona transported to the United States was at first derogatory and continued to be so until Hibernians themselves were able to manage their images, both onstage and off, through the process of Americanization (W. Williams 1996, 134–36). Sheer numbers helped power that process. By the 1880 US Census, the City of New York contained 21.5 Irish persons for every one African American (Rosenwaike 1972, 73, 77), surely an indicator that the Irish had acquired great influence by then, while African Americans had relatively little.

The commonality of class inherent in much of Tony Pastor's work supports the idea that Irish workers were beginning to integrate into mainstream, blue-collar New York during the Civil War. *Tony Pastor's "444" Combination Songster* (1864) contains forty-two songs. Of these, ten are Irish themed, while only one other piece, a comic German dialect song, adopts an immigrant persona. There is no reason to assume that this ratio of one Irish to three other songs is accidental, for it corresponds exactly with the population makeup of Manhattan during the Civil War. The extent to which Pastor played the Irish card is significant, in that it recognizes the degree to which he believed they were integral to New York City life, particularly its musical life. Noticeable too is a strong, antiestablishment bias in Pastor's song selection, also reflective of Irish attitudes and supportive of their interests. Through colonization and repression in Ireland, Catholics learned to be deeply hostile to authority. By late 1862 and early 1863, the direction of the war, the looming military draft, war profiteering, the perceived threat posed by emancipation, reduced employment, and further socioeconomic worries diminished respect for authority among working-class New Yorkers. At this time of great stress, American, German, and Irish workers had more in common than they had previously thought. "The White House," a "444" songster lyric by G. R. Edeson, casts life at the center of power—alien, Republican Washington—in its worst light:

There are lawyers, statesmen, soldiers, contractors by the score,
With scheming politicians, and every kind of bore;
From Barnum down to Cassius Clay they round Old Abe do stand,
A-listening to the anecdotes he's got at his command.

(Pastor 1864, 25)

Poole's "Our Grandfathers' Days," on the other hand, contrasts the perceived image of respectful democracy of yesteryear with materialistic contemporary times:

> In our grandfathers' days men were judged but by merit,
> And those that were sound got their measure of praise;
> But now-a-days folks judge of men by their money—
> That wasn't the case in our grandfathers' days.
>
> (Pastor 1864, 55)

Henry De Marsan's great store of Irish songs includes sentimental pieces, such as "Aileen A Roon," "Aileen Astore," "The Dear Irish Boy," and "I Think of Old Ireland Wherever I Go," as well as nationalist songs like "The Escape of Stephens, the Fenian Chief" and "The Croppy Boy." The latter song alludes to the 1798 Rebellion and generally references the consequences of resistance to colonial oppression—similar to the retribution that was endured by patriots during the American Revolution:

> It was early in the spring,
> The small birds whistled sweet did sing,
> Changing their notes from tree to tree,
> The song they sung was old Ireland free.
>
> It was early last Thursday night,
> The yeoman cavalry gave me a fright,
> The yeoman cavalry was my downfall,
> When I was taken to Lord Cornwall.
>
> It was in his guard house where I was laid,
> And in his parlor where I was tried,
> My sentence passed and my spirits low
> When to New Guinea I was forced to go.
>
> (LC amss.as102550)

Many humorous Irish songs composed during the Civil War can be found in the De Marsan catalogue; few if any are mean-spirited.

Gleeful mention of the potato has long sent chills up the spines of many Irish immigrants, but "The Last Potato" is not directly related to the Great Hunger and possesses a benignly playful feel even if the title is dubious:

> 'Tis my last, last potato!
> Yet boldly I stand,
> With the calmness of Cato,
> My fork in my hand.
> Not one in the basket?
> Must you also go?
> (With sorrow I ask it:)
> Shall I peel ye or no?
>   (LC amss.sb20264a)

"The Irishman" is a sincere depiction of the Hibernian male as a flawed, yet warm and honest, laborer—a "solid man," in nineteenth-century local parlance, or a "regular guy" today. It further situates the Catholic Irish within the mainstream of New York workers:

> His hand is rash, his heart is warm
> But honesty is still his guide;
> None more repents a deed of harm,
> And none forgives with nobler pride;
> He may be duped, but wont be dared—
> More fit to practice than to plan;
> He dearly earns his poor reward,
> And spends it like an Irishman.
>   (LC amss.as201670)

The "444" where Tony Pastor worked represented the high mark of New York concert saloons. Below the "444" and a handful of other first-class establishments rested a plethora of raunchy and seedy houses, such as the Santa Claus Bar on Broadway, "a long, narrow and cheerless looking hall with sawdust on the floor, and a very dingy and forlorn aspect generally," and Gudney's Saloon on Grand Street. Both were immortalized in a page 1 article in the *New York Times* on 3 December 1858. The reporter writes that the entertainment at the Santa Claus "comprised songs, Caucasian and Ethiopian—and that most contemptible and inane of exhibitions known as negro dances. . . . The male singers were seedily, and the female singers shabbily-genteelly attired, and with the exception of one little man, who did his part respectably in an Irish duet, all sang miserably, vilely ill." The man from *The New York Times* disliked Gudney's even more:

> The room was of the dirtiest kind; the music, if I might use so dignified a term, was of the most discordant; the attendant women of the boldest; the stage the smallest and rudest; the guests of the most ordinary and noisiest; the songs of the commonest, and, in some instances, were obscene. A Gentleman of the Jewish persuasion sang Irish songs with an accent intended to be Hibernian, but which was purely Polish. . . . [The] company applauded at every uncouth or dirty expression and gave evidences of being greatly charmed. . . . I learnt that the performers earned, at this degrading work, from 75 cents to $1 per night, and that the women receive $3 per week, depending, for the rest, on the chances of remuneration for other more debased employment after the place is closed for the night.

That Irish songs were featured in both venues is important, for in one instance the reporter finds the performance satisfactory, the only approving words written about any aspect of either saloon, and in the second instance, he finds the idea of a Polish man singing an Irish song absurd. The article from its conception was intended to be snidely amusing, but the *New York Times* reporter, an ear of the most conservative newspaper in the city, chooses in both instances to defend the integrity of Irish song. The implication must be that he finds it somehow artistically reputable, belonging to a song corpus that he associates with New York culture and from which he clearly excludes blackface minstrelsy. And what of the singer with the "purely Polish" accent struggling precariously to hold the attention of an unruly audience at Gudney's Saloon? With approximately one-quarter of Manhattan's population then Irish-born, and Gudney's a dodgy place patronized by rowdy, low-wage earners, he likely perceived singing Irish songs as a safe modus for connecting with what could easily become an abusive audience threatening both his limbs and meager livelihood.

The immensely popular Italian American singer Tony Pastor, commanding the high stage on Broadway, also chose an Irish identity for its audience connectivity. Pastor could nudge Irish listeners in the ribs to signify that everyone in the house (himself included) was "in" on a joke about a Hibernian peculiarity but also to show that he was demonstratively on their side, *and* he had the advantage of sharing with them the Roman Catholic religion (Zellers 1971, 111). Another example of nonnative "ethnic" Americans adopting Irish identity is seen in De Masan's broadside of "Dublin Bay," "as Sung by M. Solomon" (LC Digital ID sb10097b).

Hellish Battles

The war songs of the New York Irish dating from the first year and a quarter of the conflict were remarkable both for their number and for their sincere enthusiasm, which was at least equal to that of mainstream American war lyrics:

> 'Twas then the Gallant Sixty-Ninth with spirits light and gay,
> Cheered by the ones they dearly loved, when marching down
> Broadway,
> Went forth to meet the Rebel foe, who would destroy the land
> That gave them birth and nurtured them, the dastard rebel band.
> ("Return of Gen. Corcoran of the Glorious 69th,"
> LC amss.sb40538a)

New York Hibernian males who had rushed to join the Union army viewed service both as a civic duty and as an opportunity to prove the worth of their community. On 29 August 1861, at Jones's Wood picnic ground, a hundred thousand New Yorkers "paid twenty-five cents admission to a Grand Festival for the benefit of the widows and orphans of the 69th," and fifty thousand remained afterward to hear Thomas Francis Meagher ask, "Will the Irishmen of New York stand by this cause—resolutely, heartily, with inexorable fidelity?"

Later, the group sang "Corcoran to His Regiment, or I Would Not Take Parole" en masse. Song created an emotional bond as the Grand Festival morphed into a recruiting rally for Meagher's newly formed Irish Brigade, which by mid-November 1861 had three regiments—the Sixty-Third, Sixty-Ninth, and Eighty-Eighth New York Volunteers—numbering twenty-five hundred men (Jones 1969, 98–99).

The summer of 1862 brought reports to New York of hellish battles during the Peninsula Campaign. The Irish Brigade had been within sight and sound of Richmond before being ordered to retreat. The Sixty-Ninth alone lost "222 men, killed, wounded, or missing after the battle," and the Sixty-Third and Eighty-Eighth New York together lost 238 (Wylie 2007, 158). When Meagher returned to Manhattan to recruit in mid-July 1862, he found the city's mood had "shifted dramatically from the previous year," and his efforts produced only three hundred of the thousand men he had expected (Wylie 2007, 158–60). More community demoralization followed. At the Battle of Antietam on 17 September 1862, 512 soldiers were lost, over half of those who remained of the three New York regiments. At Fredericksburg on 13 December, the brigade charged up a steep hill known as Marye's Heights, meeting "a blinding fire of musketry" from behind a stone wall at the top (Wylie 2007, 174–75). Colonel Robert Nugent soon realized that the mission was hopeless: "By virtue of the commanding position of the enemy no attack could have been successful" (quoted in Bruce 2006, 129). Nugent's first-hand report of the carnage substantiates Miller's (1985, 324) claim of "the unnecessary, if not intentional, waste of Irish regiments in hopeless combat situations."

As war became synonymous with slaughter, enlistments dropped off, and the buoyant, optimistic anthems of the past disappeared and were replaced by lyrics bearing pain and protest. The Emancipation Proclamation further reduced enlistments and sapped the morale of large numbers of men already in uniform. The draft inducted many Irish Americans. Others whose numbers were not drawn by lottery were later induced—less through ethnic loyalty or patriotism and more by lofty enlistment bounties and the high price of inflation in New York—to volunteer. Veteran soldiers lucky to have survived their terms of service were then wooed with reenlistment bonuses.

Immigrants straight off the boat from Ireland were targeted too. An epic broadside ballad, "The Glorious Victory of the Seven Irishmen over the Kidnapping Yankees of New York," was already in circulation in Ireland. It pictured the scene thusly:

> He brought them to an ale-house and gave them drink galore
> I am sure—such entertainment—they never got before
> When he thought he had them drunk he unto them did say
> You are listed now as soldiers—to defend our country
>
> They looked at one another—and unto him did say –
> Its not to list that we did come unto America
> But to labour for a livelihood—as many done before
> That we have emigrated from the lovely Shamrock shore
>
> .   .   .   .
>
> Our Irish boys got to their feet which made the Yankees frown
> As fast as they could strike a blow they knocked a soldier down
> The officer and his men—they left all in their gore
> They proved themselves St Patricks sons thro' Columbia shore.
> (Bodleian 2806 c.8 [291])

Not all greenhorns were so wise and so quick. A folk song, "By the Hush, Me Boys," found by collector Edith Fowke (1965, 52–53, 172) in the Ottawa River Valley of Ontario tells a different story. Fowke believed it was carried there by "some wandering Irish American who visited" after the Civil War. Her premise is supported because North American lumbermen were known for paying little or no regard to the international border and Irish immigrants were penetrating the logging woods during that time (Doerflinger 1990):

> Oh, it's by the hush, me boys, I'm sure that's to hold your noise.
> And listen to poor Paddy's narration.
> I was by hunger pressed and in poverty distressed,
> So I took a thought I'd leave the Irish nation.
>
> Here's you, boys, do take my advice,
> To Americay I'd have yous not be coming.

There is nothing here but war where the murdering cannons roar,
And I wish I was at home in dear old Eree-in.

Then I sold my horse and plough, me little pigs and cow,
And me little farm of land and I parted,
And me sweetheart Biddy Magee I'm afeared I'll never see
For I left her on that morning broken-hearted.

Then meself and a hundred more to Americay sailed o'er,
Our fortune to be making we were thinking.
When we landed in Yankee land, shoved a gun into our hand,
Saying, "Paddy, you must go and fight for Lincoln."

General Mahar [sic] to us said, "If you get shot or lose your head,
Every murdered son of you will get a pension."
In the war I lost me leg; all I've now is a wooden peg;
By me soul it is the truth to you I mention.

The bitter graveyard humor of "By the Hush, Me Boys," coupled
with the inference that its source was an Irishman who had seen too
much of the United States during the Civil War years, underscores the
extreme hardship posed by successive trials of the Great Hunger, anti-
Irish discrimination, Know-Nothing violence, and the terror and carnage of armed conflict. It closes with the astounding observation that,
for all its faults, life in Ireland was not so bad when compared with
mid-nineteenth-century America:

Now I think meself in luck to be fed upon Indian buck
In old Ireland, the country I delight in,
And with the devil I do say, "Curse Americay,"
For I'm sure I've got enough of their hard fighting.
                                        (Fowke 1965, 52–53, 172)

On 2 January 1864, the three New York regiments of the Irish
Brigade returned home to an "indifferent" city, to be met only by immediate relatives and an escort of two state militia companies (Conyngham 1867, 424–25; Jones 1969, 215–16). Two weeks later, at a banquet

in Irving Hall, the officers feted 250 enlisted men and noncommissioned officers who served with the brigade. Meagher led the postdinner speeches, blasting the rioters, "who raised an infamous revolt in the city against the Government, while they were fighting the battles of the Union." Calling them "Traitors to the Republic," he asked the ranks not to entertain "a disrespectful word against the President, the Commander of the Army in which they so nobly served" (*NYT*, 17 January 1864, 8). Colonel Nugent, who had supervised the draft and battled rioters the preceding July, offered a defiant toast: "No negotiation, no compromise, no truce, no peace, but war to the last dollar and the last man, until every Rebel flag be struck between the St. Lawrence and the Gulf, and swept everywhere, the world over, from land and sea." Colonel O'Mahony spoke of General Corcoran, "one of the noblest and best of men, whether considered an Irishman or an American," requesting, "May you bear a part in fulfilling, under the leadership of the dauntless Meagher, the two dearest hopes of his heart — the Restoration of the American Union and the liberation of Ireland!" (Conyngham 1867, 426–37; Jones 1969, 217). This sincere display of patriotism was prominently reported in the *New York Times*, the city's conservative paper-of-record, but it was not clear how long or how well it would be remembered.

In the presidential election of 1864, Democratic candidate George B. McClellan garnered more than twice as many votes in New York City than Abraham Lincoln, receiving large pluralities in predominately Irish areas — 90 percent in the Sixth Ward! (Spann 1996, 208). Still the president won New York State, if only by the slim margin of 1 percent. Nationwide, Lincoln won by a landslide, receiving 55 percent of the popular vote, and 212 electoral votes out of 233. Republicans also prevailed in the New York gubernatorial race. Now in full control, the ruling party viewed Irish who supported McClellan as disloyal, and their commonly held antiwar, antiabolition position as traitorous.

On 9 April 1865, General Robert E. Lee surrendered the Confederate states army of Northern Virginia to General Ulysses S. Grant at Appomattox Court House, bringing the Civil War to a close almost exactly four years after it began. Only five days later, on 14 April 1865, President Abraham Lincoln was assassinated. Coming so soon after the long-anticipated victory, his death deeply shocked the North, which quickly came to view him as a martyr. Cynical New Yorkers who had previously decried and ridiculed the nation's leader now mourned him (McKay 1991, 303–8). Though most New York Democrats had opposed Lincoln's policies, the city's Irish Catholics were especially vilified for their opposition, as though they were somehow to blame for his death. That 140,000 Irish had served the Union during the Civil War often went unremembered (Bruce 2006, 231–32).

On 9 April 1864, one year to the day before the surrender at Appomattox, Henry De Marsan wrote to a client, "I have published about 290 different songs . . . since the present Civil War commenced," continuing by noting that Michael Corcoran was "one of the most celebrated and sung-about figures of the day" with at least a score of ballads mentioning him, and Thomas Francis Meagher behind only by "a few verses" (Wolf 1963, iv–v).

The personae and behavior of these two famous Irish generals make for an interesting contrast. Both were ambitious and were seemingly marooned in America forever. Corcoran was more deliberate in his decisions, weighed his words more, was more democratic in his management, and could subordinate himself fully to the chain of command integral to survival in military life and party politics. Each held an intense love of Ireland but in Meagher that love has been seen as often compromised by self-promotion (Wylie 2007, 118). He was also the subject of rumors regarding his suitability as a leader; accusations were made that he was drunk leading his men into battle, that he deserted them in the field, and that he had recklessly exposed his officers and men to danger (Bruce 2006, 128–29; Conyngham 1867, 234). Meagher died under suspicious circumstances on 1 July 1867, at Fort Benton, Montana, soon after his term as acting governor of the territory expired (Spann 1996, 209; Wylie 2007, 304–31).

While both men were variously embroiled in controversy, only Michael Corcoran understood how to emerge from it successfully. He was a hero who largely lived up to his legend. Had Corcoran survived the war, his greatest challenge would have been the same as the Catholic Irish community at large—resolving dual loyalties to Ireland and the United States. As a committed officer in the American Fenian Brotherhood, his inclination would have been to return to the task of liberating Ireland; but the Fenian movement had factional-ized during the war years and many dedicated idealists who enlisted with the aim of learning the military skills necessary to free Ireland had died on American battlefields. He had been in ill-health at least since the Prince of Wales incident, so Corcoran's days of military cam-paigning may well have been over. Without question, he would have been proposed for political office at the local, state, perhaps even the national level, and it is hard to envision his being defeated, a situation that would have been a tremendous catalyst for the integration of Irish Catholics in the immediate postwar period. But Corcoran, an excel-lent horseman, died unexpectedly at the age of thirty-six in a riding accident just three days before Christmas 1863, greatly, dishearten-ing the city and the nation at large (Daly 1962, 270–71; Jones 1969, 215; Lane 1997, 32). It can only be imagined in what ways a longer life might have influenced the fortunes of New York's Irish Catholic community.

CHAPTER FIVE

The Road to Respectability

It's Ireland and Italy, Jerusalem and Germany,
Oh, Chinamen and nagurs, and a paradise for cats,
All jumbled up togather in the snow and rainy weather,
They represent the tenants in McNally's row of flats.

"McNally's Row of Flats" premiered in realist playwright, lyricist, and actor Edward Harrigan's 1882 musical comedy *McSorely's Inflation*. Composed as a nostalgic retrospect on lower-class New York life, its chorus, above, contains a list in broad period ethnic humor of Manhattan's most visible minority groups at the time of publication. By then, the city had substantially accommodated its Old Immigrants, the Irish and Germans (Kahn 1955, 68), and consigned its largest nonwhite populations, African and Chinese Americans, to underclass status. New mass migrations were already in the making, not as previously from northern and western Europe, but from the continent's southern and eastern reaches. The first of these, which began in the 1870s, was linked to overpopulation in the Mezzogiorno region of Italy and posed stiff occupational competition for Irish laborers. The second, mainly of Russian Jews, ensued with pogroms and restrictive polices enforced after the assassination of Tsar Alexander II in 1881 and greatly affected the availability and cost of housing in

Lower Manhattan (Burrows and Wallace 1999, 1112-26; Lankevich 1998, 122–25; Rosenwaike 1972, 82-85). The scale of the new immigration was truly huge, "twice that of any previous decade" (Lankevich 1998, 122). But while it brought distress to Irish low-wage earners, it actually conferred long-term benefits on Hibernians as a whole. New York Brahmins, many of whom had previously dreaded, hated, and railed at the Irish, were now confronted by more foreign fears, which included unintelligible languages, an increase in crime, and the propagation of radical theories of wealth distribution.

The vast influx from Italy and the Russian Empire placed another large social layer below the Catholic Irish, allowing them to elevate accordingly; for, facing this alarming alteration in European immigration patterns, many Protestant elites softened their attitude toward the city's burgeoning Irish American middle class (Miller 1985, 495–96; W. Williams 1996, 239). This attitudinal shift was accompanied by modifications within the Irish community itself, both buttressed by changes in city demographics. In 1865, the Census of New York State enumerated the population of Manhattan at 726,386. By 1870, the count thrust up to 942,292 (Rosenwaike 1972, 55–56). By 1880, with nearly one in every eight urban dwellers in the United States residing in Greater New York (Hammack 1982, 33), the aggregate of the city proper reached 1,206,299. Irish-born New Yorkers now numbered 198,595 of the total; however, when combined with their American-born children, the first- and second-generation total reached 423,159 persons (Rosenwaike 1972, 72–73). This in-group population shift significantly altered the city's Irish Catholic constituency. With over 53 percent of New York's Hibernians now American-born, the essence of what it meant to be "Irish" in Manhattan changed forever. While the overriding aspirations of the second-generation were not dramatically different from those of their parents—both wished to share in New York's prosperity and integrate into its society while maintaining important group cultural tenets—the second-generation frame of reference was far more imbedded in the island of Manhattan:

> You see I belong to New York, my boys,
>   Oh dear old Manhattan Isle,
> Famed for its wealth and its beauty, boys,
>   Its darling dear girls and their style;

On Broadway, my boys, or the Bowery,
    No stranger e'er met with a frown;
Take my word, I belong to the city,
    And hail from the East Side of town.
("The East Side of Town," Harrigan and Hart 1875, 56)

At the same time, the second-generation's conceptions of Ireland were increasingly formed more from made-in-America accounts that were idealized caricatures of the far-away heritage land as in the romantic "Cushlamachree":

Dear Erin, how sweetly thy green bosom rises,
An emerald set in the ring of the sea;
Each blade of thy meadows my faithful heart prizes,
Thou queen of the west, the world's Cushlamachree.
      (*Johnny Roach's Bold Irish* 1870, 63–64)

Affection for Ireland was great, but, when asked to choose between the United States and Ireland as the better place to live, America won out even among the first generation. Ireland lay close to the hearts of many, and they expressed their love with idealistic sentimentality, but because they believed they had been banished politically and economically (Miller 1985, 3–8), they accepted the reality of a new home in a more promising country. In William J. Scanlan's "Recollection," the speaker romanticizes about his youth in Ireland, but taking him literally, it is a part of Ireland he wishes to bring to America rather than to return himself:

When e'er I think of bygone days,
And the happy times we had
At home in dear ould Ireland,
It makes my heart feel glad.
When I think of my poor ould mother,
And my father, ah! how dear
That sweet recollection is to me,
How I wish they were here.
      (Emmet 1882)

To be clear, the post–Civil War Catholic Irish of Manhattan were diverse. Individual station was determined by a combination of factors such as affluence, age, application, class, connections, education, gender, nativity, occupation, and wealth (Miller 1985, 494). Historian David N. Doyle (2006, 214) writes that Irish Americans "were found at all social levels of the burgeoning commercial as well as factory cities," of which New York was the foremost. Immigration from Ireland, of course, continued even as the percentage of American-born Irish increased. However, down at street level, those who had arrived as laborers and had not materially progressed, and recent immigrants without marketable skills in an increasingly sophisticated urban economy, had a hard time, owing both to competition from New Immigrants and to increased mechanization in the construction industry; the combination of these factors lowered pay for unskilled manual work that was also harder to get. At the same time, savvier immigrants rose through the trades to become proprietors of businesses, while others entered politics. Harrigan's Timothy McNally successfully worked both angles:

> Its down in Bottle Alley lives Timothy McNally,
> A wealthy politician and a gentleman at that,
> The joy of all the ladies, the gosoons and the babies,
> Who occupy the buildings called McNally's row of flats.

The song elevates McNally for comic effect. Ironically, he was a small cog in the Tammany machine and only *relatively* wealthy, because Bottle Alley (later famously photographed by Jacob Riis) was one of the lowest addresses in all New York—home to stale beer saloons, where last night's flat dregs were sold today to the poorest inmates of Five Points. But McNally's tenants respected him both for his political connection and for the life-sustaining power he held over them as their slumlord. The polyglot diversity of the "new" New York is stressed in a pair of snapshot images:

> The great conglomeration of men from ev'ry nation
> The Babylonium tower, oh! it could not equal that;
> Peculiar institution, where brogues without dilution,
> Were rattled off together in McNally's row of flats.

Its bags of rags and papers, with tramps and other sleepers,
Italian Lazzarones, there was lots of other rats,
A-lying on the benches and dying there by inches
From open ventilation in McNally's row of flats.

Lacking a governmental social safety net, Tammany attempted to ameliorate the suffering of its most endangered supporters, but it was not McNally's responsibility to do so at his personal expense. Those who could not provide rent when it was due were sent scattering for other shelter on moving day:

It never was expected that the rent would be collected
They'd levy on the furniture, the bedding and the slats!
You'd ought to see the rally and battle in the alley
A-throwing out the tenants in McNally's row of flats.
                    (*Snow and Mott's* [1883?])

Irish men of both generations were moving up, driving streetcars and directing traffic, while some of the second generation were entering administrative and managerial fields. By 1890, 18.4 percent of greater New York Irish males performed white collar work, 46 percent had skilled and semiskilled trades, and 29.2 percent were employed as laborers (Hammack 1982, 83), though in that same year Irish men made up a scant, yet growing, 4.3 percent of the area's professionals (67). Irish women did better. They were increasingly employed as nurses and educators (Barrett 2012, 129–32), so that by the first decade of the twentieth century, "one-fifth of all public-school teachers in northern cities . . . were Irish-American Catholics" (Miller 1985, 496). That trend was observed in song in 1879, when William A. Pond published Edward Harrigan's "Such an Education Has My Mary Ann," a comedic lyric based on the manner in which an Irish-born father perceives his American-born daughter, a teacher at a city-administered school:

My Mary Ann's a teacher in a great big public school,
She gets one thousand dollars ev'ry year.
She has charge of all the children, You'd never find a fool,
For Mary gives them all the proper steer.[1]

Irish New Yorkers of the post–Civil War period also included a modicum of super-rich citizens. Belfast-born Hugh O'Neill came to New York as a child and began working at 16. Immediately after the Civil War, he opened a dry goods store on Broadway, just north of Union Square, among merchant firms such as Tiffany and Company and Brooks Brothers. In 1887, he relocated to a purpose-built building in the Ladies Mile section of Sixth Avenue, employing twenty-five hundred people by the 1890s. On his death in 1902, O'Neill's fortune amounted to $8 million (*NYT*, 2 May 2004). Similarly, William R. Grace, shipping magnate, merchant trader, and twice mayor of New York, died in 1904, leaving a personal estate of ten million dollars (Clayton 1985, 265).

But before Grace could don the mantle of the mayoralty and the Irish could be recognized by a majority of native-born Americans, the community had to navigate traps that had characterized their settlement throughout as an advance-retreat progress—importantly, the embarrassing Fenian raids into Canada that followed the Civil War and the Orange riots of 1870 and 1871. Again, ancient animosities transferred from Ireland to Manhattan threatened to derail the group transit from alien to American. As seen earlier, many—but not all—of the events in the Irish passage from ignominy to integration are chronicled in folk and period popular song. These accounts, which often conflict with reports in city newspapers, are highly valuable because they convey the wants, needs, aspirations, and attitudes of the community base. As the Catholic Irish became more American, more involved, more hopeful, and more accepted, the content of their songs changed to reflect their new image and outlook. Representations of the previously downtrodden yet rebellious Irish and their destitute homeland do not disappear but diminish. Newer songs generally convey more realistic stories of people who are an integral part of the Empire City, people who remember where they came from and are able to effect change for the better in the new home they helped build, figuratively and literally. This is not to suggest that by the end of the hundred-year integration era in 1883 that the Catholic Irish community had achieved 100 percent parity with Protestant Americans—that took *far* longer—rather, that they then made up more than one-third of the city's population, held the leadership of the city's largest religious group (Lankevich 1998, 118), and controlled the most significant faction within the Democratic Party. In addition, their class structure had broadened significantly. The fear Protestant elites loved to dread most had come and passed benignly: an Irish-born Catholic had been elected mayor of the city and ran an open, inclusive, business-like, reformist administration that had rid city government of some of its most illicit, revenue-diverting operations. From 1883 onward, the Catholic Irish continued to improve materially and socially as they became more widely educated. The new Catholic Irish person was a highly urbanized, thoroughly Americanized "citizen patriot who drew his or her strengths from a mythical land known as the Emerald Isle" (W. Williams 1996, 239).

Fenian Raids

The issue of independence for Ireland, temporarily set aside during the Civil War, gained front and center position in New York during the summer of 1865. On 25 July, a crowd of "at least 30,000" attended a Fenian Brotherhood picnic and rally at Jones's Wood (*NYT*, 26 July 1865, 8) on the Upper East Side. The *New York Times* published a report the next day, written mostly in a snide tone intended for the amusement of its elite readers; however, from it can be drawn the image of a picture-perfect event, a "monster" political gathering of like-minded Irish Americans preceded by an enormous family picnic. The article describes the men in attendance as mainly "uneducated and youthful, impulsive, hard working Irishmen": most American born or immigrants who came to the United States at an early age. Despite the large crowd, the scene is even-tempered: "This will seem strange to those who regard our Irish friends as mere warriors, but the fact is, that many of them went to the war, where they got all the fighting they cared for and now they are on their good behavior. . . . They smoked fearfully vile cigars, drank much rum and danced themselves wet. They had a real jolly time."

Five years earlier as the Sixty-Ninth Regiment set off for Washington and war, working-class Irishwomen in the crowd had been styled as "Biddies"; now they were described as having "ladylike" comportment. They were quite normal, being "some of the prettiest, some of the homeliest we ever saw. . . . The young Irish girls who danced, and flirted, and talked, and romped, and sat in the swings, and played pretty little games on the greensward, were mainly shop girls and work girls of various degrees. To their credit it should be said that their conduct was in eminent good taste, their demeanor as ladylike as their actions proper" (*NYT*, 26 July 1865, 8).

The *New York Herald*, which competed with the *New York Times*, also reported on the peaceful and fun-filled picnic mood, mentioning "singing and swinging, dancing and 'all sorts iv divarshun'" (26 July 1865, 8). The article links the day's good nature to the positive effect of Americanization on the Irish, contrasting it with the negative effects of their dark history of colonization at home. If fault lay with the Irish, it reasoned, it was put there by the English:

> It is also said that Irishmen can never come together without having a row. . . . This is a thoroughly English idea, and, like everything pertaining to 'perfidious Albion,' is entirely false. . . .
>
> [Here] in America, there is no opposition offered to the naturally jolly nature of the Celt. He is untrammeled by laws in which he had no voice in making, and is allowed to enjoy himself as he may. . . . He becomes a rational being and indulges his feelings in a rational way. He becomes a member of respectable society, takes a prominent position in politics, becomes educated, and rises to a point of distinction he could never hope to attain in his own unhappy country—at least while under the influence of English rule. The free institutions of the American republic remodel his whole character.

Here lies the contrast—while the *New York Times* envisions the Irish at their proper level within city society, the *New York Herald* places no upward limit on them. The *New York Times* seeks to maintain elite control of the Irish, while the *Herald* seeks to free them.

The core reason behind the event—raising recruits and funds for an American-engineered uprising intended to bring independence to Ireland—led both reporters to position it as an *Irish* affair. However, with "Irish" demographics in a state of change, it can also be viewed as an *American* function held in connection with an Irish cause. The *New York Times* (26 July 1865, 8) clearly identifies most male attendees at the picnic as rooted in the United States. When a beau caters to his sweetheart, he runs for "two plates of ice-cream and two tumblers of cobblers" — a treat as American as apple pie. The newsman observes, "A dance is a dance the whole world over, and as far as we could see there is no difference between the heeling and the toeing of a Fenian couple than any other." He briefly describes dancers stepping out the "Virginia reel," perhaps not realizing they were actually swirling to a forerunner dance brought to America from Ireland. The picnic also contains trappings of American officialdom with uniformed militia and a police detail benignly present. Why, then, is the affair *Irish* and not *American*? For the *New York Times*, it is partly because by 1865 the majority of its readers had not yet endorsed the idea that the Catholic Irish could be regarded as Americans and partly that the Jones's Wood merrymakers were, unlike the elite newspaper's readers, mainly members of the working class. They were, therefore, alien in education, social standing, and wealth; class reinforced their foreignness and contributed to their segregation. Conservative *New York Times* readers would have preferred little-to-no social change, but the Irish had "helped to change working-class culture" in New York by this time (Gordon 1993, 8–9), meaning that certain Irish cultural hallmarks were already incorporated into the city's nonelite norm. As Moloney (2006, 384–87) mentions, the highly musical, highly verbal, more English-speaking Irish of the postfamine period were at the forefront in American variety theater. Emulation was another indicator; as seen in chapter 4, it was commonplace for non-Irish entertainers to sing Irish songs. Conversely, the *New York Herald* reporter wrote that the roughness previously apparent in Irish immigrants resulted from their deprivation under English rule; but he also clearly believed fair treatment had brought them to the brink of full integration into the city's culture and society. While these views differ considerably, they are not directly opposed; rather, each newspaper perceives the same phenomenon according to the social philosophy and political alignment of its readers. The *New York Times* has modified its tone somewhat from the prewar years, not just because the Irish have changed, but also because an initiative was at work to seek reparations from the British government for having materially aided the Confederacy (*NYT*, 26 October 1865, 1–3). That the Irish might now deal a blow to the British is interpreted positively.

The main event of this "first really great demonstration on the part of the Fenians" in the City of New York came at the end of the day (*NYT*, 26 July 1865, 8). The chief orator was William R. Roberts, a County Cork immigrant, who was so successful in the Manhattan dry goods trade that he retired as a millionaire at age thirty-nine to pursue a career in politics (Glazier 1999, 810). He spoke in "plain common-sense talk," saying, "We require facts not fancy, dollars as well as sympathy, muskets not advice, and bullets in place of words" (*NYT*, 26 July 1865, 8), making it clear that the picnic was over and the time for business had now arrived. That enterprise was the liberation of Ireland with American arms and money and expertise provided by Irish American Civil War veterans. Curiously, the *New York Times* article does not comment on Roberts's speech, though it was printed in full. It is strangely mute on whether a fighting force should be raised on American soil to invade what the United States government recognized as an integral part of the United Kingdom.

The grand transoceanic scheme had numerous problems. Its likely commander, General Michael Corcoran, had died in December 1863, and no one of similar experience, great reputation, and high governmental connections existed to take his place. In addition, many battle-hardened Irish American troops had been killed or disabled during the Civil War or were otherwise disinclined to further service. A rift had occurred within the organization that produced two opposing policies—an uprising in Ireland versus an invasion of Canada—and many Fenian organizations both in the United States and in Ireland were infiltrated by spies. Timing was somewhat auspicious in America. Many Northerners remained angry about Britain's favoritism toward the Confederacy during the Civil War, particularly regarding damage caused by the commerce raider the CSS *Alabama*. A Fenian songwriter identified only as "J. C. P." attempted to use the issue as a wedge in a new version of "The Wearing of the Green":

Oh! Paddy dear, and did you hear the news that's going round,
They say, the Alabama claims John Bull will not pay down,

The Yankee wears a hostile look, John Bull, a dogged mein,
So we shall have another chance for the Wearing of the Green.
(*Wearing of the Green* 1869, 114)

However, conditions for an uprising were inopportune in Ireland, where much of the Catholic population lived in grinding poverty and heavy subjugation.

"The Green Fields of America" is a classic, old emigration song still widely sung today. A version published on a circa 1810 broadside expresses the hopelessness of life in Ireland, the grief of parting and the optimistic promise of the New World:

My father is old and my mother is feeble,
To leave their old cottage their hearts they are sore
The tears down their cheeks in large drops are falling,
To think they must die on a far foreign shore;
But little I'd care where my bones should be buried,
If in peace and in comfort I should spend my life,
The green fields of America gaily are blooming,
And we shall never know misery or strife.

Oh! who could stay here in want and vexation,
To hear their poor children crying out for bread,
And many poor creatures without habitation,
And without a shelter to cover their head;
Come pack up your store and consider no longer,
Six dollars a week is no very bad pay,
No taxes or tithes will devour up your labour,
When you're in the green fields of America.
(Moulden 1994, 6–7)

Zimmermann (2002, 17) writes that the condition of Irish peasants was still desperate in 1870, as the price of agricultural products spiraled downward while the cost of livestock rose. These market changes persuaded landlords to further convert farmland into pasture and resulted in the eviction of many small tenant farmers. Thus, for much of the nineteenth century, whether through blight, rent, tax increases, or agricultural restructuring, Irish small farmers, cottiers, and journey-men farm laborers endured near-constant misfortune. The perception of a bleak future permeates many Irish songs, including the later "Kenmare Committee":

> Since the prices are so low and the taxes are so high,
> The farmers of this country to America they must fly,
>
> .   .   .   .
>
> The landlords they are waiting to seize upon their crops;
> The taxman comes next morning and at your door he raps.
> (Zimmermann 2002, 17)

Life in Manhattan was especially tied to capital. Thus, Irish songs popular in ever-more urban, commercial, and industrial New York diverged over time from those being sung in rural Ireland. Irish "comique" Watty Morgan gave sound advice on thrift to his immigrant audience in the title song of *Watty Morgan's Don't Keep the Working Man Down Songster* (Morgan, n.d.):

> Now when you are working your money you spend,
> Along with your comrades each day;
> And before the week comes to an end
> Your wages will soon pass away.
> And if you'd only lay by one dollar or two,
> And place it in some bank in the town,
> You could then wink your eye, tell the boss on the sly,
> You can't keep the workingman down.
>
> If we take the theatre, 'tis no impropriety
> To compare it for that is my plan:
> The roof is the aristocrat the walls are society,
> The foundation is the poor laboring man.
> If you take off the roof the walls still remain
> Move the walls the foundation's still sound,
> If you move the foundation, that's the poor working class,
> And the whole thing comes to the ground.

New York was no haven, but it showed increasing promise. The discrimination, intimidation, and physical hostility with which most Protestant Americans countered large-scale immigration from Ireland in the first half of the nineteenth century had caused Irish Catholics to coalesce as a national group. Between 1845 and 1870, the Catholic Church achieved great influence as "the American hierarchy, led by New York's John Hughes and other bishops of Irish birth or descent, made massive efforts to church the emigrants, bolster and modernize their faith, and insulate them from Protestant scorn and proselytizing." As clerics "became progressively more Irish in composition, the church itself seemed more familiar, a link rather than a break with home" (Miller 1985, 332). Parishes that were overwhelmingly Irish in membership often became "the center of the people's universes" as families committed to devotional Catholicism (Dolan 2008, 115). The parish school was a second structure that promoted bonding. "By the 1860s the Catholic Church in the United States was committed to the establishment of the parish school" as an alternative to the city-funded elementary school, with parochial schools "mandated" in 1884 (114, 130). However, the irreconcilable differences between Catholic and Protestant educational models fanned the flames of religious antagonism (Dinnerstein, Nichols, and Reimers 1990, 120–21). Hughes's overarching response to nativist rejection of the Catholic Irish was to build an interlocking system of institutions that encompassed national origin and religion: not just churches and primary schools but colleges, hospitals—even a bank (Casey 2006, 306; fig. 27).

Group bonding was also inherent in the Tammany political machine and labor unions (Gordon 1993, 8) and was a residual of enlistment in Civil War units composed exclusively of Irishmen. Bonding on national grounds became a positive antidote to an exile mindset brought on by defeat in Ireland and an uneasy sense of belonging in America's often cold, always rapidly changing Empire City. Demonizing and plotting against England was another huge community binding agent. McCaffrey (1997, 141) expands on the last point:

Irish American nationalism was saturated with bitterness; many of its advocates harbored a deeper hatred of England than love for Ireland. Despising the English was cathartic for Irish American tensions and frustrations, a way of expressing and explaining Irish

Figure 27. Irish Depositors of the Emigrant Savings Bank Withdrawing Money to Send to Their Suffering Relatives in the Old Country, 1881. Wood engraving. New York Public Library.

failure, a means of striking out at real and imaginary enemies. Britain had to be punished and humiliated, not only as a step toward Irish freedom but as an atonement for its sins against the Irish. British laws, cruelty, religious bigotry, insensitivity, and indifference to Irish needs had contributed to the deaths and banishment of millions of Irish Catholics.

The Fenian Brotherhood, viewed with great suspicion by the Church as a competitor for the allegiance of parishioners, provided a mechanism to address group insecurities rooted both in Ireland and in America and further served in group bonding.

A lasting song artifact of the Fenian movement is the conversation ballad "Skibbereen," which is related to "The Irish Refugee, or Poor Pat Must Emigrate" (discussed in detail in chapter 3), though those who sing the lyric today mainly associate it with the Great Hunger, not Fenianism. The song was once forgotten but enjoyed rebirth and renewal in Ireland about the time of the Easter Rising. But only recently has the name of its lyricist and the milieu in which its characters speak been brought to light. In 2003, song researcher John McLaughlin (140) wrote, "The song's author is unknown but ["Skibbereen"] almost certainly originated in East Coast America and was probably written by a radical ex-patriot such as O'Donovan Rossa." In 2009, a folk song enthusiast group at an Internet forum (www.mud cat.org) identified the author through *The Poets of Ireland* (O'Donoghue 1912, 60), which cited Patrick Carpenter as the lyricist and stated his "Old Skibbereen" was included in *The Irish Singer's Own Book*, published in Boston in 1873. Carpenter was described as "a native of Skibbereen, County Cork," who "went to America many years ago" and wrote poems in the 1870s for the Boston *Pilot* and the *Irish World* of New York.

The Irish Singer's Own Book is a "good-cheap" songbook of its era. It includes a mélange of lyrics (sometimes without attribution) and, in place of musical notation, identifies melodies with the words "to the tune of." *The Irish Singer's Own Book* is actually a compilation of three earlier volumes, one of which, *The Wearing of the Green Song Book*, was published in Boston in 1869 (pages 208–10 bear what may be the first-ever printing of "Old Skibbereen"). No less surprising than the finding of the composer and original text was the discovery that the intended tune was not the woeful, minor melody that has been associated with the lyric throughout living memory but the well-known, strident, major scale, martial tune "The Wearing of the Green," called "the most famous Irish nationalistic song" by W. Williams (1996, 109). A comparison of texts shows that both start with a question and that Carpenter's "Old Skibbereen" scans to the melody as well as Dion Boucicault's "The Wearing of the Green," substantiating that what has long been regarded a famine lament was actually created as a Fenian anthem.

"Old Skibbereen" is a conversation initiated by a son who asks his father why he voluntarily left a place he still describes as idyllic:

"Oh, father dear, I've often heard you speak of Erin's Isle—
Its scenes how bright and beautiful, how 'rich and rare' they smile;
They say it is a pretty place wherein a prince might dwell,
Then why did you abandon it, the reason to me tell?"

The answer is that, while the physical setting was magnificent, conditions within it were horrid:

"My son, I've loved my native land with fervor and with pride—
Her peaceful groves, her mountains rude, her valleys green and
    wide,
And there I've roamed in manhood's prime, and sported when a boy,
My shamrock and shillelagh sure my constant boast and joy.

"But lo! a blight came o'er my crops, my sheep and cattle died,
The rack-rent too, alas! was due, I could not have supplied;
The landlord drove me from the cot where born I had been,
And that, my boy's the reason why I left old Skibbereen."

Official terrorism then intervenes to make an untenable situation unbearable:

"O! what a dreadful sight it was that dark November day;
The Sheriff and the Peelers came to send us all away;
They set the roof a-blazing, with demon smile of spleen,
And when it fell, the crash was heard all over Skibbereen.

"Your Mother dear, God rest her, fell upon the snowy ground,
She fainted in her anguish at the desolation round;—
She never rose, but passed away from life's tumultuous scene,
And found a quiet grave of rest in poor old Skibbereen."

The once-blissful father now becomes a hunted revolutionary:

"Ah! sadly I recall that year of gloomy '48;
I rose in vengeance with 'the boys' to battle against fate;
We were hunted thro' the mountains wild, as thraitors to the
    Queen—
And that, my boy's the reason why I left old Skibbereen.

"You were only two years old, and feeble was your frame;
I would not leave you with my friends—you bore my father's
    name!—

I wrapped you in my 'Cathamore' at the dead of night unseen,
We heav'd a sigh and bade good-by to poor old Skibbereen."

The conversation between "Young America and His Irish Father" (the original subtitle of "Old Skibbereen") describes a family driven from Eden by a set of natural and human forces: blight, neglect, and landlordism for certain. When the father rose with other Irishmen to reclaim his land, he was hunted relentlessly and ultimately forced to flee—effectively exiled overseas. But the last stanza makes clear the song was designed more as a polemic than a lament. Young America now addresses Old Ireland and promises that, when the time is right, Irishmen in exile as well as at home will rise together and reclaim their land through battle, all the while maintaining in the forefront of their minds the callous atrocity (considered outright genocide) committed at Skibbereen—no longer an exceptional place but now an Irish everyplace:

"O Father, Father, when the day for vengeance we will call,—
When Irishmen o'er field and fen shall rally one and all,—
I'll be the man to lead the van beneath the flag of green,
While loud on high we'll raise the cry—Revenge for Skibbereen!"
(*Wearing of the Green* 1869, 208)

"Old Skibbereen"—personal, immensely sad, stirring, defiant, and, above all, community-binding—is an outstanding nationalist lyric, as well as a fascinating case study of the origin, transmission, and transformation of Irish traditional song between the United States and the mother country, for after its publication in *The Irish Singer's Own Book*, "Old Skibbereen" appears in print only rarely in nineteenth-century America, in part because so many Fenian songs were being written concurrently. In 1873, it was included in a nationalist "dime songster," *The Favorite "Irish Sunburst" Songster, No. 3*, using the text and attributions printed in *The Wearing of the Green Song Book*. In its original form, it is somewhat literary and slightly long to be widely embraced as a performance song, particularly when set to "The Wearing of the Green" melody, which is simply too fast and bright. However, in 1875, "Skibbereen" was printed on a song sheet at the Poet's Box in

Glasgow, its text condensed and unattributed, its currency described as "very popular," and its tune cited as "original." One credible explanation for these discrepancies is that the song arrived at the broadside publisher orally, with no reference to its author, and that the well-known, major scale "Wearing of the Green" tune had already been disassociated, perhaps lost or regarded as unsuitable for a song that dealt so intimately, so gravely with the Great Hunger—but there is no clue whatsoever to the nature of the new "original" melody. However, in just six years, Carpenter's "Old Skibbereen" had achieved the high honor of being absorbed into folk tradition. In an odd export-import transaction, the now traditional song "Skibbereen" was reintroduced to America in the first quarter of the twentieth century, after its inclusion in Herbert Hughes's *Irish Country Songs* (1915, 76–84).

Fenian songs represented a mammoth outpouring of nationalism, but critically many of the lyrics lacked humanity or were otherwise unrealistic, the product of polemicists with little poetic talent. One example is "Song of the Brother-Fenians!," published by De Marsan sometime between 1861 and 1864, which is nothing more than a hearty helping of pumped-up bravado and a telegram to the enemy. It asks listeners to believe the Fenians could fund and man fleets of ironclad ships and commerce raiders and that the world's greatest military power would easily surrender its Irish possession, predicated on a timely landing of American military veterans coordinated with a joint uprising of Fenians in the British Army and farmworkers in the countryside:

> To take off those English fetters that bound us down so long,
> We'll march, on her Majesty, five hundred thousand strong.
> Arise, arise! old Grannie's sons: show them you are not dead;
> We'll see, once more, on Erin's shore, the Green above the Red.
> . . . .
> We will have Fenian Monitors, and Alabamas, too:
> And, if we catch those Red Coats, we know what we will do;
> We'll make them all be Fenians, to fight against the Queen,
> Liberty's cause for to maintain, by Wearing of the Green!
> Our Bonds, they are all ready, and our ships are fit to sail,
> Bound to the coast of Ireland, with a sweet and pleasant gale.

We are the boys that fears no noise, when cannon-balls do fly;
Our Country's Freedom is our cause, and for it we will die!

                                                (LC amss.as112830)

Though the Fenian Brotherhood was a major force in Irish
American affairs after the Civil War, it imploded mainly because its
mission was too great and its cohesion too weak. Also, the Catholic
Church forbade the organization. The rival plan to the invasion of Ireland called for the seizure of land in Canada and the holding of it for
ransom in exchange for the liberation of Ireland (Kenny 2000, 128–29;
McCaffrey 1997, 152–54). In April 1866, Fenians attempted to invade
Campobello Island off the New Brunswick mainland, but the Royal
Navy was waiting and the plot fizzled with no shots being fired. The
following month, a Fenian force of six hundred defeated a company
of Canadian volunteers and captured Fort Erie in Ontario, but they
were soon forced to retreat owing to lack of supplies and the advance
of the Canadian regular army (McCaffrey 1997, 153). Yet another raid,
this time along the Vermont–New York State border with Quebec
in May 1870, resulted in an organizational shambles. Reports of the
events carried in the *New York Times* (29 May 1870, 1, 4) display uneasiness regarding the ambivalence of American government officials
toward the fumbled incursions into Canadian sovereign territory. At
street level, response to the ineptitude of military planning and exe-
cution was direct. Back in Manhattan, broadside printer J. Wrigley
published "Mickey's Gone for a Laborer." Based on "Johnny's Gone
for a Soldier," it was a song sheet spoof of the 1866 raid and a reflection of the anti-Fenian propaganda that soon became ubiquitous on
both sides of the ocean:

Being out of work it was no fun,
So I went out and bought the "Sun;"
And down it's columns I did run—
There was a chance for Laborers.
Chorus—   Twenty thousand was the call,
          So I went down to Tammany Hall,
          I saw Kerrigan there, who loud did bawl,
          Put your name down for a Laborer!

.   .   .   .

After being out a little time,
We arrived at a place, they called it their line
Of operations, and here we did dine—
For the first time since I was a Laborer.
Chorus—　The Gineral issued an order immediately,
　　　　　Says he: we're going to make Ireland free;
　　　　　And shall strike a blow at Fort Erie—
　　　　　So be prepared all you Laborers.

Says I to the Gineral, if you want earthworks made
I'm the broth of a boy, for that's my trade;
I can dig, I can trench, I can build and grade,
But I never was born for a soldier.
Chorus—　The only way to do things right,
　　　　　Is to get Fifty thousand all ready to fight,
　　　　　You can over-run Canada, just in one night—
　　　　　By soldiers used to war, but not Laborers.
　　　　　　　　　　　　　　　　(Wright 1975, 531)

Following the Civil War, the government of the United States sought wartime reparations from the United Kingdom for building Confederate commerce raiders, and an international arbitration tribunal ruled in America's favor in 1872. The combination of American embarrassment over the Fenian raids into Canada and the settling of the *Alabama* Claims rendered the Fenians redundant to American interests.

The Orange Riots of 1871

On 8 July 1871, the *New York Times* commented it had received a query from the grand master of the Loyal Orange Institution of the United States, asking whether a parade might be held celebrating the victory of the Protestant prince, William of Orange, over the Catholic King James II at the Battle of the Boyne on 1 July 1690 (celebrated on 12 July since 1752, owing to the introduction of the Gregorian calendar). The matter needed full consideration because, one year earlier, a mixture of eight Catholic and Protestant Irishmen had been killed in Orange parade rioting (Gordon 1993, 221–22). In an editorial, "The Demands of the Orangemen," the *New York Times* wrote it had advised against the demonstration, stating, "The Orangemen themselves have apparently come to a different conclusion and it seems probable we shall have to chronicle something more than the usual amount of riot as a result of the observances of Wednesday next. As our opinions concerning the encroachments of Roman Catholicism are pretty well known . . . we point out to Protestant members of Orange societies, the false position they occupy both to our Republican Government and our national spirit of toleration."

The archconservative broadsheet then objected to the constitution of the Loyal Orange Order, which specified their "loyalty" was confined to the royal family of Great Britain, and suggested "members of the Association are therefore bound by a tie which precludes their transformation into American citizens." The Orange Order had claimed to represent "religious freedom" and attempted to identify their cause with American Protestantism, notions the *New York Times* then rejected:

> The fact that St. Patrick's Day is publicly observed under municipal patronage has been persistently put forward, in a number of letters. . . . We confess our inability to see why the existence of one abuse can make an excuse for perpetrating another. . . . The fact that, however wrongfully, their ignorant Catholic fellow-countrymen should be likely to be inflamed to the extent of armed interference with their procession, ought of itself be sufficient reason to a body of men professedly Christian, to observe the day in some less public fashion. . . . Of the two parties, we naturally expect the Protestant to lead the way in forbearance and toleration. In this case the Orange organization might cease to exist, but the cause of humanity and American civilization would have found a new triumph.

Two days later, the newspaper reaffirmed its opposition, publishing an editorial calling the parade an "anachronism . . . open to much graver objections on political grounds." Unfortunately for the Catholic

Irish, it did not stop there: "The line taken by the Roman Catholics in reference to the matter, however, is so outrageous that the Orangemen may well ask if the infamous intolerance of James II is really a thing of the past. At a 'Convention of the Irish Societies,' held last Friday evening, a delegate proposed that the Mayor should be requested to prohibit the procession, and that if he declined, the Irish Catholics should turn out and settle the dispute 'at once and forever, cutting down every Orangemen in the procession.'" (*NYT*, 10 July 1871, 4).

The *New York Times* then came down even harder on Romanists, reacting as though the heated comment was the agreed belief of all Catholic Irish, rather than an extremist view: "They are simply resolved to set up a State Church here, and to drive Protestantism to take shelter in holes and corners," and "to cut down all men, women, and children who intend to march." It concluded, "Orangemen are as much entitled to march in procession as the Papists." Entitled "Is There to Be a Riot on the 12th?," the editorial appears hastily written, for while its beginning sentence stresses that such potentially dangerous parading has no place in New York—"We have repeatedly maintained that foreign citizens have no right to introduce the discords of their own country into this"—its concluding paragraph argues, "the Police can keep order if they are made to do it. . . . [Police] Superintendent Kelso must expect to pass a bad time on the 13th if the Catholics are permitted to carry out their threats." Thus, the newspaper appears to endorse peace and confrontation simultaneously and clearly holds Catholic Irishmen responsible for any trouble that might develop. Why did it not instead renew its call on city government to ban the parade just as the *New York Tribune* had on 8 July? Probably because the *New York Times* recognized another episode of internecine Irish mayhem could be a catalyst to realize its vision of a "better" New York through the destruction of Tammany Hall, potentially leaving the vast majority of Manhattan's Catholic Irish without political sponsorship.

Five months earlier, it had published "How Long Will Protestants Endure?" (*NYT*, 2 February 1871, 4), an editorial that sheds light on the issues surrounding the Twelfth of July controversy: "There is a steady and insensible change going on in this State in the seat of political power. . . . The population of this city and the surrounding counties, owing to immigration and the prolific power of a laboring class, is increasing at an enormous rate. . . . [The] result is the governing power of this portion of the State . . . is fast centering itself in the ranks of the lowest and most ignorant class of the whole community—the Irish Catholic laborers and the tenement-house population."

Vehement objections are then made to city and state grants of land and capital funding to elements of the Catholic Church, including financial support for parochial schools. A takeover of the municipal school system is alleged: "Already some of our Ward schools are supplied entirely with Catholic teachers, and everything is 'expurgated' from the books which might seem to smack too much of liberty of conscience and of thought." Lastly, the *New York Times* issued a call to arms: "If our Protestant bodies do not arise and show some manhood, they will deserve to be trampled on and thus insulted by the delegates of the Catholic masses. . . . And they may be certain that the treatment they have thus far received from the Tammany Ring is mild and considerate next to what is in store."

The Twelfth of July event in 1871 presented an opportunity that the anti-Catholic, pro-Republican *New York Times* could exploit politically. Using Orangemen as their willing but unendorsed surrogates, and turning Catholic Irish outrage over the parade to their advantage, Protestant elites could use alarm over civil unrest to strike a blow to the already off-balance Tweed Ring (Tammany's ruling clique, headed by William M. Tweed). The 8 July 1871 issue of the *New York Times*, in which the Loyal Orange Order was criticized, also carried ominous references to Tammany fraud emanating from the rental of city armories—"Over Eighty Per Cent of the Money Stolen"—while the 9 July issue insinuated foul play in the planning of the New York Viaduct Railway, which would entail the building of 348 railway bridges and the purchase of vast amounts of valuable property. Failure by the Tammany-led city government to maintain order during the parade might be a catastrophic misstep, resulting in a fatal fall for the Democrats locally and nationally. Realizing this, the city administration opted for cancellation of the parade on the grounds of public safety. At 9 p.m. on 10 July, superintendent of police James J. Kelso issued an order to his staff officers, instructing them to "keep all streets cleared from groups and assemblages of every class of citizens, whether sympathizing with or against the proposed procession, or whether they are lawlessly disposed or otherwise" (*Herald*, 11 July 1871). The cancellation was received by most city newspapers along political lines, and page 1 opinions in most major dailies published the following morning positioned the parade ban not as prudent but cowardly: the *New York Times* led with the headline "City Overawed by the Roman Catholics"; the *Sun* with "The City Authorities Quailing before the Rioters" and "The Will of the People Stifled"; and the *New York Tribune* with "Surrender to the Mob." Taking an opposite view, the *New York Herald* (11 July 1871, 3) termed Kelso's order "mature consideration," while the *Daily Star* supported the superintendent on the basis of public safety and the *World* pointed out that Great Britain had already suppressed the Orange Order by law and with force (*Star* and *World* reprinted in *Herald*, 12 July 1871). But the harsh backlash in the majority of city newspapers carried the sway and Kelso's decision was quickly reversed. Feeling heat from the *New York Times* investigations, and wishing to distance himself from the Tweed Ring, Governor John T. Hoffman, a Tammany operative, revoked the superintendent's order on 11 July 1871 (*Herald*, 12 July 1871; Gordon 1993, 86). The parade would march off with heavy protection from the police and state militia.

Song, again showing its power to motivate, provided the blasting cap that ignited the Twelfth of July explosion in 1871. All-too-familiar melodies played by parading bands carried word sets that were intended not just to lift the Orange community but also to incite Catholic Irish bystanders by mocking their religious institutions and ethnic heritage. The song texts were familiar to the Catholics they taunted:

To William's name sound trumpet praise,
Who check'd dark Popery's vulture wing,
To him your tuneful voices raise,
And thus your Orange anthem sing—
 "Hail! glorious, pious, immortal memory
 Of Great King William, who set us free."

The nation lay in gloom and woes,
For Popery shed its with'ring blight,

Till Nassau's star for us arose,
And gave the land to Freedom's light.
(Archer 1852, 26)

Major themes were battle sites where Orange triumphed over
Green, union with Britain and allegiance to the Crown, anti-
Republicanism, and anti-Catholicism. Some songs, like "Daniel
O'Connell in Purgatory" (to the air of "Kick the Pope before Us"),
weighed in on two topics, simultaneously ridiculing Catholicism and
O'Connell, Ireland's foremost Catholic statesman, whose nonviolent,
"monster" gatherings had awakened a moribund nation two genera-
tions earlier:

Now this is Rome, the mystic whore,
Who keeps the keys of Heaven's door,
And trades in dead men's souls demure
    By Popish Purgatory.

Doctor Miley he has said,
When Dan, the Irish king, was dead,
Angels were waiting at his head,
    His soul to Heaven to carry;
Maynooth and Rome they formed a plan,
And robbed the Angels of old Dan—
The Kerry Boy, we understand,
    They have got in Purgatory.
(*Standard Orange Song Book* 1848, 141)

Anti-Catholicism was the principal theme of songs such as "John
Knox" and "The Champions of Protestantism." The Knox text was
odious to Catholics not so much for its praise of the father of Presby-
terianism but for what was deeply resented as the slander of the
Catholic Church:

Dark clouds of error spreading wide
Had hid the Light Divine,
And Rome in idol pomp and pride,
Profaned the Altar's shrine;

But from afar, these ills to mar,
And check their Monkish guile,
Arose John Knox, a glorious Star —
The Star of Scotia's Isle!
(Archer 1852, 103)

In Ireland, the Orange Order and its sympathizers had functioned historically as a colonial garrison guarding Britain's backdoor from the French, whomever else might seek to invade, and from home-grown nationalist insurgencies; but Orangemen were also regarded by the Westminster government as troublemakers who had to be kept in place. Official vacillation typically elicited signs of loyalty. One such example is "The Protestant Queens of England" (to the melody of "God Save the Queen"), which praises Elizabeth, Mary II, and Anne. Most objectionable to Catholics were Orange songs that gloried in their defeats and the massacres that often followed. Place-names of these military downfalls were both contained in the titles of songs and emblazoned on the banners that Orange lodge brothers carried as they processed purposefully through Catholic areas. Parades included bands playing the song melodies — virtual incendiary flares shot into Republican Catholic strongholds. Such titles included "The Gates of Londonderry," "The Achievements of Enniskillen," and "The Battle of Aughrim" (Archer 1852):

It may be said such sanguine scenes the muse should not relate;
But I say, yes! you must be told the deeds you'd emulate;
A holy zeal our sires fill'd to crush oppression strong,
And oh! I'd try that zeal to raise upon the wings of song.
For should the Papists coil again their adamantine chain,
As did our sires, so we their sons, should rend the yoke in twain;
And in the spirit of my song, which, with my heart must die,
I fill to Aughrim's victor fight upon the Twelfth July!
(Archer 1852, 71–72)

Anti-Catholic melodies were an integral part of Twelfth of July celebrations in New York. Under the ominous headline "A Riot Impending," the *New York Tribune* (10 July 1871, 1) reported, "The

Orangemen, fewer in numbers, have chosen to parade flaunting their favorite colors and marching to their favorite music . . . while the Ribbonmen have passionately appealed, first, to the authorities to prevent what they claim are insufferable insults . . . and, next, to muster under arms for riot. . . . [It] is believed [the Orangemen] will abstain from playing the especially obnoxious air of 'Croppies Lie Down.'" A passage of the song lyric was quoted in the same article:

Water, water,
Holy water;
Sprinkle the Catholics, every one;
We'll cut them asunder,
And make them lie under.
The Protestant boys will carry the gun.
(Chorus)—Croppies, lie down;
    Croppies, lie down;
    We'll make all the Catholic Croppies lie down.

The song emanates from the 1798 Rebellion and reportedly relates to the torture of United Irishmen. "In some districts," pitch-caps were used on "Catholics who cropped their hair short after the fashion of French republicans. Tormentors filled a brown paper cap with hot pitch, splashed it on a Catholic's head, and then ignited it" (Gordon 1993, 33). Zimmermann (2002, 296) quotes the testimony of the Earl of Gosforth before an 1835 House of Commons select committee, citing three "party" tunes commonly played in County Armagh as being highly offensive to Catholics: "Boyne Water," "The Protestant Boys," and "Croppies Lie Down," each standard repertoire in New York Twelfth of July celebrations (Gordon 1993, 32). On 10 July, a reporter from the *New York Herald* (10) interviewed a laborer working on The Boulevard, identified only as "Hibernian," asking, "Do you think there will be a riot if [the Orangemen] parade?" He received the plain and chilling answer, "If they march playing the party tunes, some of them will never march again." "The band's music touched off the first disturbances," writes Michael A. Gordon (1993, 115), whose *The Orange Riots: Irish Political Violence in New York City, 1870 and 1871* presents a full account of the events of 12 July 1871, pieced together from newspaper reports and later testimony, though the very name of the first tune played cannot be ascertained. The marchers were escorted front and back and on each side by five regiments of the state militia, as well as detachments of city police, both mounted and on foot.

If the ploy of the Orangemen (and probably the *New York Times*) was to incite Catholic Irish into violence for political ends, who among the Romanists took up the challenge and who did not? First, a large percentage of religious Catholics would have avoided the parade because their spiritual leader had ordered them to do so, and the diocesan clergy read his words at Mass on Sunday, 9 July: "The Archbishop wishes the Catholic people to absent themselves from the Orange procession on next Wednesday, the 12th inst. They should array themselves on the side of order and peace, and allow the Orangemen to walk" (*Tribune*, 10 July 1871, 1).

Second, the American Fenian Brotherhood likewise officially advised members not to disrupt the parade but instead reminded them "they were obliged to promote peace and love, to liberate Ireland, and not to perpetuate 'dead issues'" (Gordon 1993, 62–63). The day after the parade, the *New York Herald* (13 July 1871, 3) reported an absence of Fenian leaders at the event. Third, middle-class Irish people had businesses they might have to defend in case of a general riot, while managers who had good-paying jobs to protect could not take the day off lest they be suspected of being rioters. Fourth, the Ancient Order of Hibernians held meetings and drills related to contesting the marchers but apparently did not go into organized action on the Twelfth, though some members undoubtedly were at the parade site. Fifth, at least five females were counted amongst the dead, two of these were little more than children and presumably onlookers, while a third was identifiably an Orange supporter.

The anti-Orange rioters appear to have been largely composed of Irish-born laborers, as the *New York Herald* (13 July 1871, 3) headline described them the following day—"Men of the Quarry, the Sewer, the Road and the River Hurry to the Fray." At midday on 12 July, a little more than a mile from the parade marshalling area, a red-faced street paver walked to the doorway of a workingman's bar on Tenth Avenue near Forty-Seventh Street and shouted out, "Hurroo, boys, I'll give ye a song." According to a *Herald* (13 July 1871, 4) reporter, he launched into

Figure 28. Hibernian Hall (Prince Street) and Orange Head-Quarters (Twenty-Ninth Street and Eighth Avenue). New York Public Library.

> Me name it is Kelly, the rake,
> An' I don't give a damn about any mon;
> Off I had but a knife in me hat,
> Shure I'd shtick it right into an Orangeman.

That a respected, large circulation newspaper would collect and reproduce a street rant from the mouth of an enraged worker is a strong validation of the power of song as both a motivator and gauge of public opinion.

Kelly's Ulster accent, revealed in his pronunciation of "man" as "mon" and "if" as "off," is an indicator of who within the Irish community were most motivated to confront Orangemen on the streets of Manhattan. Ulster was the last province of Ireland to come under English rule and the most heavily planted by settlers from Britain. There, in certain localities, former landowning Catholic Irish rented property they once owned from planters, making competition for farmland particularly bitter and strong. Ulster was also where Protestants represented the highest percentage of the population, where discrimination against Catholics was generally more severe, and where the Orange Order was founded. Kelly likely worked on The Boulevard, Central Park, or another large construction site north of the parade route—New York was rebuilding selectively downtown but expanding greatly into the rocky reaches well beyond midtown.

He finished off his song with what the reporter perceived to be an "Irish war-whoop," but the singing did not cease:

> A friend struck him on the back and started a ballad on his own account. This gentleman's name was Moriarty, and, as he had a pretty fair voice, a good audience came around him. He had a new version of an old song; consequently he was listened to with interest. Mr. Moriarty sang:—

> An' sure we'll come again,
>   Says the Shan Van Vaugh;
> An' we'll bring ten thousan' min
>   Says the Shan Van Vaugh.
> An wid powder an' wid ball,
> For our rights we'll stan' or fall;
> D'ye think they'll hear our call?
>   Says the Shan Van Vaugh.

> If they mane to do us ill,
>   Says the Shan Van Vaugh,
> Sure we'll come from Mackerelville,
>   Says the Shan Van Vaugh;
> An' march along so gaily,
> Wid musket an' shilelah,
> In spite of Father Daly,
>   Says the Shan Van Vaugh.
>   (*Herald*, 13 July 1871, 4)

Moriarty indicates he does not intend to heed the order of Archbishop McCloskey. If he came from Mackerelville, the Lower East Side area centered around Avenue A below Fourteenth Street, where many inhabitants were employed in the distribution of fish, his local parish was St. Brigid's; but Moriarty was probably an infrequent attendee. The title of the song he sang, "The Shan Van Vocht" [*sic*], is an Anglicization of the Irish for "The Poor Old Woman," long a commentator in song on the difficulties of Ireland. The song form dates at least from 1798, the time of the United Irishmen. The Shan Van Vocht, of course, was not just aged but wise from her many years of hard experience; she was also the personification of "Mother Ireland."

Orange parades were too hot a touchstone for most first-generation Catholic Irish to bear. Regardless of whether their opposition was active or passive, they were galled at having been forced from Ireland and, now resident in what they regarded as the home of liberty, still being subjected to religious insult and cultural dominance—this despite constituting more than 21 percent of the city's total population (Rosenwaike 1972, 67). On 14 July, the *Herald* headlined the 1871 Orange Riot as "A Glorious Victory," calling it a battle "fought and won for equal rights, the constitution, liberty and law" (Gordon 1993, 164); however there was no glory in it, only gore, and any "victory" pyrrhic. McCloskey and Kelso were right. Hoffman and Moriarty were wrong. Because of political concerns, sixty-two persons were killed outright or later died of wounds received on the day, including two children on their way home from school. Fifty-five were killed as a direct result of the militia firing indiscriminately into the crowd (Golway 2014, 97–100; Gordon 1993, 113–33, 151–52). The overarching power of songs such as "Croppies Lie Down" and "The Shan Van Vocht" had heightened emotions and made the 1871 Orange Parade a major event in New York history. Their ferocious lyrics had predicted the event, but the "authorities" had turned a deaf ear.

Manhattan's Streetscape in Song

Although 12 July 1871 was one of the city's worst-ever days, overall conditions were actually improving for the Irish, who by now had imprinted their image on New York life. Two scenes in *Dick Sands' Songster* present contrasting views of Lower Manhattan in the final quarter of the nineteenth century. The first, "The Market on Saturday Night" (1882), is a colorful description of the most significant central place in any urban area, one that reached the zenith of activity on the eve of the only day of rest for many workers in the great metropolis. It centers on one small trader's pride in being a fellow entrepreneur among many stallholders in a huge bazaar. Thoroughly involved in her business, she is the picture of confidence, perfectly cast in her role:

I'm a poor market woman,
I do a fine trade,
Selling my goods at the stall;
A nate bit of money
Myself I have made
Where I sit with my back to the wall.

I sell turkeys and partridges,
Turnips and cabbages,
Crockery and tinwear so bright,
Parsnips and cresses,
And little babes dresses,
At the market on Saturday night.

The Mondays and Tuesdays
And Fridays are fine,
Wednesdays and Thursdays are light,
But thousands of people
They stand in a line
At the market on Saturday night.

We sell lemons and butterbeans
Carrots and holly greens,
Celery, so crispy and white,
Pickles and chow-chow,
And dogs that say bow-wow,
At the market on Saturday night.

In summer or winter,
Oh, when the wind blows,
Filling wid dust all our eyes,
In rain or in frost
Or terrific snow
We're shouting and yelling our cries.

We sell peanuts, bananas,
And Chinese Havanas,

It's really a beautiful sight,
It's oleomargarine,
Little pigs *crubeens*,
At the market on Saturday night.
    (*Dick Sands' Songster* [1883?], 22)

From the next page in the same songster, another character sneers provocatively across the "gutter" and stitching that separate the two lyric portraits. His song is "We're All Young Fellows Bran' New" (1883):

We're all young fellows, we travel with the gang,
All born on Manhattan Isle;
We know every twist in manufactured slang,
We lead the down town style.
We hang out of the corner to give the girls a bow,
Or dish 'em up an oyster fry or stew,
Oh, we're out all night till the sugar it is light
We're all young fellows bran' new.

We all look natty at a picnic or a ball,
We sing love songs to a T;
We look just as neat as pictures on a wall,
With pants cut tight to the knee.
If you want to get a pointer, just gaze at our shoes,
They're made to order by a German Jew,
Oh, we're out all night till the sugar it is light
We're all young fellows bran' new.

When they want heelers to colonize a ward,
They call on us, do you see?
We scoop in the soap, and make our summer board,
To vote on the strict Q. T.
We never fear a copper unless he's got a club
We like to keep respectful distance [too],
Oh, we're out all night till the sugar it is light
We're all young fellows bran' new.
    (*Dick Sands' Songster* [1883?], 23)

At first, much about these two scenes appears in direct opposition. The details of the hardworking stallholder are unknown, but we picture her as middle aged, somewhat disheveled, and certainly Irish-born because she refers to pickled pigs feet as *crubeens*. Conversely, the narrator of the second song is a young, super-stylish dandy in craft-made footwear, American-born, and an opportunist unfamiliar with hard work. Despite considerable differences, these odd neighbors are connected by certain similarities. Both are adept at what they do and are part of a New York tableau that permits them a place in the sun; similarly, both belong to organizations greater than themselves—a throng of market hawkers and a street gang—and both are secure in their positions within the city at large. She is honest and so upholds her reputation; he exists on the shady side of the law but nevertheless has a direct connection to Tammany Hall, getting out the vote on Election Day (and probably voting for whomever he is told as often as he can for monetary reward). Both are Irish—he of the second generation, hence his eagerness to point out he was born in Manhattan—and each is characteristic of the teeming downtown that is by now 80 percent populated by first- and second-generation immigrants of many nations (Rosenwaike 1972, 72).

The contrast and similarity between the two songs are heightened with the knowledge that they were written only a year apart and by the same person, Edward Harrigan (also lyricist of "McNally's Row of Flats"; fig. 29). Hardly the *quintessential* New Yorker—his father was from Newfoundland, and his mother was born in Charlestown, Massachusetts, and raised in Norfolk, Virginia (Moody 1980, 7–9)—but Harrigan was *exceptional* within the multiple meanings of the word. He was atypical, an Irish American who was half Anglo and the child of a father who had converted from Roman Catholicism to New England Calvinism (Moody 1980, 8)—though these significant discrepancies were considerably mitigated by the fact he had grown up on the Seventh Ward's heavily Catholic Irish "Cork Row," and he was a master of characterization as evidenced by his description of the stallholder. Other songwriters passed her by without noticing, but Harrigan did notice because he realized her sort mattered and was on the rise. More than any popular song lyricist before or since, Harrigan displayed an intense interest in the Manhattan cultural streetscape and wrote credibly, perceptively, artistically, and prolifically about the City of New York, not only in his song lyrics but also in sections of

Figure 29. Front cover of "Patrick's Day Parade. An Original Sketch and Song by Ed. Harrigan. Sung with Immense Success by Harrigan and Hart." Music by David Braham. New York: William A. Pond. Collection of author.

his first and only novel, *The Mulligans* (Harrigan 1901, 394–97). While many Irish Americans have penned songs about their fellow ethnics, no one has produced any that surpass Harrigan's best. An apparent outlier, in this odd way he became the ultimate insider, and the foremost name in American musical theater during his heyday.

Edward Harrigan ran away to sea as a teenager, settled in San Francisco, and did not return for the best part of a decade, meaning he spent many of his formative, most impressionable years away from the Empire City. By the time he returned from self-imposed exile, he was a professional entertainer at a critical juncture in his career. In need of inspiration and content for his skits, he rekindled his childhood interest in the human streetscape of Manhattan, which he could now view within a wider frame of reference. W. Williams (1996, 158) suggests the San Francisco experience "might have been an important factor in the development of his brand of satire, which allowed him to make fun of the Irish while celebrating them." Because the California Irish did not encounter the extreme discrimination prevalent in New York (Bayor and Meagher 1996, 534–36), Harrigan felt freer to construct a more positive Manhattan Irish group identity. But there is another window illuminating the lyricist-playwright's vision: the Catholic Irish were now reaching critical mass numerically, and Harrigan observed they were rapidly becoming Americans — albeit highly urbanized — thoroughly imbedded in their new island home but with living memory of their European origin. The realist writer then portrayed the New York Irishman as a "regular guy," who "rejected aristocratic pretension, snobbery, and the blandishments of society and stood with his own" people (Meagher 2006, 625). This "average Joe" character was not his sheer invention but more a distillation of shaping influences from the New York Catholic Irish collective experience: village life in Ireland; the embattled urban ghetto of Lower Manhattan; wartime suffering away and at home; trade unionism staving off competition; the binding atmosphere of the Catholic parish; saloons where male workers gleaned the important and incidental intelligence of the hour; and Tammany's umbrella of protection, power, and pilferage.

Politics was painted into much of Manhattan's streetscape. McCaffrey (1997, 119) writes that politics was the "only skill [the Irish] brought with them from the Old to the New World." Glazer and Moynihan (1963, 223–26) expand on the influence of Irish rural custom on New York urban politics. Because prejudices excluded Irish Catholics from many opportunities, politics (along with the church and organized labor) was one of the few viable routes to success. Tammany was an army that beginning in the early 1870s relied increasingly on a chain of command staffed by dutiful functionaries. In the best case scenario, each was regarded to be a "solid man" (a "regular guy" on the rise), a man of the people who garnered his respect by serving constituents well. Uppermost of this political type was Harrigan's fictional "Muldoon, the Solid Man!" (1874):

> I am a man of great influence,
> And educated to a high degree;
> I come here when small from Donegal,
> In the Daniel Webster, across the sea.
> In the Fourteenth Ward I situated,
> In a tenement house with my brother Dan;
> By perseverance I elevated
> And went to the front like a solid man.

Muldoon's credentials stand straight and tall among the working class, but, played for comedic effect, those of his voter-clients far less so. His electorate are frequent boarders at the Tombs, the municipal jail centrally located in the Sixth Ward adjacent to Five Points, and they are often residents of the city prison situated on Blackwell's Island, around which flows the speeding current of the East River, adding a whirlpool of additional security for the authorities:

> I control the Tombs; I control the Island.
> My constituents, they all go there
> To enjoy the summer's recreation,
> The refreshing East River air.
>   (*Cronin and Sullivan* 1882, 25)

Popularity breeds imitation—and Harrigan's "Muldoon, the Solid Man!" was very popular (Meade 1997, 6–11, 41–48)—so it spawned a host of opportunist tributes, including a spoof by Charles Davies, based on a tenuous connection to the seat of power, "My Wife Does the Washing for Muldoon, the Solid Man":

> I'm going to tell you of the luck on which I fell
> By getting married to a girl the neighbors call big Nell;

She does every bit of my washing, and a little out side too;
She turns her money in the house, and says her love is true.

I'll take in every sociable,
I'll take in every ball;
They can't refuse admitting me
Into Tammany Hall.
Should you meet a friend
And she asks you who I am,
Tell her my wife does the washing
For Muldoon, the Solid Man.

(Snow and Mott's, n.d.)

Political characters appearing in songs were usually composites
with fictitious names because of the risk involved in running afoul of
real officials, who held genuine power and who also had many ardent
supporters. Simply inventing party bosses, or making composites, was
easy and safe and allowed the public free rein to ascribe the songs' bravado and fault to whomever they wished. But in 1875 or shortly thereafter, a song entitled "Kelly, the Boss of the Gang" became popular.
Patterned after the well-known "Since Terry First Joined the Gang,"
the lament of a father about his son's errant behavior, the new song was
public criticism of "Honest" John Kelly, who in 1871 replaced William M. Tweed as the Tammany Hall leader. Kelly reconstructed Tammany with architecture based on the hierarchy of the Catholic Church,
imposing a tight rein and conservative agenda (McCaffrey 1997, 123;
Solari 2003). The song's first-person narrator is Jack Donohue, a pipe-
fitter who was "as happy as days are long, before Kelly was boss of
the gang":

He believes in the one man power,
And says we must have home rule,
And in a place call'd Tammany Hall,
He opened a weekly school.
Then every Saturday afternoon,
With many a shout and a slang,
The Kelly men are there learned how
To rule and boss the outside gang.

Figure 30. New York—The Trial of Wm. M. Tweed. Cover of Frank Leslie's *Illustrated Newspaper*, New York, February 15, 1873. New York Public Library.

One dollar-and-sixty cents a day,
He says is enough for all.
Now that is all the people get,
From the boss of Tammany Hall.
Therefore we find it very hard,
To live and pay our way,
Now Sussie and the little ones curse
Kelly the boss of the present day.
   (*Ferguson and Mack's Political Candidates*, n.d.)

John Kelly tried but could not balance the wants of American reformers and the Irish middle class with the needs of Irish workers (Golway 2014, 105–15).

That virtually impossible task became even harder during the economic depression that followed the Panic of 1873, reaching crisis level at "A Monster Mass Meeting of the Unemployed." Held at Tompkins Square on 13 January 1874 (*NYT*, 14 January 1874, 2), it was attended by between three thousand (the *New York Times*' estimate) and twenty thousand people (the workers' Committee of Safety's estimate). Many were arrested. The mayor subsequently attempted to placate the unemployed demonstrators but, along with the *New York Times* (20 January 1874, 2), branded their leaders as idle loafers and Communists. Kelly at first sided with the workers but in July turned about-face after he had the folk hero and former boxer, gambler, congressman, and race track entrepreneur John Morrissey expelled from the Democratic Party for challenging his authority, much to the chagrin of Morrissey's staunch working-class supporters (Gordon 1993, 202–3). Morrissey was a "solid man" and the well-known subject of at least three Irish broadside ballads: "Morrissey and the Russian Sailor," "Morrissey and the Buffalo Boy," and "Morrissey Again in the Field" (Milner 1983, 80–82).

Just as politicians provided fodder for the variety stage, so did political issues. In 1876, A. G. Weeks composed "The Rights of Ladies," a satire on women's suffrage. The song anticipates women not just as voters but also as office holders, suggesting female politicians would "become pawns of shiftless working-class husbands," according to W. Williams (1996, 142):

An' thin whin we mate in convintion,
The ladies of course will be there,
An' may be somebody will mintion
Me Biddy to sit in the chair.
An' may be for office select her,
Wid four or five dollars a day;
It's meselif 'twould vote to elect her,
An' put in me pocket the pay.
(*J. K. Emmet's Love* 1882, 48)

But there is more to Weeks's song. Reminiscent of blackface minstrelsy, in which white men hiding behind burned cork assumed black persona to make cutting comments they may not have wished to present directly, Weeks used an alias, Dennis McFlinn, and a bumpkin brogue to voice a view that was not just sexist but also nativist. During the post–Great Hunger era, Irish American women actually held an important advantage over their male counterparts, in that they generally fared better occupationally. Diner (1983, 71) writes, Irish women "suffered less overt job discrimination" in their chosen fields of "teaching, nursing, stenography, and clerical and sales work," adding "schoolteaching for the second-generation was what domestic service had been for the first" (Diner 1983, 96–97). Weeks's lyric thus is doubly demeaning, portraying well-educated Irish women as gullible and underemployed Irish men as lazy connivers.

The campaign season was a propitious time for male voters to earn free drinks and other rewards. For the office seeker, buying a goodwill round of lager at a bar was a trifling expense compared to the lucrative "opportunities" associated with electoral office. Municipal employees who were beneficiaries of patronage typically paid their political sponsors for the privilege, but even more money was made from advance knowledge of city planning that provided 100 percent sure investments, a situation later termed *honest graft* by Tammany politician George Washington Plunkitt (Klinghard 2011, 489–90; Riordon 1963). Overly greedy politicians who stole outright from city coffers intrigued in "dishonest graft," according to Plunkitt, and fell hard when caught out by reformist elements. Such was the fate of the Tweed Ring in 1871–72. "Mulcahy's Gone Away" by Joseph P. Skelly remembered Tweed's lieutenants. It appeared in 1874 and was popularized by comic singers Johnny Roach and James O'Neill:

He won our pride and won our praise,
And he deserved it too!
Sure many a time for nights and days
We stuck to him like glue;
He held an office of the State,
And faith he made it pay;
But for such a place he was too great,
And now he's gone away!

.   .   .   .

He was as sound a Democrat
As ever filled a chair,
But he lost his position,
And it drove him to despair;
We know not where to seek him;
He must have crossed the say;
O, it grieves us just to think of it—
Mulcahy's gone away!
   (*James O'Neill's Candidate* 1876, 58–59)

An oft-trod route into politics and the middle class was through the police force. Cops who walked a beat were highly visible fixtures on neighborhood streets. Those who functioned with diplomacy and proved popular could rise locally, and with luck might ascend to the Common Council. The city's municipal force was still fairly new, but sensational crime stories in tabloid newspapers and the *National Police Gazette* had raised their visibility. William Scanlan's "O'Halleran, the Brave Policeman" presents an immigrant who swells with pride because of the advancement he has made following his arrival in New York:

My name is O'Halleran, and from Ireland I came,
And since I came here I've gained great fame;
The captains and aldermen all know me quite well,
And my heroism and bravery they can easily tell;
If at night on my beat as I walk to and fro,

The blackguards they see me, arrah, from me they'll go,
To an alleyway or bar-room they'll run if they can,
For they all know well I'm a brave policeman.

> For as I promenade my beat at night through the street
> I'm admired by every young lady I meet;
> You'll hear them all sigh as hard as they can,
> For they're all deep in love with this brave Irishman.

I was very soon promoted to a roundsman you see,
And respected no matter where'er I might be;
They put the sthripes on my arms to look solid and grand,
For they knew I was a hero from dear Paddy's land.
(*Johnny Roach's Best Songster* 1877, 14)

In actuality, many immigrants carried with them across the Atlantic a negative view of the police. In Ireland, the constabulary were regarded as the agents of an alien government and the landed class—informers and evictors—so public distrust was inbred, and there was a burden on patrolmen to prove themselves. Evidence of suspicion is glimpsed in Richard Madden's "He's on the Police Force Now":

The man that I will sing about
His name is Pat O'Brien,
He came over to the country
Upon the White Star Line;
He came here to America
A week ago to day,
He says he likes this country
And here he's going to stay.

> And he's on the police force now,
> A smile on his heavenly brow,
> With a club in his hand;
> Oh, doesn't he look grand!
> He is on the police force now.

A poor old aged mother,
Who only had one boy,
She did her best to raise him,
He was her pride and joy;
But when he grew to manhood,
From labor he would shirk;
To tell the truth he was
Too tired for to work.

He's on the police force now;
He's better off you must allow
Up the alley he will sneek,
At twelve o'clock he's fast asleep,—
He's on the police force now.
(*E. J. Hassan's* [1889?], 26)

Self-admiration and laziness were only mildly adverse characteristics when compared with official corruption. Kahn (1955, 48–49)
outlines the modus operandi of Alexander S. Williams, who, when
promoted to captain in 1876 and charged with the pacification of Manhattan's "recreational district," quickly devised a system for personal
enrichment, bringing a new geographic moniker, "The Tenderloin
District," into the American lexicon: "On receiving news of his assignment, which placed him in gratifying proximity to most of the city's
saloons, whorehouses, restaurants, theatres, dance halls, and other
promising benefactors, he exclaimed, 'No more chuck steak for me.
Now I'll get a little of the tenderloin.'. . . After he had been nudged off
the police force, he denied having engaged in racketeering. He had
just got rich, he said blandly, from shrewd investment in building lots
in Japan."

But the song "Dissolving Views," sung by the popular Irish entertainer Johnny Roach, bares far more sinister corruption laid on the
community. The harm it propagated was directly linked to social ills
caused by dangerous workplaces, poor sanitary conditions, gross overcrowding, high rates of disease, endemic alcoholism, overly high rents,
and family desertion (Diner 1983, 107–19), hideously aggravated by
state and municipal neglect and official misconduct:

The next was a police court; two prisoners were led in;
One, a well-dressed swindler, and the other a boy ill-fed;
The boy had stolen, and confessed his guilt, and for pardon did
    entreat;
He said, 'I am an orphan boy; and had nothing to eat;"
Three months hard labor was his doom—the tears ran down his
    face;
While he who swindled many a man walked out with a good grace;
He paid for counsel with his spoil—his money put him through,
That ends the case, and he gets free in this dissolving view.
                    (*Johnny Roach's Best Songster* 1877, 43)

Roach was a comic singer but, like Tony Pastor, one with a conscience and a desire to influence moral change in public thought. He
also wished to present variety onstage, and the occasional serious
song that cried out for social justice fit well with his own "solid man"
image. In Frank Melville's "Don't Put Your Foot on a Man When He's
Down," another from his darker repertoire, Roach takes the middle
ground to encourage charity during the Gilded Age:

The poor laboring man, who tries all he can
To battle his way through life's throng,
Oft finds to his cost, that the cold winter's frost
Impedes much his getting along.
The working men strive in the industrial hive,
Something to put by from their trade,
Commercial depression brings stern retrogression,
And swallows the little they made.

    .   .   .   .

Misfortune's cold shade visits every shade,
The rich man as well as the poor,
Then hesitate not, while wealth you have got,
To help whom you can from your store.
                    (*Johnny Roach's* 1870, 56)

Despite advances made by the Irish in the postwar period, the absence of a government-administered welfare system could make single parenting a sentence to penury or worse. "A Dollar a Dozen for Shirts" by William Ashcroft, possibly a street cry heard by the lyricist and brought to the stage, is a snapshot of life in an edgy, drudge existence:

If ye's please, sirs, I'm a young widdy,
A large family I have to maintain;
For meself, sure I don't care a penny,
For my children their bread I must gain.
I'm looking around for such labor
As a strong, hearty woman can do;
For reference — ax all me neighbors,
Your patronage I ax of you.

    Collars, dresses, undershirts,
    Frocks, frills and underskirts,
    Gowns, cuffs and handkerchiefs,
    Arrah, a dollar a dozen for shirts.
               (Ashcroft 1874, 8)

Why some Irish New Yorkers were mired in poverty while others rose is an important question. Without doubt, a significant number were not equipped for the hard life of the city — less intuitive, intelligent, or responsible. Others were simply less lucky, more sickly, or with no form of support. Gross population statistics can be misleading. Richard Stott (1990, 84–86) writes there was a churning in migratory flow: "80 percent of the city's growth was due to in-migration"; however, that represented only a fraction of those who landed at Castle Garden, for the majority continued their journey immediately after disembarking while thousands of others stayed "for a few months or years before moving" to places as close as Brooklyn or Jersey City or to states as distant as Michigan and California. In essence, year over year, a significant portion of the Irish population, who had tried their luck in New York City over time and who were dissatisfied, lifted stakes and ceded ground to new immigrants. Manhattan's Catholic Irish thus were segmented into the relatively successful, chronic underperformers, and recent arrivals. On Saturday night, those who led content, family lives stayed at home, or visited relatives and friends, attended social affairs at the parish hall or elsewhere, or shopped at the market; while those who were single and restless went instead to the main thoroughfare of working-class Manhattan. Shortly after Edward Harrigan composed "The Market on Saturday Night," Charley Davies parodied it with the altogether different "The Bowery on Saturday Night":

> I'll vocalize and a history relate
> Of the Bowery on Saturday night,
> Where there's always a racket, there's always a scrimmage,
> There's always a row or a fight;
> Where there's sailors and whalers and jailors and tailors,
> And toughs that are ready to fight
> For the daisies who powder their face with clam chowder,
> On the Bowery on Saturday night;
> Where's there's sweat men and banco men, Italians and Chinamen,
> Fenians and Bohemians, all tight;
> Where there's fighters and biters and sleep out-all-nighters,
> On the Bowery on Saturday night.
>
> (*Snow and Mott's*, n.d.)

On the Bowery, farmland in the days of the Dutch, the indigenous, transitory, and entirely unrooted populace perused, passed by, or bounced off one another. There at the dynamic, nocturnal center of working-class New York, a city like only a handful of others in the world, the Irish played highly significant roles as publicans, policemen, and performers.

Songs about Employment

Located 125 miles west of Manhattan, Pennsylvania's Wyoming Valley anthracite mining region was directly connected to the economy of New York City as its chief supplier of energy. So close was the interdependence that, when business activity in New York cooled,

Scranton, Wilkes-Barre, and the surrounding area descended into a deep freeze. Likewise, a strike in coal country might threaten lives and livelihood in the Empire City. In 1892, former mayor William R. Grace thought sufficiently of the Wyoming Valley that he journeyed there to address a gathering of miners on Saint Patrick's Day (*NYT*, 18 March 1892). There was a cultural connection too. The song "When the Breaker Starts Up Full Time" (Glazer 2001, 189, citing *Con Carbon's Own Songster*) accurately conveys Irish working-class aspirations in the last quarter of the nineteenth century not just in the anthracite region but also in mercantile-manufacturing Manhattan. The "breaker" is the "building where anthracite is prepared for market" (Korson 1964, 312), making it analogous to New York's factories. Desires expressed are for steady employment, financial solvency, and a modicum of creature comfort, plus a few daydreams of relative luxury; but these goals were often thwarted by unexpected downturns caused by supply-and-demand gyrations and other imbalances inherent in the economy of a megacity:

> Sure the Boss he told Mickey this morning
> When he's 'bout to enter the mine,
> That the coal was quite scarce down 'bout New York
> And the breaker would start on full time.
>
> And it's, oh, my, if the news be true,
> Me store bill's the first thing I'll pay.
> And a new parlor suite and a lounge I will buy
> And an organ for Bridgie, hooray.
> Me calico shirt I will throw in the dirt
> And in silk ones won't I cut a shine?
> Cheer up, Mrs. Murphy, b'damn, we'll eat turkey
> When the breaker starts up on full time.

These desires were consistent with those of Irish laborers in Manhattan. In rapidly expanding New York, steady work for reasonable pay might have seemed a given, but that was hardly the case. Though the Irish had replaced African Americans on the Hudson and East River docks by the Civil War, black longshoremen returned to compete as strikebreakers. Even in times of labor peace, the amount of work available for Irish dockworkers was often insufficient for the numbers who sought it (Man 1951, 392–93, 395), in part because the immigration of unskilled Irish workers continued throughout the late 1800s (McKivigan and Robertson 1996, 303). The final quarter of the nineteenth century brought yet another threat to New York laborers—the arrival of New Immigrants, especially men from Italy. New York's earlier Italian residents were primarily from Rome and the north; but the far larger wave, who began landing in the 1870s, came from poorer southern regions such as Abruzzo, Calabria, Campania, and Sicily. Unexpectedly, yet understandably, they bore certain commonalities with the city's Irish laborers, including agricultural origin, foreign customs, and the Catholic religion (Lankevich 1998, 122–23). These points (and others) were not lost when Irish song lyricists began to write about their Mediterranean competitors. "The 'Longshoremen" by P. J. Downey demands preference for the proud Irish dockworkers, claiming a stronger work ethic and higher efficiency:

> Our enemies, Italians,
> They work for lower pay,
> We're sure the bosses lose on them,
> They're only in the way.
> But take the men from Erin's isle,
> And give them a decent pay,
> You'll not go far, you'll find they are
> The men to clear the way.
>
> Dock yard clerks we claim to be.
> The cotton hook is our pen,
> When we turn out the people shout:
> "Three cheers for the 'longshoremen.'"
>   (*Sheehan and Coyne's* 1881, 16)

Here, the Irish demand respect. They are aware many Italian laborers are "birds of passage," not immigrants but seasonal workers intending to return home with the arrival of winter (Lankevich 1998, 122–23), in contrast to the Irish, who came on a one-way ticket, embedded themselves in Manhattan, and served in the Civil War. The majority of them planned to remain forever.

Figure 31. Saint Patrick's Cathedral, New York. Collection of author.

The rise of the organized labor movement, in which Irish leaders were highly represented, and invigorated Irish nationalism temporarily diminished the influence of Tammany, which was forced to take a broader and deeper interest in the community, realizing it "could no longer appease working-class voters with coal, food baskets, and political blarney" (McCaffrey 1996, 227). Patronage was the grease that lubricated the political machine, and it was dispensed largely to individual voters through employment. Political connection carried great weight in determining the hierarchy in which jobs were bestowed. The Gilded Age was an epoch of great public works projects, such as the Grand Central Depot—1871, the second Saint Patrick's Cathedral—1879, the Metropolitan Museum of Art—1880, the Brooklyn Bridge—1883, and the Statue of Liberty—1886. Another huge construction project was The Boulevard, the continuation of Broadway beginning at Central Park and extending nine miles far-

ther north, much of it over Manhattan's rocky backbone. In "The Boulevard, or One Sixty a Day" ($1.60 daily pay), another variety theater
song, a newly arrived "greenhorn" secures a job through a Tammany-
connected relative:

> GOOD evening to ye's, one and all,
> You're looking well, I see,
> I took a trip in a great big ship,
> Across the raging sea.
> I've been out of work a month or more
> And you know that's mighty hard,
> But now I've got a job to do,
> Beyont on the Boulevard.
>
> Arrah! here I am an Irishman,
> And of work I am not afraid,
> While Dan does carry the pick, me boys,
> And I do carry the spade.
> For Uncle Dan is an alderman,
> And he carries all the ward,
> 'Twas him that gave us tickets all,
> For to work on the Boulevard.
>
> Now fare ye's well, one and all,
> And it's time I was away,
> For if I keep singing here for you
> Sure I'll loose a half a day
> I'm going down to the City Hall,
> For to try and get a card,
> And put my uncle's brother to work
> Beyont on the Boulevard.
>   (Harrigan and Hart 1875)

The spoils system, through which Tammany conducted business,
is treated as common knowledge to the extent the song becomes an
advertisement to potential voter-clients. Though The Boulevard provided a great reservoir of patronage-directed work, it did not flow in

a steady stream but more like a water tap, which could freeze solid in cold weather. In the throes of winter, snow and ice might bar access to building sites and concrete could not be poured. It was, therefore, the most challenging season for construction workers, for when income was lowest they faced additional expenses for heating coal and heavy clothing. A second song about The Boulevard, Jim O'Neill and Jack Conroy's "When McGuiness Gets a Job" (1880), focuses on the seasonality of outdoor construction work and, like "The 'Longshoremen," comments on interethnic competition and the cultural differences between Irish and Italian laborers. In theater performance, it was a clothesline conversation sketch between two women commiserating over their spouses' lack of work: therefore a mechanism for providing dramatic testimony in support of worker complaints. The huge infrastructure improvement included "two capital roadways . . . separated by a central strip of lawns, trees and flowers" (King 1894, 134) and would provide years of employment; however, construction was halted. Significantly, the titles of "When McGuiness Gets a Job" and "When the Breaker Starts Up Full Time" start with the same word. They are about surviving the economic consequences of inactivity, getting by on an alternating diet of rumors and dreams, and the expectation that springtime (both actual and figurative) is not far off:

Last Winter was a hard one, Mrs. Reilly, did you say?
Well, 'tis myself that knows it, for it's many's the day
Your husband wasn't the only one sat behind a wall;
There's my old man McGuiness didn't get no job at all;
The Politicians promised him work on the Boulevard,
To handle a pick and shovel, and throw dirt on the cart.
Ah, six months ago they promised him work he'd surely get,
But believe me, my good woman, they are promising him yet.

Then cheer up, Mrs. Reilly,
Don't give away to the blues,
You and I will cut a shine,
New bonnets and new shoes;
As for me, I'm done a crying,
No more will I sigh and sob,

> I'll wait till times gets better,
> When McGuiness gets a job.

> The Italians, the devil take them, why don't they stay at home,
> Sure we had plenty of our own class to ate up all our own;
> They come out like bees in the Summer time and sworn for to stay;
> The contractors they have hundreds for forty cents a day.
> They work upon the railroad, they shovel snow and slush,
> But there's one thing in their favor, Italians they never do get lush;
> No, they always bring their money home, taste no gin or wine,
> And that's one thing I'd like to say of your old man and mine.

Unlike African American "others" portrayed in earlier Irish American songs, Italians are credited with a small portion of respect in "When McGuiness Gets a Job." That Italian men saved their wages, while Irishmen were more likely to dally overlong in a saloon, is an important admission. But it does not confer superiority. Hostility is still justified in Mrs. McGuiness's opinion; for despite some questionable habits her husband still excels at his trade:

> Ah! the Spring time now is coming we'll all have plenty work,
> McGuiness will go back to his trade, shure he's a handsome clerk.
> You should see him climb the ladder as nimble as a fox,
> Faith he's the boy can handle the ould three-cornered box.
> The boss is always bawling, Hi! there don't you stop,
> Keep your eyes turned upward, don't let no mortar drop;
> Ah! the old man he is always careful, nothing he let's fall,
> The divil a word you'd hear him say to my old man at all.
>
> (*Edwin Joyce* 1883, 48)

Like Tim Finigan, McGuiness's occupation was as a hodman, the unskilled laborer who scampered up a ladder bringing bricks and mortar to the skilled bricklayer. His employment was seasonal and temporary, dependent on weather, and tied to project funding. A third bricklayer's mate was the shadowy, immensely interesting, and gravely threatened Dennis Morgan, whose employment insecurity resulted from a sea change in construction methodology. Weather could be fickle and upsetting, but the advance of mechanization in the building industry was unyielding and inescapable. The first-person narrator of "The Hodman's Lament" tells of the ruination brought to his trade:

> My name is Dennis Morgan. I was born in the County Mohicon.
> Where a nice nate farm I lived upon. that was in days gone by:
> I came over to this country along with my small family.
> Where rich and poor were on equality, my fortune for to try.
> I am a long time from that good old sod. many miles of this broad land I trod.
> My occupation was carrying the hod. but those days will nevermore be seen:
> For they've cut our wages down so small a poor man can scarce live at all.
> For the hod, the mortar, bricks and all they're hoisting up by steam.

Despite being composed about local circumstances and printed in New York, "The Hodman's Lament" is an intensely Irish song. Indeed, it follows its model, "The Irish Refugee or Poor Pat Must Emigrate," not just in melody but also in lyric structure, including an internal rhyming scheme based on the assonance of Irish-language poetry. The typesetter seems to have played havoc with the first line, for we must conclude that the narrator's birthplace is in County Monaghan (not Mohicon). It is also possible his surname might have been Morrigan or Corrigan, though the name Morgan is not an unknown in Monaghan. Once in the City of New York, and thirsty to drink from the cup of equality, he found the brotherly beliefs championed by Thomas Paine (1737–1809) had died with their author; that America was a changed country now powered by unbridled, individual capitalism rather than fraternal, collective republicanism; and that he had also landed too late to savor prosperity, for his hod-carrying trade soon became diminished with the introduction of the steam hoist. Morgan's dilemma was common for the time. Indeed, "about 1870," writes folklorist Alan Lomax (1960, 551), a man of "pure African blood" working on the Big Bend Tunnel in West Virginia contested a steam drill to see which could advance the excavation fastest. According to legend, six-foot-tall, two-hundred-pound John Henry swung two twenty-pound hammers for thirty-five minutes and "beat the machine handily, drilling two holes seven feet deep, while the steam drill only made one of nine feet." As one version of the ballad recalls, Henry "beat that steam drill down," but "he hammered his fool self to death" (Lomax 1960, 561). Through death-inducing triumph, the man who raged against the machine achieved immortality. The hodman's situation was far worse. He could never move the volume of bricks and mortar the steam hoist could lift, and he had come to America to live decently and modestly—just as Tom Paine had promised.

Gordon (1993, 203–4), Miller (1985, 330–31), and W. Williams (1996, 141) each reprint sections of "The Hodman's Lament," primarily in connection with the mention of William M. "Boss" Tweed in the second verse. Gordon (1993, 204–14) also points out "the new alliance between capitalists and government" that brought down Tweed was inclined to nativism, calling up for examination of the use of public funds to support Catholic parochial schools and "alleged papal influence." This suggested that the hodman's discontent, while centered on employment, stemmed from systemic political complaints. In fact, each verse of "The Hodman's Lament" focuses on a separate yet interrelated issue. The song itself indicates it was composed while Tweed was absent from the city scene—presumably between late 1871 and his death in April 1878, during which time he was variously on trial, incarcerated, or on escape from prison:

> Long life and health to you, Bill Tweed, whate'er your nation or your creed.
> For you always helped the poor in need when you were a Senator;
> No soup-house paupers then did lurk, and less poor men were out of work.
> For you fought the wolf just like a turk when hunger did occur.
> But if e'er you should come back again you'll meet the help of honest workingmen,
> For no matter who may you condemn, you were poverty's best screen;
> But now your loss we do deplore and none will say much less, I'm sure
> Tho' you robbed the rich you fed the poor, and never acted mean.

It is estimated that Tweed and his associates illegally diverted between thirty and two hundred million dollars from city coffers; but also vague is the portion of the total that wound up in the hands of needy rank-and-file constituents.

Tweed was anything but a perfect Robin Hood, but under him Tammany Hall offered patronage employment to those who supported it, as well as a network to deliver necessities, such as emergency food, coal, and rent money—whereas the upper-class political and philosophical opponents of the Irish offered nothing. It is against the latter that the hodman rails in the last verse, calling on the memory of "Father of the Nation" George Washington to put right the wrongs, especially the unfair distribution of wealth, that has risen since he led the colonies to independence. The narrator is no doubt inspired by the rise and fall of the Paris Commune in the spring of 1871, but he feels free to speak as he does because he and his fellow immigrants regard themselves as American stakeholders, who, owing to political, religious, and economic discrimination in Ireland, cannot envision a set of circumstances in which they might return to the country of their birth. As such, they seek to hold America to the words "land of the free, home of the brave" and not succumb to the economic slavery engendered by laissez-faire capitalism:

> I could recall many facts here in my rhymes, but God be with them
>   good old times.
> When in New York we had less crimes, and labor got its pay;
> But we daily see before our sight that capital still backs up might,
> And still do strive to cheat the rights up to the present day.
> But pull together, show our power and wash out might with a right-
>   ful shower.
> And heaven's blessing every hour will help the poor man's cause;
> For if Washington was here to-day his eloquence he would display.
> And grant the poor man still fair play, and put down thievery and
>   fraud.
>   (*Delaney's Irish Song Book No. 4*, 1894)

"The Hodman's Lament" and "When McGuiness Gets a Job" are exceptional songs by any measure. Their vibrancy brings to life two-dimensional census entries and motionless photographic images of laboring people. Neither is solely a complaint; rather, both are rallying calls that end on hopeful notes. Interestingly, the two songs differed greatly in circulation within their time period. "McGuiness" was well known on the New York stage, while "The Hodman's Lament" appears to have been published only twice and without reference to a performance context: once in *Wehman's Collection of Songs No. 23*, printed in 1889 (Atkinson and Roud 2016, 169), and again in *Delaney's Irish Song Book No. 4*, impressed in the 1890s and quoted here. The hodman narrator writes with the voice of a self-educated man from the teeming streets. Almost certainly, he was one of the "Communist" protestors at the Tompkins Square demonstrations of 1874 reported by the *New York Times*:

> There is a vast hydra-headed class here, made up of very ignorant and poor people, with many who have grown up to youth and manhood in the life of the streets, who if urged by hunger or stimulated by what they fancied a great wrong—as great as the draft of 1863— would fill our streets with a great throng and strike at property and order, and all we most value. . . . We advise the Police to keep a sharp eye on this class, now and at all times. Its leaders ought to be closely watched, instead of being petted by the Mayor. (*NYT*, 20 January 1874, 4)

And what did these "very ignorant and poor people" like the hodman poet want? According to the *New York Times*, it was "work for the unemployed, the enforcement of the Eight-hour law, the reduction of house-rent for the benefit of the unemployed, and the abolition of the contract system by the City Government" (*NYT*, 9 January 1874, 2). This is largely the basis of what New York City's progressive administration attempts to provide today. Here, street song lyrics illuminate accounts in period newspapers by offering important, contrasting person-in-the-street perspectives.

"Laboring was regarded not as a profession so much as a temporary expedient while the laborer tried to find a better job," writes Stott (1990, 60–61); "Savings were the most obvious way out of unskilled labor. . . . Construction laborers often saved to buy a horse and cart, and many longshoremen hoped to buy a saloon." After the mid-1850s, by which time Germans had taken over much of the grocery store businesses (Burrows and Wallace 1999, 740), Irishmen concentrated on operating saloons, a Manhattan transformation of the city's traditional tavern that served the newly introduced "lager beer as the principal drink"; distinctively, saloons borrowed "much from Irish rural drinking places" with a "long, straight bar along one wall" and few chairs (Stott 1990, 217–22). Starting a new saloon required a large amount of cash. In the "row and ruction" music hall song "Duffy's Opening Night," a neophyte loses everything quickly, through a too-generous marketing plan:

> Did you ever here tell of Pat Duffy?
> He came from the County Mayo.
> Last week, shure, he started a bar-room
> Down in the Fourth Ward below.
> There was lager, free lunch and whiskey,
> Faith, indeed 'twas an elegant sight;
> But the boys, one and all, they got frisky
> On Duffy's grand opening night.

> Ah, but Duffy sold horrible liquor,
> It would knock you up high as a kite
> And the bar I'm sure never looked sicker
> Than on Duffy's grand opening night.

> Poor Duffy sent out invitations,
> And invited his neighbors to come.
> He told them he'd treat them all dacent,
> And give them their fill of good rum.
> They came there in droves and by dozens,
> And got into a terrible fight.
> They broke all the doors and the windows
> On Duffy's grand opening night.

> They stole all the stock that he had there.
> And drank all his whiskey so sweet;

They took both his clothes and his money,
And threw him out into the street.
They scattered his family, and left him
To roam in a terrible plight.
Poor Duffy now lives on free lunches
Since he gave his grand opening night.
              (*Dick Sands' Songster* [1883?], 58)

The successful saloonkeeper held a key social position in his neighborhood—in some regards, he was the secular counterpart of the parish priest. His "store" was a main connection point, place of exchange, and "cornerstone of political activity. . . . Prominent politicians flattered and aided him. Sometimes they presented him with political office, enabling him to dole out jobs and privileges to his neighbors and to increase his political prestige as well as the patronage of his establishment" (Ernst 1965, 163). He also extended credit and made loans, so it was in his best interest to structure his patron relationships with defined borders. He was *from* them but could not continue to *be* one of them, a class difference that further signifies the upward mobility of the times and its reflection in popular song. This cordial detachment is evident in Edward Harrigan's "I Never Drink behind the Bar":

I used to own a fine saloon,
With mirrors on the wall,
The finest class would never pass
But just drop in and call.
"Good morning, Pete," they'd say to me,
"You're looking slick—ta-ta!
Will you jine?" "I must decline
While I'm behind the bar."

    I never drink behind the bar,
    But I will take a mild cigar,
    Or a sip of Pollinar,
    I never drink behind the bar.

Like a pink I'll mix a drink
And toss the glass in style,
"The round on you? a dollar due,"
I'd whisper with a smile.
"Don't go home, I'm quite alone,
You've time to call a car;
Try one with me, oh, don't you see
That I'm behind the bar?"[2]

Thus, Peter McSorley (whose Old Ale House still stands at Fifteen East Seventh Street) knew well what Pat Duffy did not have time to learn—that the saloonkeeper was only his client's second-best friend, one who would faithfully sustain him when their interests coincided but who foremost would look after himself, not the least because it was he who took the risk and had to bring in the necessary capital to continue operating. A less grandiose, more cautious management approach than Duffy's is displayed in "I'm Going to Have My Name above the Door," which appears in *Wylie and Sanford's Songster*, published in 1888:

When I bought out from Flynn, he went out and I went in,
There was no one knew the difference I am sure,
For the bus'ness didn't stop at my little liquor shop,
Where I'm going to put my name above the door.
For the trade remained the same, though I never changed the name,
They took me for a bartender I am sure,
But I'll have you all to know, I'm the boss down here below,
Where I'm going to put my name above the door.
                    (*Wylie and Sanford's Songster* [1888?], 10–11)

The proprietor then daydreams about rapid expansion and even a career in politics before returning to his senses: "But I think I'd better stop at my little liquor shop / Where I'm going to have my name above the door."

Wylie and Sanford's Songster contains a joint biography of the married duo. William Wylie was born in Brooklyn in 1851 and made his first public appearance as a "German Comedian" at sixteen. Two years later, he "went into the vaudeville profession, and was the first one to introduce to the public what is now known as the North of Ireland business." The exact meaning of "North of Ireland business" is not known, though it might relate to a comedic theater act centering on Catholic-Protestant competition in Ulster. Kate Sanford was born in Philadelphia in 1861 and had spent fourteen years "as an actress and vocalist, having sustained all the leading roles in all of the comic operas of the present day." Wylie managed theaters in Tennessee, Colorado, Nebraska, and Maine; together, they toured Europe for three years, during which they were "personally complimented" by the British royal family and "appeared in Dublin before Lord Mayor Sullivan." Thus are presented two highly ambitious American performers anxious to play diverse roles that furthered their careers. Consistent with a new paradigm emphasizing escapism, with songs safe for performance nearly anywhere, there is no urban grime, and their Irish political songs bear no bloodstains. This entertainment model, less community-based and more indicative of the twentieth century, sought to lull rather than involve or incite the audience.

Greater New York (Manhattan and its suburbs) was by 1880 a large manufacturing hub, employing 274,939 industrial workers, 30 percent of whom were women working in the garment business and 11 percent men occupied in metal working (Hammack 1982, 40). It is, therefore, at first surprising that virtually no industrial folk songs seem to have survived. A large part of the reason relates to Manhattan's position as the center of America's entertainment industry, making it difficult for community-based folk song to endure the drowning onslaught of commercial music in a megacity that was becoming ever larger and more impersonal. "Maloney, the Rolling Mill Man," by J. W. Kelly, was sung on variety stages in Manhattan, but it was a pop song mostly about politics. Kelly was from Philadelphia, and his millwork experience was gained in Pittsburgh and around the south shore of Lake Michigan (Cullen, Hackman, and McNeilly 2004, 625). "Scovill's Rolling Mill," one of America's industrial folk song gems, may be as close as we can come, with the caveat it was composed in Waterbury, Connecticut, a cultural outpost of Manhattan some seventy-five miles away — New York is even mentioned in the text. Many Waterbury immigrants landed in New York and returned there occasionally for "big nights," visiting family and friends; also, much of the Connecticut recreational shoreline was inaccessible to the general public in summer because it was under private or municipal ownership, so some Waterbury Irish traveled to amusement parks and beaches at Coney Island and Rockaway. Waterbury had a large and active Irish community, many of whom worked in the brass industry at some time in their lives (Brecher et al. 1982). The song is included here for the above reasons, and because it tells eloquently what it was like to be an immigrant worker in a toxic factory, where, a century before the Occupational Health and Safety Act (1970), brass workers stood in close proximity to baths containing the 10 percent sulfuric acid solution used as an agent to remove scale from rolled metal sheets (Swift 1921, 395). Its frankness speaks volumes.

"Scovill's Rolling Mill" begins with a journey on the Great Southern and Western Railway from Tralee, County Kerry, to Queenstown (now Cobh), County Cork, to make connection with a transatlantic sailing. The immigrant train was taking away its regular daily share of the excess population of rural Ireland. The postfamine custom of impartible inheritance (Miller 1985, 403) dictated that, for those with little chance of taking over a family farm, emigration provided the best opportunity for a successful life:

Figure 32. Works of the Scovill Manufacturing Company, Waterbury, Connecticut. Collection of author.

The half past ten from Tralee town to Queenstown on its way
Brings thousands of our boys and girls off to Amerikay.
They leave the places of their birth and that's against their will
And they labor for their bread in Scovill's Rolling Mill.

You may work at the pickle tub, you may work in the yard.
You may work at the scratching machines, for that's not very hard.
But when Wednesday comes around again, your belly with beer
   you'll fill
And you'll spend the money you earned hard in Scovill's Rolling
   Mill.

"Good morning, Mr. Wilcox." "Good morning," he will say.
"Have you e'er a job for me Willie at a dollar and a half a day?"
He will give you a bag and a piece of wire and your eyes you'll begin
   to rub,
For your daily occupation is beside the pickle tub.

You may work at the muffles. They say that it is swell.
But take a tip from me, boys, I'd rather be in hell.
If he gave me a broom to sweep the floor, I'd do it with a will
But I'll be damned if I'd work at the pickle tub for Wilcox in the
   Mill.

The pickling tub was inescapable because it was intrinsic to the
production process. So too for many was the habit of hard drinking
to waft away the heat and poisonous vapors of the plant. The drinking
life also fit into a form of secular celibacy that kept alive the dream of
one day returning to Ireland. Having no nuclear family in America
meant one could remain flexible. But when the dying man decides to
go back to his home place, it is the community (his greater family) that
provides his ticket:

You may go down to Randolph's. You may go over to Booth's.
You may go to Benedict's and Chase's is no use.
And when payday comes around again, your belly with beer you'll
   fill
And you'll curse the day you sailed away to Scovill's Rolling Mill.

You may go down to New York, my boy, and hear the ocean roar.
You may imagine you see your mother standing at the cabin door,
Crying "Darling Jack, come back again and the old farm you can till,
Then no more you'll roam from your native home to work in the
    Rolling Mill."

And when your health and wealth are gone and you think you'd like
    to go home,
Your friends will get a raffle up to ship you across the foam,
Your mother will greet you with a smile but tears her eyes will fill.
She knows your health was broken down in Scovill's Rolling Mill.

And when you arrive in Ireland, the boys and girls to see,
They will ask you all about the land you call the brave and free.
You will answer them quite modestly though it's against your will.
You know your health was broken down in Scovill's Rolling Mill.

Now when you are six months in Ireland and feeble is your walk,
Your friends you knew while in your youth, to them you'll scarcely
    talk.
Your dance is gone, your voice is still, six feet of earth you'll fill
And they'll lay you away in the burying ground due to Scovill's
    Rolling Mill.

                                (Brecher et al. 1982, 9)

    The importance of "Scovill's Rolling Mill" derives from its fidelity to real life. Composed by a chronicler intimately familiar with the conditions it describes, it is completely honest and accurate, intensely sad without being maudlin; and the song is universal within the working-class Irish of the era. What happens to the protagonist could occur to anyone in nineteenth-century industrial America; however, it is clear that those who take better care of themselves are likely to last longer. One of the central functions of traditional song, seen here, is to present life-changing advice evidenced by example.

Mayor Grace

Like Thomas Francis Meagher, eight years his senior, William Russell Grace came from one of Ireland's distinguished Catholic families (fig. 33). His forbearers were landowners who could trace patrilineal descent from a Norman noble present at the Battle of Hastings (1066). But the similarity ends there, for while Meagher departed Ireland to attend England's foremost Roman Catholic educational institution, Stonyhurst College,[3] Grace instead "ran off to sea" (James 1993, 10, 14–15; Wylie 2007, 24–25). If the two were from the same cloth, they were not of the same cut: Meagher was impulsive, drawn to lofty heights at which he sometimes dizzied and fell, while Grace rose steadily to attainment and great wealth through tireless application, keen imagination, respect for others, and calculated risk taking. Grace was a self-made, independent man not unlike Edward Harrigan and Judge Charles P. Daly, both of whom also sailed off to see the world and later gravitated back to New York, where opportunities were numerous and rewards were huge.

Figure 33. William Russell Grace. Mayor of New York. Print. Notable New Yorkers of 1896–1899: A Companion Volume to King's Handbook of New York City. New York Public Library.

Grace was away from Ireland for two years, spending much of that time in Manhattan, working at several jobs, including cobbler's helper, apprentice printer, assistant in a dry goods shop, and shipping house clerk (James 1993, 14). The last two positions were formative. In 1850, at the age of eighteen, he opened an emigrant packet ship brokerage in Liverpool, booking passages on the White Cross Line in conjunction with a Dublin agent (James 1993, 15). In 1851, Grace traveled to Peru, where he parlayed his experience in shipping and merchandising at a ship chandlery in Callao, becoming a junior partner by 1854. The firm repaired and provisioned Pacific Ocean whalers, California clippers, and cargo ships filled with guano, bird dung accumulated over thousands of years, "whose extraordinary value as fertilizer had been discovered by the world at large" about ten years before Grace's arrival (James 1993, 21). On his initiative, the guano operation was later moved to the extraction site, the Chincha Islands, where the satellite, literally a hulk strategically anchored among the large fleet of transport ships, became a highly successful enterprise (James 1993, 20–26). Grace left Peru for good in 1865, withdrawing his stake in the ship chandlery but leaving behind a younger brother, who kept watch for further business prospects (James 1993, 46). Following a sojourn in Ireland and England, he headed to New York either later that year or early in 1866 and began to look for opportunities. Grace sensed that the commercial hub of the United States was the place to be and that the timing—during the post–Civil War rebuilding—was excellent (James 1993, 14–46).

In *Grace: W.R. Grace & Co., The Formative Years, 1850–1930*, an official history of the founding and evolution of the multinational trading and shipping company, Clayton (1985, 84) muses on the unique status W. R. Grace held in Gilded Age American politics: "Not only was he foreign-born, but his business experiences were international. . . . [He] was one of the first Roman Catholics elevated to high office in the United States . . . a businessman who chose to enter politics when most of the more celebrated figures in American trade and industry . . . consistently sought their fortunes in private life with precious little service volunteered in the public orbit."

Grace's position was unique but so were the personal traits and talents he had accumulated through broad experience. In South

America, he dealt regularly with Peruvian and foreign officials, and so was no stranger to politics and its sister, diplomacy. He knew how to make deals and realized agreements had to be honored: the shipping business operated worldwide, often on promises and involving weighty sums of money. Grace was also highly social, having joined in many evenings of "singing, dancing and feasting" in the Chinchas and frequently entertaining ships officers from the principal seagoing nations—foremost of which was the United States (James 1993, 22–32, 37). In Peru, he read the *New York Herald* consistently, so he was familiar with events in New York and the nation (James 1993, 36). With regard to religion, it is significant that Grace (like Daly and Meagher) married a Protestant, for successful interfaith marriage connotes an open urbanity, opposed to narrow interests, which allowed Grace to interact effectively in cosmopolitan, yet Protestant-dominated, New York City.

Highly successful in business, W. R. Grace first found broader prominence in Manhattan in February 1880, when he responded generously to a newspaper fundraising campaign meant to alleviate a new instance of mass hunger in Ireland (*Herald*, 4 February 1880). But it was entirely unexpected when the *Tribune* reported on 19 October 1880 that the bitterly opposed Irving Hall and Tammany Hall factions had met and jointly decided to nominate Grace as the unified Democratic candidate for mayor. The *New York Times* (19 February 1880, 4) reacted quickly with a scathing editorial:

> Mr. Grace is a wealthy commission merchant, Irish by birth and Roman Catholic in religion . . . as far as we know, of no particular ability or knowledge of public affairs. . . . Though neither his birth nor his religion can be held to be of itself a disqualification for the office of Mayor, there will be a natural desire on the part of reflecting men of both parties to have his position defined on certain public questions that the Church to which he owes allegiance has dealt with in a way that does not meet with the approval of the majority of his fellow-citizens. . . .
>
> The chief objections to Mr. Grace will, however, arise from the character of the influences which have contributed to his nomination. Mr. Kelly accepted the nomination of Mr. Grace because he

was the one man on the Irving Hall list who would best serve as a figure-head for the Tammany "Boss." His election would mean a continuance of Mr. Kelly at the head of the Finance Department and his restored supremacy in all departments of the City Government. Mr. Grace is the choice of a set of men who live by politics, and who regard the Municipal Government of New York simply as a rich placer [*sic*] of patronage and plunder. He would discharge the functions of the Executive office only by the permission of the men who have nominated him.

The *New York Herald* (19 October 1880), stating it spoke for "the great mass of Catholics," wisely observed that religion would henceforth pervade the campaign, while the *New York Tribune* (19 October 1880, 4) intimated that Irving Hall had been duped by Kelly. These claims further encouraged the *New York Times* (20 October 1880, 4), which continued its attack the following day in an editorial entitled "Roman Catholicism in Politics." In it, the conservative Republican standard-bearer warned if the Democratic ticket were to be elected that Catholics would control "the expenditure of every dollar of taxes and assessments raised . . . [and] the appointment of every head in the local Government." Though the article mostly berated Kelly, it did demand, "speaking on behalf of the non-Catholic majority of New York voters," that Grace define "his position in regard to questions affecting the disposal of public money on which the leaders of his Church have pronounced in a sense not reconcilable with the principles of American freedom."

The *New York Times'* one-sided, xenophobic attack on Grace, about whom it admitted to know very little, speaks for itself. Clearly, the greatest objection to the combined Democratic candidate was far more his religion than his ethnicity. Catholicism was and continued to be the greatest roadblock to Irish integration and advancement. The puppet-puppeteer relationship the *New York Times* wrongly presumed Grace to have with John Kelly of Tammany (even though he was proposed by the conservative, "good-government" Irving Hall wing of his party) was a practical, political issue based on class and privilege; but, for the nativist broadsheet, the United States was still a nation rooted in a British Protestant heritage, and leadership of its business, cultural, and social center by a Roman Catholic was simply insufferable.

Grace considered his formal acceptance and released a carefully worded letter to appear in the city's newspapers on 24 and 25 October. In it, he thanked Irving and Tammany Halls and simultaneously declared his independence. But his tribulations did not end there. On 26 October, the *New York Herald* questioned his citizenship. Two days later, the *New York Tribune* (28 October 1880, 4) reported the candidate had been an agent of the New York Board of Marine Underwriters in Callao between 1865 and 1871 and had engaged in gross fraud, resulting in false insurance claims. Grace denied both charges, in the latter instance stating he had left Peru before the period of the alleged scheme; but he was in an awkward position, unable to produce any proof until 1 November, the day before the election. Characteristically, bad news not only travels fastest but lingers longest, so the Democratic candidate was still under suspicion as votes were being cast. At 11 p.m. on 2 November, "the managers of Mr. Grace's canvass" admitted defeat (*NYT*, 3 November 1880, 5). However, when all electoral returns were tallied, he had squeaked in with a slim majority of 2,904 votes among the 200,802 cast (*Tribune*, 4 November 1880, 1). It was a most uncomfortable victory, however—tragic for the Democratic Party— because the adverse publicity given Grace was regarded as costing Winfield S. Hancock the national presidency, and Grace by now had gathered the distrust of both Democratic factions that had united to elect him.

The mayor-elect set out quickly to clear his name and to declare the policies of his administration, which would take office in less than two months. On the first count, Grace sent a mutual friend to *Tribune* editor Whitelaw Reid, with the personal message that he was gathering proof. Owing to the absence of his brother from Callao, confirmation was delayed until the new year; however, on 6 January 1881, the *New York Tribune* (2–3) reproduced in full the new mayor's inaugural message, which occupied more than a full page of the broadsheet. Its analysis commented that Grace's plan "shows the result of a careful study of city affairs" (*Tribune*, 6 January 1881, 2), while an editorial on page 4 concluded with a retraction of the insurance fraud accusations. Meanwhile, the *New York Times* (6 January 1881, 4) gave the Mayor's Message faint praise.

The same issue of the *Tribune* (6 January 1881, 3) contained the report of a stalemate within the Board of Aldermen concerning the selection of its presiding officer. The two Democratic factions were now in direct, hostile opposition, while Republican members stood back coolly and enjoyed the Democratic debacle. Grace could have ended the standoff by giving Kelly sufficient patronage to buy Republican members but declined to do so, thereby undermining the Tammany "boss" and supporting his own "good government" cause. For three decades, the Board of Aldermen had been known as the "Forty Thieves" (Burrows and Wallace 1999, 825–27) for their proclivity to switch positions in exchange for patronage or personal bribes. Edward Harrigan offered this characterization in "The Aldermanic Board":

> Behold these statesmen bold, who never yet were sold,
> We handle from one million up to ten;
> The makers of your laws, each section and each clause,
> The people's choice, the Board of Aldermen.

> As rulers of New York we have a right to talk,
> Supreme in district, precinct or in ward;
> From the Captain to a Cop we bring them to a stop,
> The ornamental Aldermanic Board.

> .   .   .   .

> To stop all future strife, just put us in for life,
> Upon that point we members all accord;
> We'll save the City's cash when the banks they go to smash,
> This intellectual Aldermanic Board.[4]

The *New York Times* (30 October 1880) had earlier reported on a rally against Grace's candidacy, claiming that if elected he would fail to carry out his campaign promise to keep the city's public schools independent of the Catholic religion. To end this prejudiced suspicion, Grace appointed William Wood, a "strict Scotch Presbyterian," as president of the Board of Education, a hugely important action that "brought the remainder of the good-government element to the

Grace standard, some of them shamefully anxious to atone for their earlier distrust" (James 1993, 163). The mayor's alignment with substantial public-spirited Brahmins, his repudiation of Tammany boss John Kelly, and his honest steadfastness in following his campaign promises reflected well on him—moreover, because his even-keeled navigation of the rocky shoals of New York politics was effectively disproving nativist claims and casting his Irish Catholic fellow citizens in a warmer light.

Grace then turned attention toward issues raised by him in the department-by-department analysis contained in his Mayor's Message (*Tribune*, 6 January 1881, 2–3). Beginning after less than a month in office, he became immersed in the city's street cleaning operation, which was inexplicably within the purview of the Police Department (rather than the Board of Health) and was a major source of patronage and graft. Ultimately, Grace was unable to gain full responsibility for street cleaning, but a compromise bill passed into law allowing the mayor partial control (*Herald*, 29 January 1881; *NYT*, 23 January 1881, 26 January 1881, 29 January 1881, 5 February 1881, 20 February 1881; *Tribune*, 29 January 1881, 22 February 1881, 24 February 1881).

During 1882, Grace locked horns with railroad "robber baron" Jay Gould, who manipulated share prices to acquire ownership of the three companies that composed Manhattan's overhead railway system ("The Elevated," or simply "The El," in common usage) and later sought to have property taxes greatly reduced or eliminated. Through a combination of skill and exceptionally good timing, the mayor was able to persuade the Republican state governor—for regulation of the city's transportation network was in the purview of the state rather than of city government—to defeat a bill that would have amounted to "legislative robbery," with the resident-taxpayers of the City of New York as its victims (*Herald*, 1 June 1882; James 1993, 167–68)).

A combined review of Grace's first year in office and his 1882 Mayor's Message printed by the *New York Times* (3 January 1882) presented a politically based assessment that found his year forward plan hardly "remarkable for originality of conception." It contained, however, "many just and forcible strictures on the working of our present system of Municipal government and some eminently judicious suggestions for its improvement." Both mayor and the newspaper agreed on the need for a stronger chief executive, but the *New York Times* dashed any hope of political peace when it wrote, "invested with actual power and responsibility, the office would be worthy of the ablest men in the community, and that, under such circumstances, neither party would dare to go before the community with a mere serviceable politician like Mr. William R. Grace." Considering the hostility of the previous campaign, Grace could have received far worse treatment. While he was effectively declared second class, no Democratic Party officeholder could have expected more; and with the review coming from what was still a nativist newspaper, the Catholic Irish mayor actually received approval.

On his retirement, Grace was praised in many city newspapers but not in the Tammany-controlled *Mail and Express* (James 1993, 176–77). The *New York Tribune* (2 January 1883), conservative but with a high regard for accuracy, found the mayor particularly praiseworthy: "Mr. Grace retires to private life with the good will and respect of substantial and public-spirited citizens. . . . He would not submit to Tammany dictation and he would not make terms with the Republican machine. . . . We thought very ill of him when he was elected; and it gives us the greater pleasure to be able to speak thus of him as he goes out of office." Three days earlier, the *New York Times* (30 December 1882) extended itself as far as it could in summarizing Grace's two-year term: "The course of Mayor Grace has . . . exhorted the approval of those who labored to prevent his occupancy of the mayor's chair . . . returning to private life far stronger in the confidence of the people, without distinction of party, than he was when he invited their support." Neither Grace's religion nor ethnicity were mentioned in the editorial.

The election and successful first mayoral term of William Russell Grace stands as the watershed episode in the integration of the Catholic Irish population into the mainstream of New York City society. Irish "bosses" controlled Tammany after the downfall of Tweed, but Grace's selection by the populace at large was completely different. An Irishman could be elected to the mayoralty of the nation's primate city only with the support of many non-Irish, non-Catholic voters; not only did that occur but Grace managed the city well. Nativists and pope haters would continue to rant (McCaffrey 1997, 114–15), mainly because the City of New York was so large that no new paradigm could gain unanimity; however, by the time Grace left office on 2 January 1883, those intransigently opposed to the Catholic Irish could no longer construct a serious argument that Irish Americans were *incapable* of holding positions that required complex skill sets, working cooperatively and fairly with people of all backgrounds, displaying sober behavior consistently, upholding American law over Church interests, and favoring the public good over group and personal benefit. Grace, Irish Catholic Democrat, had disproved such claims to the satisfaction of New York's two most conservative Republican newspapers. Unquestionably, his pioneering example helped clear the way for children of hodmen and laundresses to move into skilled and white-collar positions. Considerable credit is also owed to organizations that promoted group economic advancement, such as the diocesan educational system and labor unions (often headed by Irish immigrants), which had fought from antebellum times for the fair pay Catholic Irish families needed to function as stable, respectable units of city society (Burrows and Wallace 1999, 750–51; McCaffrey 1997, 114; McKivigan and Robertson 1996).

Following the Panic of 1873 and the depression that ensued, employment and living standards for immigrant Irish workers began to improve and continued to do so for the next two decades (Hammack 1982, 324–25). The elevation of American-born Irish was even more pronounced and was related to population geography. While the number of New York residents increased greatly after the Civil War, the percentage of Irish-born to total population actually declined — 22.2 percent (161,334 of 726,386) in 1865 versus 16.5 percent (198,595 of 1,206,299) in 1880. However, the total "Irish" count in the 1880 census more than doubles to 423,159 when the second generation is added (Rosenwaike 1972, 67, 73). In practical terms, the Irish community had to be accommodated meaningfully based on sheer numbers. Luckily, as the prosperity of the city grew and its population expanded, more white-collar positions were created in education, commerce, civil service, and the general supervision of every aspect of the busily expanding metropolis, now growing up and out simultaneously. As educated, fluent, and native-born New Yorkers, Irish *Americans* were well placed to fill these positions, and as Democrats were politically connected.

A second improvement in the overall lifestyle of the Empire City Irish relates to changes in transportation geography, specifically the construction of a fast and affordable rapid transit system with its own right-of-way. Before this era, most of New York's working class were forced to live in or close to the downtown central business district, in crowded conditions greatly exacerbated by Manhattan's wedge-like shape, which allowed for expansion over land in only one narrow direction—to the north-northeast. Paying high rents in tight, antiquated accommodations, they typically walked to work because vehicular transportation was both highly expensive and very slow. Inexpensive rapid transit lines freed the denizens of Lower Manhattan tenements to relocate to the open air of newly developing neighborhoods uptown, "where their influence was noticeable but not predominant." And by 1890, the once-teeming Irish wards around the central business district were "thinly settled" (Rosenwaike 1972, 83). The first such network was built quickly, mostly between 1878 and 1880, on elevated trestles in areas where relatively few people lived, so construction was generally unhindered by preexisting structures. Pulled by steam-powered locomotives, the trains made their way up and down Second, Third, Sixth, and Ninth Avenues with crosstown links at Thirty-Fourth and Forty-Second Streets (Derrick 2001, 30). The elevated railroad (fig. 34) was an instant sensation. It greatly expanded the usable acreage of Manhattan, allowing the New York Irish to spread to healthier, more spacious locales (Lankevich 1998, 119). Coincidentally, it provided a new form of entertainment, for as the trains moved between stations, passengers could peer into third-floor apartments, "feasting their eyes on endless rows of *tableaux vivants* featuring men in undershirts and women in housedresses" (Sante 1991, 51). For New York Irish wage earners, the overall effect was akin to finding the leprechaun's pot of gold, for they not only got to build The El and live in the new housing congregating around its stations but also got to work on the trains that rolled overhead (McCaffrey 1996, 229–31):

> There's the fireman, Blake
> And O'Brien, on the brake,
> And our great engineer, Pat McGan,

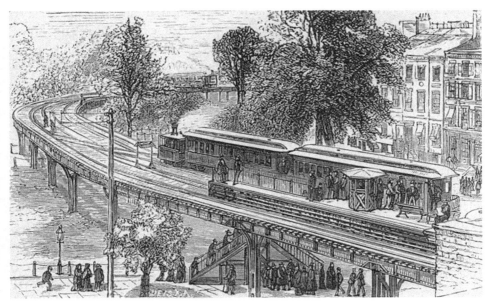

Figure 34. Elevated railway at The Battery. New York Public Library.

> Who can sing like a thrush,
>   Or a bird on the bush,
> You can bet he's a great ladies' man.
>   But we're the conductors,
>   So don't interrupt us,
> We're dainty, the ladies do say,
>   As they hand out the cash
>   Us conductors they mash
> On the great elevated railway.
>   ("The Great Elevated Railway," *Happy Dick Turner's*, 36)

The new suburban space gave the Irish an air of respectability. Paddy, shovel in hand, and Bridget, scrubbing at the washtub, would continue to exist mainly as immigrant figures laboring hard to earn their way in the Empire City; but, among Irish *American* New Yorkers, such foreign caricatures were on the wane. In place of Paddy and Bridget, there stood, increasingly, clerks, police and firefighters, skilled workers, managers, entrepreneurs, and even some professionals — men and women addressed as "mister" and "miss," "sergeant," "nurse," and "teacher." Going forward, the new Irish Americans increasingly wore dresses, suits, or uniforms, rather than soiled aprons or raggedy dungarees, working for a municipal department or in company offices or running their own businesses (Hammack 1982, 79–86). Importantly, they valued being American even more than being Irish, and the great, throbbing metropolis of which they were an intrinsic part came to regard them as such.

Conclusion

If I have given undue prominence to the Irish and negro, it is because they form about the most salient features of Gotham humanity, and also because they are the two races who care the most for song and dance.
— Edward Harrigan, *Harper's Weekly*, 2 February 1889

The central relationship throughout this book has been that between New York's American Protestant elites and its Irish Catholic immigrants, because it was the former who determined the value of the latter and, consequently, were the grantors of acceptance into the Manhattan mainstream. Chapter 1 established that the Act against Jesuits and Popish Priests, made law in 1700, effectively prohibited the settlement of Catholic Irish in the city, while at the same time Protestant Irish were admitted freely and their status weighed on the bases of class and wealth. Chapter 2 showed that various influential Founding Fathers believed the rights proclaimed in the Declaration of Independence, and later guaranteed by the US Constitution, accrued to all white males, while certain others argued that allegiance to a recognized form of Protestant Christianity was essential for full citizenship and societal participation. Though the more liberal view eventually prevailed legally, the existence of statutory protection did not result in tolerance and inclusion. Chapters 2, 3, 4, and 5 made clear that bias was often displayed overtly—through intimidating rituals, such as

Pope Day bashing; riotous acts, such as church burning; official Civil War policies that were arbitrary and discriminatory; demeaning cartoons and insulting editorials in elite periodicals; and Twelfth of July Orange parades that incorporated songs ridiculing Catholic Irish history and religious beliefs. The great hostility faced by Irish Catholics was principally attributable to the tenacious loyalty with which they held to their ostracized religion and to their burgeoning numbers, both perceived as threats to the security of all non-Catholics within the city.

Wherever possible, from a disillusioned Irish colonial soldier's sad musings in "Dear Molley" to an ultraconfident Irish American train conductor's proud proclamation in "The Elevated," songs have displayed a wide range of sentiment and purpose. In displaying feeling, they have enhanced the understanding of what it meant to be Catholic and Irish in the City of New York during the integration epoch. Over a century of community-voiced song, Paddy morphed from being an outcast in his own country, and a pariah in what is known as "the land of the free and the home of the brave," to a likeable, reliable, indispensable Empire City functionary. Likewise, Bridget rose from backbreaking scrubbing at a laundry tub in "When McGuiness Gets a Job" to the chalkboard at the head of a classroom in "Such an Education Has My Mary Ann," teaching Manhattan's schoolchildren to read, write, count, multiply, and envision a faraway world, through maps of green and brown and blue that worked like window blinds. In among the seas and continents lay a little land pointed out lovingly — the Emerald Isle.

The Civil War presented an important opportunity for Manhattan's Hibernians to integrate into the mainstream city population. Their quest had been thwarted twice previously — initially by a large inflow of rural workers made redundant by a changeover in land use practices in Ireland following the Napoleonic Wars and later during the disastrous Great Hunger. Each caused the unanticipated and unwelcome arrival in New York of too many strangely clad, often poverty stricken, sometimes contagious, overwhelmingly Catholic immigrants, the specter of whom greatly alarmed and angered the city's American Protestants. During the Civil War, enlistment by Manhattan's Irish was crucial to the Union cause. The Sixty-Ninth Regiment responded quickly and wholeheartedly. It and other units of Meagher's Irish Brigade and Corcoran's Irish Legion performed valiant service throughout, helping to bolster patriotic spirit nationally, though the significance of their sacrifice was painfully compromised during the brutal draft riots of 1863 (fig. 35).

But even at that dire time—some of New York's darkest days— nascent integration was observable in the New York press. On 1 August 1863, *Harper's Weekly* printed Thomas Nast's illustration *Charge of the Police on the Rioters of the "Tribune" Office.* In it, Irish mayhem-makers are sketched as rampaging apes. That the image focused on rioters, who engaged in what might be described as animalistic behavior, is both undeniable and highly important. But Nast, a German immigrant, who may have sought to displace his own foreignness onto another immigrant group, worked for a historically nativist publisher—and not *all* insurrectionists were pictured as simian. The drawing shows what might be termed "good rioters" and "bad rioters," with the latter intended to be Irish Catholics. However, the most conflicted aspect of the illustration is noticeable in the police force subduing them—they are handsome, dashing, dutiful, and mostly *Irish*. Then in the same issue, the news magazine included the following passage in its appraisal of what was America's bloodiest riot, pointing out that "[in] many wards of the city, the Irish were during the

Figure 35. Thomas Nast, *Charge of the Police on the Rioters of the "Tribune" Office.* Collection of author.

late riot staunch friends of law and order; that Irishmen helped to rescue the colored orphans in the asylum from the hands of the rioters; that a large proportion of the police, who behaved throughout the riot with the most exemplary gallantry, are Irishmen; [and] that the Roman Catholic priesthood to a man used their influence on the side of the law."

The divergence of these representations indicates the city was simultaneously in the throes of Irish integration and that *Harper's Weekly*, a conservative, elite periodical, was having difficulty finding its footing within that shift.

Eight years later, in 1871, members of the Catholic Irish community engaged in their last major physical confrontation in New York City, pitting themselves against a combine of Loyal Orange Order members and latter-day American nativists (Golway 2014, 96–100; Gordon 1993, 104–48). The encounter needlessly took the lives of at least sixty-seven New Yorkers. They were women and children as well as men—businesspeople, students, passersby, and onlookers. They were not just the Irish and their anti-Catholic adversaries but ethnic outliers, including a lone Australian, an African American, and four Germans. Two police and three of the militia also died (Gordon 1993, 224–37). One upshot was a swell in nativist activism. A second was the recasting of Tammany in a more businesslike, middle-class mold. The new model persuaded many in the working class to think beyond party politics and to envision greater brotherhood within radical labor unions (Golway 2016, 140–44; Gordon 1993, 188–89). The divergence occurred during a period that included the depression that followed the Panic of 1873, the setting for the stunning anticapitalist song "The Hodman's Lament." By 1883, when William R. Grace left office as the first Irish Catholic mayor of the City of New York, life as an immigrant laborer was still chancy, but the community's socioeconomic position had broadened considerably. Second-generation Irish *Americans* now outnumbered their parents. Life by then was getting good and would get even better.

How did the Catholic Irish finally manage to climb the ladder and integrate into the New York populace, while African Americans—likewise a long-standing, long-demeaned, and long-deprived group—remained on the bottom rung? The first factor is that, bigoted anti-

Irish imagery and quack physical anthropology aside, the former were undeniably "white," and color still mattered greatly in what remained a "white man's city." The second is that, though they had been dispossessed and impoverished in Ireland, and sorely abused in America, the Irish did not have an actual slave legacy. Third, by the 1880s, many Irish Catholics were projecting a new, Americanized image, partly based on their service in the Union army, partly as preservers of law and order during the 1863 draft riots, and largely because so many of them were now Manhattan-born. This persona was prominently expressed in the lighter, genial profile they now displayed as popular entertainers and sportsmen. They were now no longer just buffoonlike, stage Irish comedians and bestial boxers but also slick song-and-dance artists and heroic baseball stars. Fourth, transatlantic immigration patterns were changing, and Manhattan demography was beginning to undergo structural and material changes. The arrival of large numbers of New Immigrants from southern and eastern Europe meant Manhattan elites needed to find a basis of commonality with Irish Catholics if they wished to continue having a hand on the rudder that steered the city. The Irish were politically astute and by that time well placed politically to enroll and organize New Immigrants. Fifth, entirely contrary to the expectation of American Protestants, William R. Grace performed well in his initial term as mayor of the City of New York—and their newspapers were forced to admit it. Sixth, Irish Catholics were simply far more numerous than African Americans. The 1880 US Census determined the population of New York City to be 1,206,299. African Americans represented only a small portion of that total—19,663, or 1.6 percent—while the combined first- and second-generation Irish aggregate amounted to a massive 423,159, or 35 percent (Rosenwaike 1974, 73, 77).

The answer, then, lies within a combination of factors, but it is certainly clear that large numbers, an aspect that had long-inhibited Catholic Irish integration, actually aided in their acceptance. The more understandable Irish *Americans* now appeared as useful allies to New York's select citizens because of their huge presence and the political power they possessed. Now a fixture in the firmament, their star was rising. In a word, the Irish were *unstoppable*.

NOTES

Introduction

1. Padraic Colum's books *Cross Roads in Ireland* (1937) and *The Road Round Ireland* (1931) present lifelike word portraits of ballad singers in Ireland.

ONE Prologue

1. The Duke of York was the future King James II.

2. The first Methodist congregation in North America was founded on 12 October 1766 by Irish Palatine immigrants Barbara Heck and Philip Embury. It evolved into John Street Methodist Church.

THREE Irish Famine and American Nativism

1. "Swate Castle Garden" is collected in Robert L. Wright's *Irish Emigrant Ballads and Songs*, 494.

2. Discussed in chapter 5.

3. Daniel Cassidy (2007, 129) suggests Dead Rabbits may be a mixture of American and Irish-language slang: *dead* meaning "very" and *ráibéad* meaning "big galoot."

4. Militant clubs that marched in torchlight parades wearing white hats and robes or capes.

FOUR   The Civil War and the Draft Riots of 1863

1. Kathleen O'Neil, a singer and actress born in Dublin in 1840, has also been credited with authorship of "No Irish Need Apply." O'Neil, who performed extensively both in Ireland and England before her arrival in the United States, made her New York debut in 1862 (http://blarneystar.com/Kitty_Optimized-080817.pdf). Her rendition of the song was published in Cleveland, Ohio, by S. Brainard and Co. in 1863. O'Neil's version employs a motif strongly related to Poole's, but the details are localized to the British experience:

> Now what have they against us, sure the world knows Paddy's brave,
> For he's helped to fight their battles, both on land and on the wave,
> At the storming of Sebastopol, and beneath an Indian sky,
> Pat raised his head, for their General said, "All Irish might apply."

Poole's 1862 text was included in *Tony Pastor's New Irish Comic Songster*, where it is credited as "An Original Song by John F. Poole. Written for and sung with immense success by the great Comic Vocalist of the age, Tony Pastor. (Secured by copyright.)"

2. *Colored* was commonly used and was not considered a pejorative term at the time.

3. Zouaves were soldiers garbed in French Colonial uniforms.

FIVE   The Road to Respectability

1. Sheet music for "Such an Education Has My Mary Ann" (New York: William A. Pond, 1879).

2. Sheet music for "I Never Drink behind the Bar" (New York: William A. Pond, 1882).

3. Stonyhurst's alumni include three saints and a signatory to the US Declaration of Independence.

4. Sheet music for "The Aldermanic Board" (New York: William A. Pond, 1885).

BIBLIOGRAPHY

Primary Sources

Archival Document Sources and Private Collections

AAS	American Antiquarian Society, Worcester, MA.
Bodleian	Bodleian Library, University of Oxford.
Duke	Duke University, Durham, NC.
Hay	Hay Library, Brown University, Providence, RI.
ITMA	Irish Traditional Music Archive, Dublin.
LC	Library of Congress, Washington, DC.
Levy	Lester S. Levy Sheet Music Collection, Johns Hopkins University, Baltimore.
Madden	Madden Collection, Cambridge University Library, Cambridge.
Milner	Collection of author.
Moloney	Mick Moloney Irish American Music and Popular Culture Collection, New York University.
NYHS	New York Historical Society.
NYPL	New York Public Library.
NYSL	Manuscripts and Special Collections, New York State Library, Albany.
PPL	The Williams and Potter Collection on Irish Literature and Culture, Providence Public Library, RI.
Spencer	Frances G. Spencer Collection of American Popular Sheet Music, Baylor University, Waco, TX.
Trinity	Trinity College Library, Hartford, CT.
Watkinson	Watkinson Library, Trinity College, Hartford, CT.

Books, Pamphlets and Songsters

The American Comic Songster: A Collection of All the Wit, Humour, Eccentricity, and Originality in Song, Which the Present Day Has Produced. 1834. New York: J. G. Shaw.

Archer, William, ed. 1852. *The Orange Melodist.* Dublin: J. Kirkwood.

Ashcroft, William. 1874. *Billy Ashcroft's "Irish Character" Songster.* New York: R. M. De Witt.

Beddoe, John. 1971. *The Races of Britain: A Contribution to the Anthropology of Western Europe.* London: Hutchinson.

The Blackbird: Consisting of a Complete Collection of the Most Admired Modern Songs. New York: Christian Brown.

Browne, Junius Henri. 1868. *The Great Metropolis: A Mirror of New York.* Hartford: American.

Cavanagh, Michael. 1892. *Memoirs of Gen. Thomas Francis Meagher Comprising the Leading Events of His Career.* Worcester, MA: Messenger Press.

Conyngham, D. P. 1867. *The Irish Brigade and Its Campaigns: With Some Account of the Corcoran Legion, and Sketches of the Principal Officers.* New York: William McSorley.

Corby, William. 1992. *Memoirs of a Chaplain Life: Three Years with the Irish Brigade in the Army of the Potomac.* Edited by Lawrence Frederick Kohl. Bronx: Fordham University Press.

Corcoran, Michael. 1864. *The Captivity of General Corcoran.* Philadelphia: Barclay.

Crockett, David. 1835. *An Account of Col. Crockett's Tour to the North and Down East.* Philadelphia: E. L. Carey and A. Hart.

Croker, Thomas Crofton. 1839. *The Popular Songs of Ireland.* London: Henry Colburn.

Cronin and Sullivan's Grand Songster. 1882. New York: A. J. Fisher.

Daly, Maria L. 1962. *Diary of a Union Lady.* Edited by Harold Earle Hammond. New York: Funk and Wagnalls.

Delaney's Irish Song Book No. 4. [1887?]. New York: Delaney.

Dickens, Charles. 1842. *American Notes, and Reprinted Pieces.* London: Chapman and Hall.

Dick Sands' Songster. [1883?]. New York: New York Popular.

Dwight, Timothy. 1822. *Travels in New England and New York.* 3 vols. N.p.

Edwin Joyce & Verona Carroll's Face to Face Songster. 1883. New York: William J. A. Lieder.

Emmet, J. K. 1882. *J. K. Emmet's Love of the Shamrock Songster.* New York: A. J. Fisher.

English, Joe. 1864. *Joe English's Irish and Comic Songster.* New York: Dick and Fitzgerald.

Happy Dick Turner's Sea Side Aquarium Songster. 1885. New York: New York Popular.

Harrigan, Edward. 1901. *The Mulligans.* New York: G. W. Dillingham.

Harrigan, Edward, and Tony Hart. 1875. *Harrigan & Hart's Hildebrand Montrose Songster.* New York, A. J. Fisher.

Hassard, John R. G. 1866. *Life of the Most Reverend John Hughes, D.D. First Archbishop of New York.* New York: D. Appleton.

Hugill, Stan. 1961. *Shanties from the Seven Seas: Shipboard Work-Songs from the Great Days of Sail.* London and Henley: Routledge and Kegan Paul.

The Irish Singer's Own Book. N.d. N.p.

James O'Neill's "Candidate for Alderman" Songster. 1876. New York: A. J. Fisher.

Jameson, J. Franklin, ed. 1909. *Narratives of New Netherland, 1609–1664.* New York: Charles Scribner's Sons.

Johnny Roach's Best Songster. 1877. New York: Clinton T. DeWitt.

Johnny Roach's Bold Irish Pat Songster. 1870. New York: Frederic A. Brady.

Kendal, Joseph, Jr. 1783. "Copybook Containing 22 Topical Song-Texts." Music MS 4, 25–26. Watkinson Library, Trinity College, Hartford, CT.

King, Moses. 1894. *King's Handbook of New York City: An Outline, History and Description of the American Metropolis.* Boston: Moses King.

Lyons, W. F. 1869. *Brigadier-General Thomas Francis Meagher: His Political and Military Career; with Selections from His Speeches and Writings.* Glasgow: Cameron and Ferguson.

Moore, Thomas. 1818. *Irish Melodies.* New York: A. T. Goodrich.

Morgan, Watty. n.d. *Watty Morgan's Don't Keep the Working Man Down Song Book.* N.p.

The New-York Remembrancer, or the Songster's Magazine. 1802. Albany, NY: Daniel Steele.

O'Donoghue, Daniel James. 1912. *The Poets of Ireland: A Bibliography and Bibliographical Dictionary of Irish Writers of English Verse.* Dublin: Figgis.

Pastor, Tony. 1864. *Tony Pastor's "444" Combination Songster.* New York: Dick and Fitzgerald.

Poole, John F. 1862. *The Double-Quick Comic Songster: Containing a Choice Collection of Comic Songs Never Before Published.* New York: Dick and Fitzgerald.

Ranson, Joseph. 1948. *Songs of the Wexford Coast.* Enniscorthy, Ireland: Redmond Bros.

Riordon, William L. 1905. *Plunkitt of Tammany Hall.* New York: McLure, Phillips.

Semmes, Raphael. 1996. *Memoirs of Service Afloat during the War between the States.* Baton Rouge: Louisiana State University Press.

Shea, John Gilmary, ed. 1878. *The Catholic Churches of New York City, with Sketches of Their History and Lives of the Present Pastors.* New York: Lawrence G. Goulding.

Sheehan and Coyne's "An Everyday Occurrence" Songster. 1881. New York: DeWitt.

Snow and Mott's Down in Mobile Songster. [1883?]. New York: Popular.

The Songster's Repository. 1811. New York: Nathaniel Dearborn.

Standard Orange Song Book. 1848. Armagh, Ireland: Armagh Guardian.

Strong, George Templeton. 1952. *The Diary of George Templeton Strong: The Civil War 1860–1865*. Edited by Allan Nevins and Milton Halsey Thomas. New York: Macmillan.

The Wearing of the Green Song Book. 1869. Boston: Patrick Donohoe.

Wehman's Irish Song Book, No. 2. 1889. New York: Wehman Bros.

Wilson, H. 1856. *Trow's New York City Directory*. New York: John F. Trow.

Wright, Robert L., ed. 1975. *Irish Emigrant Ballads and Songs*. Bowling Green: Bowling Green University Popular Press.

Wylie and Sanford's Songster. [1888?]. New York: Popular.

Government Reports

Superintendent of Police. (1861) 1862. *Report of the Superintendent of Police to the Commissioners of Police, 31 December*. Reprint, *New York Times*, 5 January.

US Census Bureau. 1998. "Population of the 100 Largest Cities and Other Urban Places in the United States: 1790 to 1990." Population Working Division Paper No. 27. Washington, DC: US Census Bureau.

——. 2010. *American Community Survey*. Washington, DC: US Census Bureau.

Newspapers and Other Periodicals

BDE	*The Brooklyn Daily Eagle*
Harper's	*Harper's Weekly*
Herald	*The New York Herald*
Mail	*The Mail and Express*
NYT	*The New York Times* and *The New York Daily Times*
Star	*The Daily Star*
Sun	*The Sun*
Times	*The Times* (London)
Tribune	*The New York Tribune* and *The New York Daily Tribune*
TT	*The Truth Teller*
World	*The World*

Secondary Sources

Books and Book Chapters

Adams, William Forbes. 1932. *Ireland and the Irish Emigration to the New World from 1815 to the Famine*. New Haven, CT: Yale University Press.

Albion, Robert Greenhalgh. 1984. *The Rise of New York Port, 1815–1860*. Boston: Northeastern University Press.

Allen, Robert C. 1991. *Horrible Prettiness: Burlesque and American Culture*. Chapel Hill: University of North Carolina Press.

Anbinder, Tyler. 2001. *Five Points*. New York: Free Press.

Anderson, Bern. 1962. *By Sea and by River: The Naval History of the Civil War*. New York: Alfred A. Knopf.

Atkinson, David, and Steve Roud, eds. 2016. *Street Ballads in Nineteenth-Century Britain, Ireland, and North America: The Interface between Print and Oral Traditions*. London: Routledge.

Ballagh, James Curtis. 1969. *White Servitude in the Colony of Virginia: A Study of the System of Indentured Labor in the American Colonies*. New York: Burt Franklin.

Barrett, James R. 2012. *The Irish Way: Becoming American in the Multiethnic City*. New York: Penguin Press.

Bayor, Ronald H., and Timothy J. Meagher. 1996. *The New York Irish*. Baltimore: Johns Hopkins University Press.

Bennett, William Harper. 1909. *Catholic Footsteps in Old New York: A Chronicle of Catholicity in the City of New York from 1524 to 1808*. New York: Schwartz, Kirwan and Faust.

Bernstein, Iver. 1990. *The New York City Draft Riots: Their Significance for American Society and Politics in the Age of the Civil War*. New York: Oxford University Press.

Bilby, Joseph G. 1998. *The Irish Brigade in the Civil War: The 69th New York and Other Irish Regiments of the Army of the Potomac*. Conshohocken, PA: Combined.

Billington, Ray Allen. 1964. *The Protestant Crusade, 1800–1860: A Study of the Origins of American Nativism*. Chicago: Quadrangle Books.

Bolster, Jeffrey W. 1997. *Black Jacks: African American Seamen in the Age of Sail*. Cambridge, MA: Harvard University Press.

Bornstein, George. 2011. *The Colors of Zion: Blacks, Jews, and Irish from 1845 to 1945*. Cambridge, MA: Harvard University Press.

Bottigheimer, Karl S. 1982. *Ireland and the Irish: A Short History*. New York: Columbia University Press.

Bourgeois, Maurice. 1965. *John Millington Synge and the Irish Theatre*. Bronx: B. Blom.

Brecher, Jeremy, Jerry Lombardi, Jan Stackhouse, and Brass Workers History Project. 1982. *Brass Valley: The Story of Working People's Lives and Struggles in an American Industrial Region*. Philadelphia: Temple University Press.

Brodhead, John Romeyn. 1853–87. *Documents Relative to the Colonial History of the State of New-York*. Edited by E. B. O'Callaghan. 15 vols. Albany: Weed, Parsons.

Brown, Thomas N. 1958. *Social Discrimination against the Irish in the United States*. New York: American Jewish Committee.

Bruce, Susannah Ural. 2006. *The Harp and the Eagle: Irish-American Volunteers and the Union Army, 1861–1865*. New York: New York University Press.

Brunvand, Jan Harold. 1986. *The Study of American Folklore*. New York: W. W. Norton.

Burrows, Edwin G., and Mike Wallace. 1999. *Gotham: A History of New York City to 1898*. New York: Oxford University Press.

Casey, Marion R. 2006. "Refractive History: Memory and the Founders of the Emigrant Savings Bank." In *Making the Irish American*, edited by J. J. Lee and Marion R. Casey, 302–31. New York: New York University Press.

Cassidy, Daniel. 2007. *How the Irish Invented Slang: The Secret Language of the Crossroads*. Petrolia, CA: Counter Punch.

Cazden, Norman, Herbert Haufrecht, and Norman Studer. 1982. *Folk Songs of the Catskills*. 2 vols. Albany: State University of New York Press.

Clark, Dennis. 1979. *The Irish in Philadelphia: Ten Generations of Urban Experience*. Philadelphia: Temple University Press.

Clayton, Lawrence A. 1985. *Grace: W. R. Grace & Co., The Formative Years, 1850–1930*. Ottawa, IL: Jameson Books.

Coldham, Peter Wilson. 1988. *The Complete Book of Emigrants, 1607–1660*. Baltimore: Genealogical.

Colum, Padraic. 1930. *Cross Roads in Ireland*. New York: Macmillan.

———. 1937. *The Road Round Ireland*. New York: Macmillan.

Connolly, S. J., ed. 2002. *The Oxford Companion to Irish History*. Oxford: Oxford University Press.

Conyngham, D. P. 1867. *The Irish Brigade and Its Campaigns*. New York: William McSorley.

Coogan, Tim Pat. 2000. *Wherever Green Is Worn*. New York: Palgrave.

Cook, Adrian. 1974. *The Armies of the Streets: The New York City Draft Riots of 1863*. Lexington: University Press of Kentucky.

Crawford, Richard. 2001. *America's Musical Life: A History*. New York: W. W. Norton.

Crimmins, John D. 1902. *St. Patrick's Day: Its Celebration in New York and Other American Places, 1737–1845*. New York: John D. Crimmins.

Cronin, Mike, and Daryl Adair. 2002. *The Wearing of the Green: A History of St. Patrick's Day*. London: Routledge.

Cullen, Frank, Florence Hackman, and Donald McNeilly. 2004. *Vaudeville Old and New: An Encyclopedia of Variety Performers in America*. Vol. 1. New York: Routledge.

Cullen, Jim. 1996. *The Art of Democracy: A Concise History of Popular Culture in the United States*. New York: Monthly Review Press.

Davis, Thomas J. 1985. *A Rumor of Revolt: The Great Negro Plot in Colonial New York*. New York: Free Press.

Demeter, Richard. 2002. *The Fighting 69th: A History.* Pasadena: Cranford Press.

Derrick, Peter. 2001. *Tunneling to the Future: The Story of the Great Subway Expansion That Saved New York.* New York: New York University Press.

Diner, Hasia R. 1983. *Erin's Daughters in America.* Baltimore: Johns Hopkins University Press.

———. 1996. "'The Most Irish City in the Union': The Era of the Great Migration, 1844–1877." In *The New York Irish*, edited by Ronald H. Bayor and Timothy J. Meagher, 87–106. Baltimore: Johns Hopkins University Press.

Dinnerstein, Leonard, Roger L. Nichols, and David M. Reimers. 1990. *Natives and Strangers: Blacks, Indians, and Immigrants in America.* New York: Oxford University Press.

Doerflinger, William Main. 1990. *Songs of the Sailor and Lumberman.* Glenwood, IL: Meyerbooks.

Dolan, Jay P. 1983. *The Immigrant Church: New York's Irish and German Catholics, 1815–1865.* Notre Dame, IN: University of Notre Dame Press.

———. 2008. *The Irish Americans: A History.* New York: Bloomsbury Press.

Doyle, David Noel. 2006. "The Remaking of Irish America." In *Making the Irish American*, edited by J. J. Lee and Marion R. Casey, 213–52. New York: New York University Press.

Duncan, Jason K. 2005. *Citizens or Papists? The Politics of Anti-Catholicism in New York, 1685–1821.* New York: Fordham University Press.

Ellis, David M., and New York State Historical Association. 1967. *A History of New York State.* Ithaca, NY: Cornell University Press.

Ellis, Edward Robb. 1966. *The Epic of New York City.* New York: Old Town Books.

Emerson, Ken. 1997. *Doo-dah! Stephen Foster and the Rise of American Popular Culture.* New York: Simon and Schuster.

Ernst, Robert. 1965. *Immigrant Life in New York City, 1825–1863.* Port Washington, NY: Ira J. Friedman.

Flanders, Helen Hartness, ed. 1963. *Ancient Ballads Traditionally Sung in New England.* Vol. 3. Philadelphia: University of Pennsylvania Press.

Fleming, Thomas. 1997. *Liberty! The American Revolution.* New York: Viking Books.

Foner, Eric. 1988. *Reconstruction: America's Unfinished Revolution, 1863–1877.* New York: Harper and Row.

Foster, R. F. 1989. *Modern Ireland.* London: Penguin Books.

Fowke, Edith. 1965. *Traditional Singers and Songs from Ontario.* Hatboro, PA: Folklore.

Fowke, Edith, and Joe Glazer. 1960. *Songs of Work and Freedom.* New York: Dolphin Books.

Fox, William F. 1889. *Regimental Losses of the Civil War, 1861–1865.* Albany, NY: Albany.

Galvin, Patrick. 1962. *Irish Songs of Resistance.* New York: Oak.

Gibney, Matthew J., and Randall Hansen, eds. 2005. *Immigration and Asylum from 1900 to Present.* Santa Barbara: ABC-CLIO.

Gibson, Florence E. 1968. *The Attitudes of the New York Irish toward State and National Affairs.* New York: AMS Press.

Gilje, Paul A. 1987. *The Road to Mobocracy: Popular Disorder in New York City, 1763–1834.* Chapel Hill: University of North Carolina Press.

———. 1996. "The Development of an Irish American Community in New York City before the Great Migration." In *The New York Irish*, edited by Ronald H. Bayor and Timothy J. Meagher, 70–83. Baltimore: Johns Hopkins University Press.

Glazer, Joe. 2001. *Labor's Troubadour.* Urbana: University of Illinois Press.

Glazer, Nathan, and Daniel Patrick Moynihan. 1963. *Beyond the Melting Pot: The Negroes, Puerto Ricans, Jews, Italians, and Irish of New York City.* Cambridge, MA: MIT Press and Harvard University Press.

Glazier, Michael. 1999. *The Encyclopedia of the Irish in America.* Notre Dame, IN: University of Notre Dame Press.

Golway, Terry. 2014. *Machine Made: Tammany Hall and the Creation of Modern American Politics.* New York: W. W. Norton.

Goodfriend, Joyce D. 1996. "Upon a Bunch of Straw: The Irish in Colonial New York City." In *The New York Irish*, edited by Ronald H. Bayor and Timothy J. Meagher, 35–47. Baltimore: Johns Hopkins University Press.

Gordon, Michael A. 1993. *The Orange Riots: Irish Political Violence in New York City, 1870 and 1871.* Ithaca, NY: Cornell University Press.

Gray, Peter. 1995. *The Irish Famine.* New York: Harry N. Abrams.

Hammack, David C. 1982. *Power and Society: Greater New York at the Turn of the Century.* New York: Russell Sage Foundation.

Hammond, Harold E. 1954. *A Commoner's Judge: The Life and Times of Charles Patrick Daly.* Boston: Christopher.

Handlin, Oscar. 1974. *Boston's Immigrants: A Study in Acculturation.* New York: Atheneum.

Harte, Frank. 1993. *Songs of Dublin.* Cork: Ossian.

Hennesey, James. 1981. *American Catholics: A History of the Roman Catholic Community in the United States.* New York: Oxford University Press.

Hershkowitz, Leo. 1996. "The Irish and the Emerging City: Settlement to 1844." In *The New York Irish*, edited by Ronald H. Bayor and Timothy J. Meagher, 11–34. Baltimore: Johns Hopkins University Press.

Hirota, Hidetaka. 2017. *Expelling the Poor: Atlantic States and the Nineteenth-Century Origins of American Immigration Policy.* New York: Oxford University Press.

Hodges, Graham Russell. 1996. "'Desirable Companions and Lovers': Irish and African Americans in the Sixth Ward, 1830–1870." In *The New York Irish*, edited by Ronald H. Bayor and Timothy J. Meagher, 107–24. Baltimore: Johns Hopkins University Press.

———. 1999. *Root and Branch: African Americans in New York and East Jersey, 1613–1860.* Chapel Hill: University of North Carolina Press.

Hotten, John Camden. 1874. *The Original List of Persons of Quality; Emigrants; Exiles; Political Rebels; Serving Men Sold for a Term of Years; Apprentices; Children Stolen; Maidens Pressed; and Others Who Went from Great Britain to the American Plantations 1600–1700.* London: John Camden Hotten.

Howes, Marjorie. 2009. "How Irish Maids Are Made: Domestic Servants, Atlantic Culture, and Modernist Aesthetics." In *The Black and Green Atlantic: Cross Currents of the African and Irish Diasporas,* edited by Peter D. O'Neill and David Lloyd, 97–112. New York: Palgrave Macmillan.

Hughes, Herbert, ed. 1915. *Irish Country Songs.* Vol. 2. London: Boosey and Hawkes.

Huntington, Gale, and Lani Hermann. 1990. *Sam Henry's Songs of the People.* Athens, GA: University of Georgia Press.

Ignatiev, Noel. 1995. *How the Irish Became White.* New York: Routledge.

Jackson, Kenneth T., ed. 1995. *The Encyclopedia of New York City.* New Haven, CT: Yale University Press.

James, Marquis. 1993. *Merchant Adventurer: The Story of W.R. Grace.* Wilmington, DE: SR Books.

Jay, William. 1833. *The Life of John Jay: With Selections from His Correspondence and Miscellaneous Papers.* Vol. 1. New York: J. and J. Harper.

Jones, Paul. 1969. *The Irish Brigade.* Washington: Robert B. Luce.

Kahn, E. J., Jr. 1955. *The Merry Partners: The Age and Stage of Harrigan and Hart.* New York: Random House.

Kaminski, John P. 1993. *George Clinton: Yeoman Politician of the New Republic.* Madison: Madison House.

Kammen, Michael G. 1975. *Colonial New York: A History.* New York: Charles Scribner's Sons.

Kenny, Kevin. 2000. *The American Irish: A History.* Harlow, UK: Pearson.

———. 2006. "Labor and Labor Organizations." In *Making the Irish American: History and Heritage of the Irish in the United States,* edited by J. J. Lee and Marion R. Casey, 354–63. New York: New York University Press.

Knobel, Dale T. 1986. *Paddy and the Republic: Ethnicity and Nationality in Antebellum America.* Middletown, CT: Wesleyan University Press.

Korson, George. 1964. *Minstrels of the Mine Patch: Songs and Stories of the Anthracite Industry.* Hatboro, PA: Folklore.

Krappe, Alexander Haggerty. 1964. *The Science of Folklore.* New York: W. W. Norton.

Lalor, Brian, ed. 2003. *The Encyclopaedia of Ireland.* Dublin: Gill and Macmillan.

Lane, Phyllis. 1997. "Colonel Michael Corcoran, Fighting Irishman." In *The History of the Irish Brigade,* edited by Pia Seija Seagrave, 13–34. Fredricksburg, VA: Sergeant Kirkland's Museum and Historical Society.

Lankevich, George J. 1998. *American Metropolis: A History of New York City*. New York: New York University Press.

Lepore, Jill. 2005. *New York Burning: Liberty, Slavery, Conspiracy in Eighteenth-Century Manhattan*. New York: Alfred A. Knopf.

Lewis, Robert M. 2003. *From Traveling Show to Vaudeville: Theatrical Spectacle in America, 1830–1910*. Baltimore: Johns Hopkins University Press.

Lhamon, W. T., Jr. 1998. *Raising Cain: Blackface Performance from Jim Crow to Hip Hop*. Cambridge, MA: Harvard University Press.

Lomax, Alan. 1960. *The Folk Songs of North America*. Garden City, NY: Doubleday.

Lott, Eric. 1993. *Love and Theft: Blackface Minstrelsy and the American Working Class*. New York: Oxford University Press.

Lowens, Irving. 1976. *A Bibliography of Songsters Printed in America before 1821*. Worcester MA: American Antiquarian Society.

Maginniss, Thomas Hobbs, Jr. 1913. *The Irish Contribution to America's Independence*. Philadelphia: Doire.

Martin, Felix. 1885. *The Life of Father Isaac Jogues, Missionary Priest of the Society of Jesus, Slain by the Mohawk Iroquois, in the Present State of New York, Oct 18, 1646*. Translated by John Gilmary Shea. 3rd ed. New York: Benzinger Brothers.

McBride, Jimmy. 1988. *The Flower of Dunaff Hill*. Buncrana, Ireland: Crana.

McCaffrey, Lawrence J. 1996. "Forging Forward and Looking Back." In *The New York Irish*, edited by Ronald H. Bayor and Timothy J. Meagher, 213–33. Baltimore: Johns Hopkins University Press.

———. 1997. *The Irish Catholic Diaspora in America*. Washington, DC: Catholic University Press.

McGreevy, John T. 2003. *Catholicism and American Freedom*. New York: W. W. Norton.

McKay, Ernest A. 1991. *The Civil War and New York City*. Syracuse: Syracuse University Press.

McKivigan, John R., and Thomas J. Robertson. 1996. "The Irish American Worker in Transition, 1877–1914: New York City as a Test Case." In *The New York Irish*, edited by Ronald H. Bayor and Timothy J. Meagher, 301–20. Baltimore: Johns Hopkins University Press.

McLaughlin, John. 2003. *One Green Hill: Journeys through Irish Songs*. Belfast: Beyond the Pale.

McNamara, Brooks. 2002. *The New York Concert Saloon*. Cambridge: Cambridge University Press.

Meagher, Timothy J. 2005. *The Columbia Guide to Irish American History*. New York: Columbia University Press.

———. 2006. "The Fireman on the Stairs: Communal Loyalties in the Making of Irish America." In *Making the Irish American: History and Heritage of the Irish in the United States*, edited by J. J. Lee and Marion R. Casey, 609–48. New York: New York University Press.

Miller, Kerby A. 1985. *Emigrants and Exiles: Ireland and the Irish Exodus to North America*. New York: Oxford University Press.

———. 1999. "'Revenge for Skibbereen': Irish Emigration and the Meaning of the Great Famine." In *The Great Famine and the Irish Diaspora in America*, edited by Arthur Gribben, 180–95. Amherst: University of Massachusetts Press.

Milner, Dan. 1983. *The Bonnie Bunch of Roses*. New York: Oak.

Moloney, Mick. 2006. "Irish-American Popular Music." In *Making the Irish American: History and Heritage of the Irish in the United States*, edited by J. J. Lee and Marion R. Casey, 381–405. New York: New York University Press.

Monaghan, Frank. 1935. *John Jay*. New York: Bobbs-Merrill.

Moody, Richard. 1980. *Ned Harrigan: From Corlear's Hook to Herald Square*. Chicago: Nelson-Hall.

Morash, Chris. 1995. *The Hungry Voice: The Poetry of Irish Famine*. Dublin: Irish Academic Press.

Morison, Samuel Eliot. 1965. *The Oxford History of the American People*. New York: Oxford University Press.

Moulden, John. 1994. *Thousands Are Sailing: A Brief Song History of Irish Emigration*. Portrush, Northern Ireland: Ulstersongs.

Moylan, Terry. 2000. *The Age of Revolution: 1776 to 1815 in the Irish Song Tradition*. Dublin: Lilliput Press.

Mulholland, St. Clair A. 1903. *The Story of the 116th Pennsylvania Volunteers in the War of the Rebellion*. Philadelphia: F. McManus, Jr.

Murphy, Richard C., and Lawrence J. Mannion. 1962. *The History of the Society of the Friendly Sons of St. Patrick in the City of New York, 1784 to 1955*. New York: J. C. Dillon.

Nathan, Hans. 1962. *Dan Emmet and the Rise of Early Negro Minstrelsy*. Norman: University of Oklahoma Press.

Nelson, Paul David. 2005. *Francis Rawdon-Hastings, Marquess of Hastings: Soldier, Peer of the Realm, Governor-General of India*. Madison, NJ: Fairleigh Dickinson University Press.

O'Brien, Kevin E., ed. 1996. *My Life in the Irish Brigade: The Civil War Memoirs of Private William McCarter, 116th Pennsylvania Infantry*. Campbell, CA: Savas.

———. 1997. "Sprig of Green: The Irish Brigade." In *The History of the Irish Brigade*, edited by Pia Seija Seagrave, 59–94. Fredericksburg, VA: Sergeant Kirkland's Museum and Historical Society.

O'Callaghan, E. B. 1849. *The Documentary History of the State of New York*. Vol. 1. Albany, NY: Weed, Parsons.

———. 1858. *Documents Relative to the Colonial History of the State of New York*. Albany, NY: Weed, Parsons.

Ó Gráda, Cormac. 1999. *Black '47 and Beyond: The Great Irish Famine in History, Economy, and Memory*. Princeton, NJ: Princeton University Press.

Ó hAllmhuráin, Gearóid. 1999. "The Great Famine: A Catalyst in Irish Music Making." In *The Great Famine and the Irish Diaspora in America*, edited by Arthur Gribben, 104–320. Amherst: University of Massachusetts Press.

O Lochlainn, Colm. 1960. *Irish Street Ballads*. Dublin: Three Candles Press.

Ó Tuathaigh, Gearóid. 1990. *Ireland before the Famine*. Dublin: Gill and Macmillan.

Palmer, Roy. 1988. *The Sound of History: Songs & Social Comment*. London: Pimlico.

Pomerantz, Sidney I. 1938. *New York: An American City, 1783–1803*. New York: Columbia University Press.

Post, Jennifer C. 2004. *Music in Rural New England: Family and Community Life, 1870–1940*. Durham: University of New Hampshire Press.

Riker, David M. 1999. *Genealogical and Biographical Directory to Persons in New Netherland from 1613 to 1674*. Vol. 1. Salem, NH: Higginson.

Riordan, William, ed. 1963. *Plunkitt of Tammany Hall*. New York: Dutton.

Rodgers, Nini. 2009. "Green Presbyterians, Black Irish and Some Literary Consequences." In *The Black and Green Atlantic: Cross Currents of the African and Irish Diasporas*, edited by Peter D. O'Neill and David Lloyd, 33–46. New York: Palgrave Macmillan.

Rosenwaike, Ira. 1972. *Population History of New York City*. Syracuse: Syracuse University Press.

Ryan, Leo Raymond. 1935. *Old St. Peter's: The Mother Church of Catholic New York (1785–1935)*. New York: United States Catholic Historical Society.

Sacks, Howard L., and Judith Rose Sacks. 1993. *Way Up North in Dixie*. Washington, DC: Smithsonian Institution Press.

Sante, Luc. 1991. *Low Life: Lures and Snares of Old New York*. New York: Farrar, Straus and Giroux.

Schecter, Barnet. 2002. *The Battle for New York: The City at the Heart of the American Revolution*. New York: Walker.

———. 2009. "The Culture of Opposition in New York." In *Lincoln and New York*, edited by Harold Holzer, 47–73. New York: New York Historical Society.

Selden, John. 1892. *Table Talk*. Edited by S. H. Reynolds. Oxford: Clarendon Press.

Shannon, William V. 1966. *The American Irish*. New York: Macmillan.

Shaw, Richard. 1977. *Dagger John: The Life and Unquiet Times of Archbishop John Hughes of New York*. New York: Paulist Press.

Sherif, Carol. 1996. *The Artificial River: The Erie Canal and the Paradox of Progress 1817–1862*. New York: Hill and Wang.

Simpson, Claude M. 1966. *The British Broadside Ballad and Its Music*. New Brunswick, NJ: Rutgers University Press.

Snyder, Robert W. 2000. *The Voice of the City*. Chicago: Ivan R. Dee.

Southern, Eileen. 1997. *The Music of Black Americans: A History*. New York: W. W. Norton.

Spann, Edward K. 1981. *The New Metropolis: New York City, 1840–1857*. New York: Columbia University Press.

———. 1996. "Union Green: The Irish Community and the Civil War." In *The New York Irish*, edited by Ronald H. Bayor and Timothy J. Meagher, 193–209. Baltimore: Johns Hopkins University Press.

———. 2002. *Gotham at War: New York City, 1860–1865*. Wilmington, DE: Scholarly Resources.

Spencer, Scott B. 2012. *The Ballad Collectors of North America: How Gathering Folk Songs Transformed Academic Thought and American Identity*. Lanham, MD: Scarecrow Press.

Spottswood, Richard K. 1990. *Ethnic Music on Records: A Discography of Ethnic Recordings Produced in the United States*, vol. 5, *1893–1942*. Urbana: University of Illinois Press.

Stillwell, William H. 1887. *William H. Stillwell's Printed Gravesend Notes and Other Printed Matter*. *F 128K .62 .G7 S75. Newspaper clippings from *Kings County Journal*. New York Historical Society.

Stockwell, A. P. 1884. *A History of the Town of Gravesend, New York*. Brooklyn. Reprinted from "The Illustrated History of Kings County. Edited by H. R. Stiles. New York: W. W. Munsell.

Stott, Richard B. 1990. *Workers in the Metropolis: Class, Ethnicity, and Youth in Antebellum New York City*. Ithaca, NY: Cornell University Press.

Tchen, John Kuo Wei. 1999. *New York before Chinatown: Orientalism and the Shaping of American Culture, 1776–1882*. Baltimore: John Hopkins University Press.

Truxes, Thomas M. 1988. *Irish-American Trade, 1660–1783*. Cambridge: Cambridge University Press.

Walsh, Walter J. 1996. "Religion, Ethnicity, and History: Clues to the Cultural Construction of Law." In *The New York Irish*, edited by Ronald H. Bayor and Timothy J. Meagher, 48–69. Baltimore: Johns Hopkins University Press.

Walton, Ivan H., and Joe Grimm. 2002. *Windjammers: Songs of the Great Lakes Sailors*. Detroit: Wayne State University Press.

Warner, Anne. 1984. *Traditional American Folk Songs from the Anne & Frank Warner Collection*. Syracuse: Syracuse University Press.

Wells, Robert V. 2009. *Life Flows on in Endless Song: Folk Songs and American History*. Urbana: University of Illinois Press.

Wilgus, D. K. 1982. *Anglo-American Folksong Scholarship since 1898*. Westport, CT: Greenwood Press.

Williams, William H. A. 1996. *'Twas Only an Irishman's Dream: The Image of the Irish in American Popular Song Lyrics, 1800–1920*. Urbana: University of Illinois Press.

Winslow, Calvin. 1998. *Waterfront Workers: New Perspectives on Race and Class*. Urbana: University of Illinois Press.

Wittke, Carl. 1930. *Tambo and Bones: A History of the American Minstrel Stage*. Durham, NC: Duke University Press.

Wolf, Edwin, 2nd. 1963. *American Song Sheets, Slip Ballads and Poetical Broadsides, 1850–1870: A Catalogue of the Collection of the Library Company of Philadelphia*. Philadelphia: Library of Philadelphia.

Woodard, Colin. 2011. *American Nations: A History of the Eleven Rival Regional Cultures of North America*. New York: Viking Penguin.

Wyld, Lionel D. 1962. *Low Bridge! Folklore and the Erie Canal*. Syracuse: Syracuse University Press.

Wylie, Paul R. 2007. *The Irish General: Thomas Francis Meagher*. Norman: University of Oklahoma Press.

Zellers, Parker. 1971. *Tony Pastor: Dean of the Vaudeville Stage*. Ypsilanti: Eastern Michigan University Press.

Zimmermann, Georges Denis. 2002. *Songs of Irish Rebellion: Irish Political Street Ballads and Rebel Songs, 1780–1900*. Dublin: Four Courts Press. First published 1967.

Dissertations and Theses

Kennedy, John H. 1930. "Thomas Dongan, Governor of New York (1682–1688)." PhD diss., The Catholic University of America.

Moulden, John Pointon. 2006. "The Printed Ballad in Ireland: A Guide to the Popular Printing of Songs in Ireland." PhD diss., National University of Ireland, Galway.

Nielands, Colin. 1991. "Irish Broadside Ballads in Their Social and Historical Contexts." PhD diss., Queens University, Belfast.

O'Flaherty, Patrick D. 1963. "The History of the Sixty-Ninth Regiment of the New York State Militia, 1852–1861." PhD diss., Fordham University.

O'Rourke, Hugh E. 2001. "Irish Immigrant Involvement in Collective Violence in New York from 1845 to 1875." PhD diss., City University of New York.

Pernicone, Carol Groneman. 1973. "'The Bloody Ould Sixth': A Social Analysis of a New York City Working Class Community in the Mid-nineteenth Century." PhD diss., University of Rochester.

Journal Articles

Andrews, Rena Mazyck. 1934. "Slavery Views of a Northern Prelate." *Church History* 3 (1): 60–78.

Charosh, Paul. 1997. "Studying Nineteenth-Century Popular Song." *American Music* 15 (4): 459–92.

Connor, Charles P. 1983. "Archbishop Hughes and Mid Century Politics, 1844–1860." *U.S. Catholic Historian* 3 (3): 167–77.

Ferris, Virginia. 2012. "'Inside of the Family Circle': Irish and African American Marriage in New York City's Eighth Ward, 1870." *American Journal of Irish Studies* 9:151–77.

Foik, Paul J. 1915. "Pioneer Efforts in Catholic Journalism in the United States (1809–1840)." *Catholic Historical Review* 1 (3): 258–70.

Fried, Rebecca A. 2016. "No Irish Need Deny: Evidence for the Historicity of NINA Restrictions in Advertisements and Signs." *Journal of Social History* 49 (4): 829–54.

Gilbert, Edmund, Seamus O'Reilly, Michael Merrigan, Darren McGettigan, Anne M. Molloy, Lawrence C. Brody, Walter Bodmer, Katarzyna Hutnik, Sean Ennis, Daniel J. Lawson, James F. Wilson, and Gianpiero L. Cavalleri. 2017. "The Irish DNA Atlas: Revealing Fine-Scale Population Structure and History in Ireland." *Scientific Reports* 7 (17199). www.nature.com/articles /s41598-017-17124-4.

Gorn, Elliott J. 1987. "'Goodbye, Boys, I Die a True American': Homicide, Nativism, and Working-Class Culture in Ante-bellum New York City." *Journal of American History* 74 (2): 388–410.

Irish Sword. 1955. "Volunteers of Ireland." *Irish Sword: Journal of the Military History Society of Ireland* 2 (6): 125–27.

Jaret, Charles. 1999. "Troubled by Newcomers: Anti-immigrant Attitudes and Action during Two Eras of Mass Immigration to the United States." *Journal of American Ethnic History* 18 (3): 10–11.

Jensen, Richard. 2002. "No Irish Need Apply: A Myth of Victimization." *Journal of Social History* 36 (2): 405–29.

Kaufmann, Eric. 1999. "American Exceptionalism Reconsidered: Anglo-Saxon Ethnogenesis in the 'Universal' Nation, 1776–1850." *Journal of American Studies* 33 (1): 437–57.

Kelly, Mary C. 2010. "A 'Sentinel(s) of Our Liberties': Archbishop John Hughes and Irish-American Intellectual Negotiation in the Civil War Era." *Irish Studies Review* 18 (2): 155–72.

Klement, Frank L. 1994. "Catholics as Copperheads during the Civil War." *Catholic Historical Review* 80 (1): 37–57.

Klinghard, Daniel. 2011. "Reading *Plunkitt of Tammany Hall* in the Context of Late Nineteenth Century Party Nationalization." *Polity* 43 (4): 489–512.

Larkin, Emmet. 1972. "The Devotional Revolution in Ireland, 1850–1875." *American Historical Review* 77 (3): 625–52.

Man, Albon P., Jr. 1951. "Labor Competition and the New York Draft Riots of 1863." *Journal of Negro History* 36 (4): 375–405.

McAvoy, Thomas T. 1948. "The Formation of the Catholic Community in the United States 1820–1860." *Review of Politics* 10 (1): 13–34.

Meade, Don. 1997. "The Life and Times of 'Muldoon, the Solid Man.'" *New York Irish History: Annual Journal of the New York Irish History Round-table* 11 (6–11): 41–48.

Meehan, Jane S. 1976. "Tim Finigan's Wake." *Wake Newslittir* 13:69–73.

Milner, Dan. 2011. "The First Irishman in New York." *New York Irish History: Annual Journal of the New York Irish History Roundtable* 25:3–11.

Moriarty, Thomas F. 1980. "The Irish American Response to Catholic Emancipation." *Catholic Historical Review* 66 (3): 353–73.

O'Connor, John P. 1989. "*The Shamrock* of New York, the First Irish-American Newspaper." *New York Irish History: Annual Journal of the New York Irish History Roundtable* 4:4–5.

O'Rourke, Hugh E. 2000. "Irish Rural Culture and the Bergen Hill Riots: Immigrant Workers and Industrial Protest in the Mid-1800's." *New York Irish History: Annual Journal of the New York Irish History Roundtable* 14:5–12.

Purcell, Richard J. 1938. "The Irish Immigrant Society of New York." *Studies: An Irish Quarterly Review* 27:583–99.

Sharrow, Walter G. 1972. "John Hughes and the Catholic Response to Slavery in Antebellum America." *Journal of Negro History* 57 (3): 254–69.

Smith, Christopher J. 2011. "Blacks and Irish on the Riverine Frontiers: The Roots of American Popular Music." *Southern Cultures* 17 (1): 75–102.

Solari, Anne. 2003. "'Honest' John Kelly: Democrat to Autocrat of Tammany Hall." *New York Irish History: Annual Journal of the New York Irish History Roundtable* 17:33–42.

Swift, Herbert D. 1921. "Manufacture of Cupro-Nickel: A Description of the Process Going in Regular Order from Casting to Packing." *Metal Industry* 19 (10): 394–95.

Vorenburg, Michael. 1993. "Abraham Lincoln and the Politics of Black Colonization." *Journal of the Abraham Lincoln Association* 14 (2): 22–45.

Walsh, Walter J. 2004–6. "William Sampson, a Republican Constitution, and the Conundrum of Orangeism on American Soil, 1824–1831." *Radharc: Journal of Irish and Irish-American Studies* 5/7:1–32.

Williams, Alfred M. 1892. "Folk-Songs of the Civil War." *Journal of American Folklore* 19 (5): 265–83.

INDEX

Page numbers in italics refer to figures.

INDEX OF SONGS AND MELODIES

DAN MILNER is an adjunct assistant professor of geography and history at St. John's University. He is the author-compiler of *The Bonnie Bunch of Roses: Songs of England, Ireland and Scotland* and has produced a number of CDs, including the twice Indie-nominated *Irish Pirate Ballads and Other Songs of the Sea*.